OUR FATHER'S PLAN

OUR FATHER'S PLAN

God's Arrangements and Our Response

FR. WILLIAM G. MOST

TRINITY COMMUNICATIONS
MANASSAS, VIRGINIA

ISBN: 0-937495-27-1 Paper
0-937495-28-X Cloth

DEDICATION

To our Father,
through the Hearts
of Jesus and Mary,
in the Holy Spirit

ABBREVIATIONS

The following abbreviations are used in the footnotes:

AAS - *Acta Apostolicae Sedis*

ASS - *Acta Sanctae Sedis*

BAC - *Biblioteca de Autores Cristianos* (Madrid)

CBA - *Catholic Biblical Quarterly*

CC - *Corpus Christianorum*

DS - H. Denzinger - A. Schönmetzer, *Enchiridion Symbolorum, Definitionum et Declarationum*

NAB - New American Bible

PG - J. P. Migne, *Patrologia Graeca*

PL - J. P. Migne, *Patrologia Latina*

RSV - Revised Standard Version (Bible)

SC - *Sources Chrétiennes*

TABLE OF CONTENTS

Introduction
To Open: A Lost Dimension

Why is it that many souls who try hard, even generously, to grow spiritually find spiritual things, even the Mass, mean little or nothing to them, so that they say they "get nothing out of it?" There are several reasons. We plan to explore all of them at various points in this book. But for now it is good to focus our attention on a lost dimension.

A great vista has fallen out of the spiritual life of many, if indeed it was ever there. The early Fathers of the Church will help us get a start. Arnobius, an early apologist for the faith, writing near the end of the age of persecutions, addressed these words to God: "To understand you, we must be silent; and for fallible conjecture to trace you even vaguely, nothing must even be whispered."[1] Similarly, an author who calls himself Dionysius the Areopagite, writing near the year 500 A. D., said that God is best known by "unknowing."[2] St. Gregory of Nyssa had expressed the same idea even earlier when in his *Life of Moses* he said that, "The true vision of the One we seek, the true seeing, consists in this: in not seeing. For the One Sought is beyond all knowledge."[3] In his treatise *On Christian Doctrine*, St. Augustine boldly stated the same fact, with pardonable exaggeration: "He must not even be called inexpressible, for when we say that word, we say something."[4]

The greatest of all theologians, St. Thomas Aquinas, near the end of his life, felt constrained to leave his monumental *Summa* of theology unfinished: "Such things have been revealed to me that the things I

---

[1]Arnobius, *Against the Nations* 1.31. PL 5. 755-56.
[2]Pseudo-Dionysius, *Mystical Theology* 1.2. PG. 3.1025.
[3]St. Gregory of Nyssa, *Life of Moses* PG. 44.376.
[4]St. Augustine, *On Christian Doctrine*, 1.6.6 PL 34.21.

have written and taught seem slight to me."[5] Once he had been given some glimpse of what God really is, Thomas felt his profound *Summa* so poor that he could not bring himself to touch it again.

Even the pagan Plato wrote that God is "beyond being."[6]

These writers had entered deeply into the immense dimension that is unknown to sterile souls. They tried to express the inexpressible by seemingly contradictory words. Nor do we blame them. We could try to explain it a little in the following way: When we speak the words red, green, blue, a person who is not color-blind grasps the sense, and gets the image of what we mean. The reason is that both we and our hearer *share a common experience*. For we have all sensed these colors. But suppose we speak of colors to one who is color-blind. We could of course tell him the frequency of vibration of the light waves—but he would not really get a mental image of those colors such as we have. They are beyond his experience.

Similarly, when we try to speak of God, we use words that normal persons do know. But we have to use them in a sense that is partly, in fact, very much different from the sense to which we are accustomed. That is why Our Lord Himself, when a young man addressed Him as "Good Master", took the occasion to teach this lesson dramatically by replying: "Why do you call me good? One is good: God" (Lk 18:18-19).

Jesus did not of course mean to deny that He Himself was God. Nor did He mean that even as man He was not good. No, He wanted to teach forcefully the truth seen by Arnobius and the other Fathers: the word good, when applied to God, is indeed partly the same as when applied to creatures. Yet there is a difference, a difference so great that we must at once correct our language and understanding by *denying* certain features that apply to creatures. Hence, God is known by "unknowing", by correcting our notions. And when we have most fully applied all the needed correctives, what positive content we have left is rather small—and yet, beyond that, is God Himself, really inexpressible. So Dionysius wrote: "We pray to see and to know that which is beyond seeing and knowing by our very not-seeing and not-knowing."[7]

Behind all these efforts to describe God the indescribable lies that fact that He is simply *transcendent*. That is, He does not fit into our categories or classifications; He is beyond all. We can try to begin to grasp this by a concrete instance. If we try to explain *how* God knows things, we run quickly into impenetrable mystery.

---

[5]*Cf.* J. Maritain, *Angelic Doctor*, S.& W. London, 1933, p.51.

[6]Plato, *Republic* 6. 509B. *Cf.* Plotinus, *Enneads* 6.8.9: "The One is other compared to all things."

[7]Pseudo-Dionysius, *Mystical Theology* 1.2. PG.3.1025.

Now there are two ways in which a creature can know things, the active way, and the passive way. In the passive way, we take in an impression from something outside ourselves, we acquire something new, data we did not have before. Of course, we cannot think of God's knowledge in this way, as if there were a lack in Him needing to be filled: nothing can be lacking in Him.

But if we try to say God can know only in the active way, we meet worse obstacles: a blind man can know a chair is moving because he, actively, is pushing it. But even a blind man can know many things he does not actively cause. Clearly, we cannot make God more limited than a blind man by saying He can know only what He causes.

So neither the active nor the passive explanations can fit Him. The reason is as we said: He is simply beyond all our categories, cannot be contained in the frameworks we set up for created things. The word that expresses this characteristic of His is *transcendence*.

Hence St. Thomas Aquinas, in trying to explain how God can know the future free decisions of humans, was content merely to say that since God is in eternity—in which all is *present*, with no past, no future, for they would imply *change*—He can know the future, *as present*. St. Thomas was driven to this conclusion by the fact that a future *free* decision is really unknowable, since it does not yet exist—nor are there any causes lined up outside the man that will make him decide this way. If so, he would not be free. Therefore St. Thomas said that since all things are present to God, He can know them, for in the present, they are decided, and so are knowable.[8]

But St. Thomas did not dare to ask, beyond this point, just how—*in what way*— does God know the things present in eternity? For then he would be caught in the active or passive dilemma we have seen. St. Thomas, in proper humility, remained silent, knowing he could penetrate no further. Nor can we understand just how the future can be present to God. We say: Christ *will* come at the end, using a future expression. But to the divine mind that is present, not future. We say: God *made* the world, using a past expression. But to the divine mind, that is present too.

An even greater mystery is this: Scripture[9] shows various instances in which God knows a different kind of future, not the kind that *really will happen*—but instead the kind that would happen, *e.g.*, what would

[8]*Cf.* W. Most, *New Answers to Old Questions*, St. Paul Publications, London, 1971 #463-79.

[9]*Cf.* 1 Sam 23:10-13; Jer 38:17-23; Mt 11:21-23; Lk 10:13. *Cf.* also St. Gregory of Nyssa, *On Infants who are Taken Away Prematurely* PG 46.184; St. Augustine, *De Genesi ad Litteram* 11.9.12. PL 34.434.

happen if I would make this move in these circumstances. (Theologians call these things *futuribles*.) Not even eternity can make these futuribles present, for they not only do not now exist, they never will exist. Yet, God does know them, as Scripture shows.[10]

Once we get some glimpse of these truths, we can see that there are two poles in our response to God. (By poles we mean centers around which things are grouped.) They are the pole of love-closeness-warmth, and the pole of a sense of awe, of majesty, of realization of His infinity and our nothingness in comparison.

We cannot, strictly speaking, overdo either of these response attitudes, since God is infinite in all respects. He is both love and infinite majesty. But we can have a distorted, even a sick condition in our souls if we cultivate one pole largely or entirely without the other.

That is what many souls do. They are so preoccupied with God as love, that we fear they have distorted love. Satan gladly helps us to distort, for he knows that people fear to speak against love, and so can be mired in various counterfeits. St. Paul was very right when he wrote (2 Cor 11:14): "Satan transforms himself into an angel of light," that is, he takes on the appearance of good—but a sick, twisted good—so that by getting us enmeshed in it, he may keep us from what really is good.

Suppose someone told me: "Joe Doaks, who lives three blocks from here, loves you." My reaction would probably be: "Ho hum. Who is that? Why should I be interested?" Similarly, if someone is told that God loves him, but lacks a perception of the immense majesty, the infinite otherness of God, he too may be little interested in God's love. He will be spiritually stunted and sick. So we need this perspective of God's infinity *vs.* our nothingness. Without it we are easily trapped in a lack of humility, the virtue that recognizes what we are in comparison to God. This humility, as we will see fully in chapter 18, is an absolute prerequisite for love: unless we have a humility as deep as our love is to be lofty, that love will be, at least in part, an illusion, a counterfeit.

An ancient Hebrew form of address to God, current in the time of Christ,[11] balances perfectly these two aspects. The prayer opens with

---

[10]Another instance of transcendence: In the Incarnation, the Divine Word takes on a human nature, yet, according to Aristotelian-Thomistic philosophy, He could not take on a relation to it—then He would be passive. He only gives the humanity a relation to Himself. Of course God cannot change, yet there must be something else in the union of God and man; we appeal to transcendence.

[11]*Cf.* J. Bonsirven, *Palestinian Judaism in the Time of Christ*, tr. W. Wolf, McGraw-Hill, N.Y. 1965, p.30.

"Avinu-malkenu"—Our Father-Our King.[12]

But it is not enough just to read or hear of this need of spiritual balance. One must also *realize* it. And so we come to the second need. Cardinal Newman proposed a famous distinction between notional and realized knowledge. Suppose I read in the news that there is a famine in Africa. I will probably believe the account, but it is not likely to move me. I will be apt to quickly turn the page of the newspaper and read another item. I have only notional knowledge. But suppose instead I were to go to the famine area and see people near death or dying, and even to feel hunger myself—then I would also know the very same fact, but in a very different way. I would have realized knowledge. Realized knowledge takes hold of us, makes us not only think deeply, but also makes us act, it transforms us. Of course, there are many degrees of realization possible. What would happen to us if we had as deep a realization of the basic truths of faith as we have of the latest sports event? We would never be the same!

So we are going to try to set out to give a balanced picture of God and our relations to Him. This book can offer that—but for real spiritual profit, the reader needs to deeply meditate on these truths, so as to try to advance many degrees in realization.

---

[12]*Cf.* the fact that St. Teresa of Avila, even with her frequent familiarity with God in visions and revelations, habitually refers to Him as "His Majesty."

Chapter 1: Avinu-Malkenu

In the beginning there was a good Father. We can speak of Him as Father, not because He, in some merely figurative way, resembles those whom we call our fathers on this earth. Rather, all others are called fathers only because, in some very imperfect way, they imitate His Fatherhood. For it is from Him, the greatest and best of Fathers, that, as St. Paul says (Eph 3:15), "all fatherhood in heaven and earth is named." Really, we should call Him *the* good Father, for in comparison to Him, no other being is good (Lk 18:18-19), no other deserves the name of Father.

Again, we really should not have said: there *was* a good Father. For while of all creatures we can correctly say: "they were" or "they will be", of Him it is only correct to say: "He is." For whatever goodness, or happiness, or even existence we creatures have, we have it piecemeal: one installment, as it were, of our existence succeeds or follows after the previous bit has ceased to be, while another waits ready to follow when our present fleeting fragment has passed. But with the Father there is no constant succession of birth and death of moments in a bit by bit existence. He *is*. All that He is and has, He possesses simultaneously, in one undying, eternal present, which never began, nor will ever cease. As we saw above, although we seem to ourselves to say rightly, for example, that He created the world, using a past tense, yet for Him that, like everything else, is present. And though we say that His Son *will come* at the end, yet for Him, that is simply now present. For with Him (Jas 1:17), "the Father of lights, there is no variation or shadow of change." If no change, then no succession of future-present-past—for time is the most restless of changes. To Him who *is*, all is present, eternally present. (We begin to see why Dionysius said that God is best known by unknowing: we must constantly correct our imperfect words when we speak of Him.)

This good Father is rightly called Father in the first place because He has one only-begotten Son. Yet this Son is not younger than He, nor lesser in dignity or power. Of Him the Eternal Father says through the Psalmist (2:7): "You are my Son, this day have I begotten you." That is, on the never beginning, never ending day of eternity. "Yours is princely power on the day of your birth in holy splendor: before the daystar, like the dew, have I begotten you." In the infinite act of knowledge of Himself that is His very being, the Father speaks but one word (Jn 1:1)—not a word that is a quickly-dying vibration of the air, such as we creatures utter, but a complete expression of Himself, so perfect, so substantial, that this Word is a Person, His eternal Son. And yet, though the Son is another Person, distinct from the Father, that same Son could correctly say (Jn. 10:30): "I and the Father are one."

From the unfathomable stream of infinite knowledge that flows between the Father and the Son, there proceeds Infinite Love. But again, it is not a love such as that which we creatures know among ourselves. We must again revise our words: this Love of the Father and the Son is a Person, a distinct Person, the Holy Spirit. Yet these three are only one, one inexpressible God.

It is right to speak of this adorable Trinity as inexpressible, for no created words can represent the divine wonders. That is why we have repeatedly found it necessary to correct our language, as we compare divine truths to things of our experience. For all our human words are dependent on those things which we have experienced in some way. To express created things, created words can suffice. But since nothing we know directly can mirror more than some fragmentary gleam of the divine perfection, we must constantly apply correctives to our words when we apply then to God.

Here in passing we might well reflect on the frightening responsibility of those of us creatures who are called *father*, be it in the natural, or the supernatural order. For since the notion a child gains of God our Father is based on the experience he has of those whom he learns to call father, what he sees in them will of necessity reflect on God Himself!

There is another important corrective we need to use in our description of God. For it is really not true to say that He *has* goodness, or justice, or love. It is correct to speak thus of ourselves, weak creatures, that we *have* goodness, love, justice, since it is not our very nature to be good, loving, or just. We are one thing; our goodness is another. But in the "one who is good, God" (Lk 18:19) there is no such real difference.

He does not really *have* goodness, He *is* Infinite Goodness. He does not have love: rather, as St. John wrote (1 Jn 4:8): "God *is* love."

Love is a desire for the well-being and happiness of another for the other's sake[1] and so involves self-giving. The Father gives Himself so fully that the Son thus has His Divine Being. The mutual giving of Son to Father and Father to Son again is another Divine Person, the Holy Spirit. So St. John did well to write "God *is* love."

These thoughts of the Father who is no greater than His Son, of the Son who is as eternal as the Father, of the three who are one, of the God who never was nor will be, but only *is*—these daze our poor minds. An eternity of face to face contemplation will not enable our minds to come to the end of amazement. J. P. Arendzen wrote well:

> God remains unfathomable even to the greatest of His saints. They see Him, but none can see to the very depths of his divine being. God is a world, a wide universe, which none of the Blessed has ever totally explored. Even after millions of cycles of ages, neither Mary, the Queen of Heaven, nor Michael, the Prince of the heavenly host, shall exhaust the greatness of the divine majesty. It is an ocean on which the little craft of created intelligence can forever press forward in all directions. For it is a sea without a shore. As a pretty many-colored insect on swift wings floats on the summer breeze and allows itself to be driven along in the seemingly boundless air; as a lark rises in the apparently boundless sky, so do the blessed roam about in the limitless wideness of God.[2]

But it is good for us to stand in powerless awe before the inexpressible abyss of the Three who are One, the God who is love.

In His incomprehensible generosity, this good eternal Father planned to become our Father. It is solely out of the most absolute generosity that He conceived this desire. For in Himself, in the boundless life in which each divine Person gives Himself so fully to the Other that all are equal, yet all are One, He neither needs nor possibly could gain anything. As St. Irenaeus said: "In the beginning, God formed Adam, not because He stood in need of man, but that He might have someone to receive His benefits."[3]

---

[1]Cf. Aristotle, *Nicomachean Ethics* 8. 2.

[2]J. P. Arendzen, *Purgatory and Heaven*, Tan Books, Rockford, 1972. pp. 60-61. St. Thomas Aquinas thinks there is no development or progression in the vision of God: *Contra gentiles* 3. 60. But *cf.* St. John of the Cross, *Spiritual Canticle*, 7. 9: "... in heaven ... those who know Him more, understand more clearly the infinity they still have to understand." From: "Vida Y Obras de San Juan de la Cruz", *Biblioteca de Autores Cristianos*, Madrid, 1950, p. 1007.

[3]St. Irenaeus, *Against Heresies* 4. 14. 1 p. 7. 1010.

It is often said that He created to manifest His own glory.[4] This is true, but only if it is properly understood. We will grasp it best if we consider the truth as it is implicitly revealed in the constantly repeated teaching of Our Lord Himself that God is our Father. An earthly Father does not desire children that he may have someone to honor him, or to give him glory. Nor does he really love and care for them because *they* are good, but because *he* is good. Yet he does will that they honor him—not for his own good, but for a twofold reason: First, because what is right in itself calls on children to honor and obey their father;[5] second, so it may be well with them, for if they obey him, they are disposed to receive all that he generously wills to give them.

Similarly, though immeasurably greater and purer[6] is the generosity of our Father in heaven. What little honor we could give Him, even if we were far more faithful than we are, is not the thing that really *moved* Him to make us. Really, when we speak of "serving God" we should put those words within quotation marks. Imagine a monastic community of a hundred of the greatest Saints "serving" God for a century by fasting, silence, the divine office, the Mass. Or think of an apostolic community of the same number of Saints, engaged in superhuman works of zeal of the apostolate for a century. At the end of that time, He would gain nothing at all from either group. As the book of Job says (2:2-3) "Can a man be profitable to God? . . . Is it a gain to Him if you make your ways perfect?"

Nothing at all can strictly *move* the Unchangeable Father. Rather, out of His Infinite Goodness and the unspeakable Love that He *is*, in unalloyed generosity, with no hope or possibility of any gain whatsoever for Himself, He freely willed to be our Father.

When we creatures love another, we are started in that direction by some good we see or think we see in another. That leads us to feel or think: "Such a fine person. I hope he/she is well off, gets what he/she needs for happiness." For that is precisely what love is, willing good to another for the other's sake. But what good did our Father see in us at the very beginning, before He made us, that led Him to love us? Nothing at all—for we were, simply speaking, nothing. Any good we were to

---

[4]Vatican I, *Canon I de Deo creatore,* DS 3025. Cf. Philip J. Donnelly, "St. Thomas and the Ultimate Purpose of Creation" in: *Theological Studies* 2 (1941) pp. 53-83, and the words of Bishop Gasser, President of the Doctrinal Commission in *Collectio Lacensis* VII. 113. Friburg, 1892.

[5]We note here the same two reasons that our Father pursues in His works towards us.

[6]The second of these reasons, His concern for objective goodness, will be developed more in chapter 4.

be or to have would be purely His gift. So we can see now: He alone is purely generous. His love needs no starter, needs not to see good in another. When we love we need such a starter, and hence we cannot match His pure unmixed generosity.

Lovingly, as a parent might prepare the room in expectation of the first child to come, our Father prepared a wondrous world for His children, that He might satisfy His deep desire to share His happiness. By an all powerful *fiat* of His will, He created the vast depths of starry space, and adorned them with a lavish profusion of diamond-gleaming galaxies, that the heavens might tell the glory of the good Father who made them.

It is good for us to contemplate these amazing works of our Father, to try to gain some small impression of His immense majesty. As Pius XII told an international meeting of astronomers:

> We are grateful to you ... because this scientific exploration and elevating contemplation of the universe lifts up our spirit ... ever higher towards the knowledge of that Supreme Goal who transcends all knowledge and impresses His own seal [some image of Himself] in every other being ... Who is "the love that moves the sun and the other stars."[7]

Let us imagine ourselves out of doors on a clear autumn night. As we turn to the southern portion of the heavens, there, close to the horizon, we see a rather small, reddish star. It is called Antares, and belongs to the constellation of Scorpio. Its small size is, of course, only apparent, for astronomers tell us that the diameter of Antares is so huge that even if the more than 93 million miles of space that lie between our earth and the sun were tripled, Antares still could not pass between them! It is many times the diameter of the sun. Still more tremendous is its distance. For although its light has been racing towards us at the staggering speed of over 186,000 miles per second, every second of every minute, every minute of every hour, every hour of every year, still, the light we see tonight has taken well over 430 years to reach us.

And yet, the great God who made all the splendor of the heavens by a mere word, loves each one of us, and wants us to call Him Father.

But now let us turn to the northern sky. There, in the constellation of Ursa Minor, we find Polaris, the star that gleams directly over the north pole of our earth. The light we see began its journey to us long before these United States were founded, in fact, long before the century in which Columbus set sail: it was about the time of the Great

---

[7]Pius XII to the International Union of Astronomers, Rome, Sept. 7, 1952. *AAS* 44. 732. The internal quote is from Dante, *Paradiso* 33. 145.

Western Schism, in the fourteenth century, that the light of Polaris began its long journey, speeding every second, day and night, for over six hundred years, at the rate of over 186,000 miles per second. If in the time of Luther, God had willed to annihilate that star, even today we would not know of the destruction, for the light that set out in the 14th century would still be coming to our eyes.

And yet, the mighty God who made all these wonders, not by great labor, not after long planning, but by merely willing them—He loves *me* and wants me to call Him Father.

But, the truth is, even Polaris lies at a relatively short distance. Nearby in the sky, as it seems, in the W-shaped constellation of Cassiopeia is a very dim patch of light which is really a world in itself, an independent galaxy or "island universe." It is Andromeda. It lies far beyond the galaxy to which our earth and sun belong, at a distance of 2.2 million light years. Nor is it the outermost lightship of creation.

Years ago, when the 100 inch telescope of Mount Wilson was first trained on the heavens, it was able to detect some one hundred million galaxies within the sphere of a billion light years, each galaxy having about one hundred billion stars. More powerful instruments since that day have greatly enlarged what we can detect. At present the most distant objects seem to be the Quasars, the farthest of which is perhaps 14 billion light years away. Only our Father knows how many more universes may lie beyond even this staggering reach. For He is "the love that moves the sun and the other stars."[8] Yet this God of awful majesty loves *me*, and not only permits, but insists that I call Him Father.

The vast splendor of the heavens tells the glory of their Lord most eloquently of all. But for him who pauses to meditate, all creation speaks of the wonders and goodness of our Father—from the majesty of snow-draped mountains and murmuring pine forests, to the crystal-bedecked caverns that lie beneath them; from the roaring ocean swells to the mysterious creatures that inhabit the lightless deeps; from the simple invisible cells that multiply themselves countless thousands of times, to the wonderful intricacy of the human brain, in which before birth hundreds of thousands of neurons develop each minute, each making hundreds of thousands of synapses (connections), to a total of about 100 trillion synapses, and about 10^{11} neurons (about 100 billion). Yet no two neurons are identical in form.[9]

Even if we look at a bit of wood or fabric—every fiber in it is teeming with atoms, each comparable to a miniature universe. The simplest atoms, like hydrogen, have just one electron and a nucleus.

[8]Dante, cited in note 7 above.

[9]*Cf. Scientific American,* September, 1979, esp. pp. 45-46, 55, 113.

More complex atoms, such as uranium, have seven orbits, or better, energy levels around them. Within the nucleus lies a complex organization whose basic building blocks we are just beginning to understand. Yes, it is right to sing in the liturgy: "The heavens and earth are full of your glory. All you works of the Lord, bless the Lord."

Aristotle, greatest of pagan philosophers, considered it unthinkable that even friendship should exist between a god and man.[10] Yet he had in mind poor beings we would not call gods at all. What would he think of the gulf between Infinite Power and Goodness, and creaturely nothingness!

Indeed, if we allow our imagination free play, we might think of some great archangel flying through outer space, and looking from afar on our globe. Any one of us might well seem to him as a tiny dark blob, which appears for but a moment on the surface of the sphere, and then sinks back, to be seen no more. He might see too that this tiny thing is not only insignificantly small and short-lived, but that it is besmirched with many a stain. Yet, he would see this inconsequential soiled speck lift up its eyes, raising them beyond the farthest stars and most distant universes to heaven itself, and say: "My Father—I love you." Unthinkable boldness! That such a being should dare not only to speak to its Creator, but to call the great God *Father*, and should dare to offer Him its love! "What is man, that You are mindful of him, or the son of man, that You visit him?" (Ps 8:4).

And yet, our Father not only allows, not only invites, but even *insists* that we love Him. And such is His love that although when we turn to look at our own weakness and sinfulness, we see that we really are soiled dust, yet by His goodness and power, our lowliness has been made capable of receiving, by grace, a real participation in the very nature of the great God Himself. As St. Peter wrote (2 Pt 1:4) we are "sharers in the divine nature."

---

[10] Aristotle, *Nicomachean Ethics* 8. 8.

Chapter 2: Sons of God

A human father, in the merely natural order, deserves his honorable title for two reasons: first, because he has been a cause of life to a new being; second, because he provides for and takes care of that child so long as the child still needs care, and so long as the father is willing and able to give it. Our Father in heaven, (Eph 3:15) "from whom all fatherhood in heaven and earth is named," deserves to be called our Father in a much fuller, higher, and even more literal sense than do our earthly fathers.

We need to take special care at this point, because most people are in the habit of making a sort of mental discount when they hear striking spiritual truths: they assume that the writer or speaker is exaggerating, or is allowing for loss in transmission. Let us have it understood that throughout this entire book we will never indulge in any exaggeration whatsoever—and so in turn we hope readers will take care not to make such discounts.

It is of the greatest importance for us to try to *realize* how strictly and truly He is our Father, for it will be a great aid to our growth in love and reverence for Him. So let us compare His Fatherhood to the two functions of an earthly father.

First, a father should be in some way a cause of a new life. An earthly father can be called a cause of the life of his child only in a restricted sense. Although he does cooperate in the production of new life, yet he is only a cooperator, not the sole, self-sufficient cause, nor even the chief cause. His very ability to cooperate is a gift of our Father in heaven. In fact, even in the very use of the gift that he has received, the earthly father is in constant need of an influx of power from our Father in heaven, in whom (Acts 17:28) "we live and move and have our being." Further, although an earthly parent is rightly said to be the father of a *person*, not just of a body, yet the soul does not in any way come from him. He merely has a share in the process by which a body is made that is fit for and calls for the infusion of a soul. But the soul itself is the direct creation of the heavenly Father alone.

It is obvious that in this respect, that of being the cause of a new life, our heavenly Father is far more fully and literally our Father than is our earthly parent.

We *belong to* our heavenly Father more really and fully than we do to our parents on earth. A comparison may help us to realize this. Suppose someone decides to make a model airplane. He takes the necessary materials, balsa wood, cloth, glue and other requisites, and, after much painstaking work, fashions them into an attractive little plane. If he has done his work well, it will be able to fly. Perhaps he even adds a small motor. The maker of the plane then feels—and rightly so—that this little plane is his in a very special way, more completely so than if he had merely bought such a plane ready-made in a store. For he is its maker. Yet he has not made the wood itself, nor the cloth, nor the other materials. But our Father in heaven has done far more: every fibre of our being is produced by Him, not out of some previously existing material, but out of absolute nothing. Surely, we *belong to* Him far more fully and literally than does a plane to its maker, or a child to its human parents.

We said the second function of a father is the care he takes of the child as long as the child needs his help, and as long as he is willing and able to provide it.

Not all human fathers do well in this part of their role: some are unable to care for their children, some die while the child is yet young. Some few are even lazy or unwilling to provide. And at best, a time surely comes when the normal child no longer requires his father's care.

Not so our Father in heaven, the best of all Fathers. He is never unable to care for His children: He is all-powerful. Nor is He ever unwilling: as St. John tells us, He not only *has* love for us; rather (1 Jn 4:8): "God is love." But neither can a time come when we no longer need His care. If an earthly father dies while his child is young, that child is still able to live without him, and though he will miss his father's care, is nevertheless apt to enjoy even a long life without him. But we not only could not live or act without our Father in heaven: we could not even exist for a single instant without Him. Life is a *moment to moment* gift from Him in whom (Acts 17:28) "we live and move and have our being." (Chapter 18 will show the deep reason for this moment to moment dependence.)

Again, suppose we put a signet ring into water: the water takes the shape of the carved design, but only so long as the ring is there. Similarly, we need the constant impress of the power of our Father in heaven.

It is difficult for us to realize how completely we depend on our Father for everything. Another comparison may help. When we see movies, the images on the screen seem very real: they appear to have color, life, and to speak and move about. They seem so real that we readily become absorbed in the drama, and forget that it is only an empty image on the screen. But if the technician up in the projection booth should throw the switch, the images on the screen would no longer exist: they would fall back into complete nothingness.

Our dependence on the constant inflow of power from our Father is much like that of the images on the screen, but with this important difference: no technician can make an image that is able to defy his will. But the omnipotence of our Father does precisely that: He is able to make us free to disobey Him, and in His unthinkable goodness He actually does give us that ability, as a means of making us—the other side of the coin—capable of receiving unimaginably great gifts from Him, if only we refrain from resisting His generosity.[1] How true are the words of His Divine Son (Lk 12:7): "Even the hairs of your head are all numbered."

Our Father's attitude to us is best described as a supreme desire to lavish His gifts on us. St. John of the Cross, a great Doctor of the Church, who knew so well the ways of our Father by His own personal experience of Him in the highest forms of mystical contemplation, compares our Father to the sun. If only we do our small part,[2] St. John tells us, "it is impossible that God would fail to do His part, in communicating Himself, at least in secret and silence.... Just as the sun gets up early to enter your house if you open the window, so God . . . will enter into the soul that is emptied and fill it with divine goods."[3]

It is important to notice that the mystical Doctor is speaking in this passage not just of the more usual sort of graces, but of the exalted and relatively rare gift of infused contemplation.[4] In his mind, if a soul fails to receive so great a favor, it could not possibly be due to any lack of generosity on the part of our Father. It is solely due to the soul's failing to "open the window," *i.e.*, to not place obstacles in itself. For God is like the sun, which cannot help but come in if the shades are not

---

[1]On this dependence, cf. chapter 18.

[2]Our part is really nonresistance, as we shall see fully in chapter 18.

[3]St. John of the Cross, *Living Flame* 3. 46-47. BAC edition, p. 1239.

[4]On infused contemplation, see chapter 22.

shut. Similarly, another Doctor of the Church, St. Teresa of Avila, wrote: "God would never want to do other than give if He found souls to whom He could give."[5]

When God gives us His love in this life, it really means He sends His Holy Spirit within us, that Spirit which *is* the love of the Father for the Son, and of the Son for the Father. To have that Spirit within our soul is to have what St. Paul calls (Eph 1:14) "the *pledge* of our inheritance." A pledge is a sort of downpayment, to assure the recipient that the rest will follow. What we have as a pledge is God Himself, the Holy Spirit, really within our souls. It is only the fact that we are hampered by the veil of flesh that prevents us from seeing Him as He is. Once that veil is removed by death, the vision will take place, if, of course, we are sufficiently purified. If not, our needs are mercifully met by purgatory. Of course, a soul that has cast out the Holy Spirit by mortal sin could be correctly said to have, instead, a pledge of hell, that is, of the loss of God. If the veil lifts on him in that state, the loss will be everlasting.[6]

By means of this presence of the Holy Spirit, as St. John tells us, (1 Jn 3:1): "We are called and are the Sons of God," in the supernatural order, just as we are His children in the natural order since He gave us life, keeps us in existence, and cares for us.

We speak of grace as a divine adoption, but here too our language is very inadequate to bring out the greatness of the reality. For adoption makes us think of human adoption, in which, through the generosity of a human pair, some orphaned child is taken into their home, and, by a legal fiction, acquires the same rights as a natural child, and receives the same loving care as if he really shared in the blood and genes of those parents. Yet, we must admit, however much this generous pair may love their adopted child, he is not really flesh of their flesh; and though he may be called, for example, a Smith, yet there is no trace of Smith genes or blood in him.

If this human pair were able to do more for their adopted child, doubtless they would do it. But our Father in heaven does not suffer from any limitation; He, in His almighty power, is able, and, in His infinite Goodness, He wills to do that of which no creature could dream: He actually makes us, as St. Peter teaches (2 Pt 1:4), "sharers in the divine nature."

We cannot, of course, make even a good beginning of realizing what this means, for we shall be able to understand fully only in the life

[5]St. Teresa of Avila, *Conceptions of Love of God* 6. (*Meditations on Canticles*). In Santa Teresa de Jesus, *Obras Completas*. Biblioteca de Autores Cristianos, Madrid, 1954. II. p. 620.

[6]Cf. 1 Cor 3. 17.

to come, in that vision of which eye has not seen, nor ear heard, nor has it entered into the heart of man what things God has prepared (cf. 1 Cor 2:9). Yet, if we do not lose sight of the fact that our words must fall far short of the reality, we can make the attempt to gain some slight beginning of realization.

Within the most Blessed Trinity, as we indicated in the preceding chapter, there flows among the divine Persons an infinite stream of infinite, indescribable knowledge. It is precisely the one word (cf. Jn 1:1) which the Father speaks that fully expresses Himself, that fully gives Himself, that is His Divine Son, the perfect image of Himself, who is one with Him. Again, between Father and Son, from this infinite knowledge, arises similarly infinite Love, which again is a Divine Person, the Holy Spirit.

To share or join in directly in this infinite knowledge and infinite love in this way is the very nature of God. Yet by grace, we are given in this life that ability, in seed as it were. The seed, when we reach our Father's house, will blossom into knowing and loving the Father and the Son and the Holy Spirit as directly—though not as infinitely—as they know and love each other. Only someone with a divine nature is capable of such a thing.

Although nothing in our experience can give us anything even approaching a satisfactory realization of what this is like, yet a comparison may help a little with one aspect of it. When in this life we know things, for example a flower, we say we know it *directly*. But yet there is a certain indirectness in our knowledge, for we do not actually take the flower itself into our mind. Rather, we form an *image* of it within us. Now in the case of a flower or any other creature, however wonderful the creature may be, an image is able to give us complete knowledge. But when we arrive in our Father's house to have what St. Paul calls a face to face vision (1 Cor 13:12), no image could possibly let us know Him as He is, for any image is a created thing, a finite thing—but He is infinite, uncreated Goodness.

Hence there must be a direct union of God with the soul, with no image coming in between, as Pope Benedict XII defined.[7] St. Thomas boldly drew the inescapable conclusion: God Himself takes the place of the image![8] Thus we, made partly divine, take part in the streams of infinite Knowledge, infinite Love. So Arendzen was obviously right with his imagery of the butterfly trying to take in the vastness of the ocean; this beatific vision is ever new, eternally inexhaustible. Only a God who is Love could conceive, and will to carry out, such a plan. How insignifi-

---

[7]DS 1000.

[8]*Summa Theologica*, Suppl. 92. 1. c

cant is the dignity of any king, president, or ruler of this earth compared to that of a son of God, a partaker in the divine nature itself!

The full effect of grace will be attained only when we enter the mansions of our Father. But even here the soul in grace becomes a wonderful thing. St. Basil the Great wrote:

> Just as shining lucid bodies, when a ray of the sun strikes them, become superlucid and send another ray out from themselves, so the Spirit-bearing souls, shone on by the Spirit, are made perfectly spiritual themselves, and send grace into others.[9]

St. Cyril of Alexandria, speaking of the same Holy Spirit, said: "He who is God and proceeds from God imprints Himself invisibly in the hearts of those who receive Him, like a seal in wax . . . restoring the image of God to man."[10] St. Cyril of Jerusalem says the Holy Spirit transforms the soul as iron is transformed into fire in a forge: at first it is cold and black, but then warms up, begins to glow, and finally the iron seems to have been changed into fire.[11]

This transformation is the result of the promise given by Our Lord Himself the night before He died (Jn 14:23): "If anyone loves me he will keep my word, and my Father will love him, and we will come to him and take up our dwelling with him." And St. Paul adds (1 Cor 3:16): "Do you not know that you are the temple of God, and the Spirit of God dwells in you?" The soul in the state of grace has, literally, all three Divine Persons dwelling within it. We rightly reverence the tabernacle, or the chalice even when they are empty, because they have contained the Body and Blood of Christ. But yet, though the tabernacle and the chalice do deserve respect, still the divine presence in them has not changed their nature. But our souls, as we have seen, are changed by grace, by the Three Divine Persons dwelling within them, making our souls into something superhuman, something sharing in the very nature of divinity.

Such, then, is our tremendous dignity. But also rightly does the liturgy place on our lips these words before we say the Our Father: "Jesus taught us to call God our *Father*, and so we have the *courage* to say. . . ."

---

[9]St. Basil, *On the Holy Spirit* 9. 22. PG 32. 109.
[10]St. Cyril of Alexandria, *Thesaurus* 4. 34. PG 75. 609.
[11]St. Cyril of Jerusalem, *Catecheses* 17. 14. PG 33. 985.

Chapter 3: Restoration Beyond Infinity

It would be foolish for us to think that everyone must always, in all ages and cultures, have used the same patterns of writing as we 20th century Americans do; for different peoples have different ways of doing things. For example, a modern historical novel about the Civil War is basically factual or historical; and the background descriptions fit the period. But we expect the author to do fill-ins, *e.g.*, to report word for word conversations of Lincoln with high officials. We do not really think the author has a word for word record of such things. But to make it more interesting, he fills in these things. Our modern historical novel is a mixture of history and fiction. But we do not for this reason say the author is ignorant, or trying to deceive us. No, there is an established pattern or *genre* of writing that we, the author, and his readers all understand, and know how it was meant, and how to take it.

Other cultures and other centuries, of course, need not have had our patterns. So we must try hard to learn how they meant things. Vatican II tells us:

> Truth is [in Scripture] presented and expressed in various ways—in texts that are in different ways historical, in prophetic texts, in poetic texts, and in other patterns of speaking. So it is necessary that the interpreter seek out that sense which the sacred writer . . . within the conditions of his age and culture, intended to express, and did express, using the literary patterns of that time.[1]

If we ignore this obvious principle, we would fall into fundamentalism, *i.e.*, acting as though Scripture were written by 20th century Americans.

---

[1]Vatican II, *On Divine Revelation* #12.

We have gone into these matters because we want to look at the first three chapters of Genesis. Pope Pius XII, in his encyclical *Humani generis*, recognizes this problem of the pattern or genre of these chapters, and yet, in a carefully balanced statement, warns us not to be too loose in handling these chapters:

> Although they do not fit with the strict rules of historical composition [such as we use today] yet in a certain sense, which needs to be further investigated and determined by scholars, they pertain to the category of history.[2]

So these chapters do tell us facts, things that actually happened, but not in the modern way of speaking. The same Pius XII even told us, two paragraphs earlier,[3] that we may consider evolution of the human body as a real possibility. The Pope could not say that if evolution clearly clashed with the true sense of Genesis.

So that sense must be such as to report facts, yet in a way quite a bit different from the 20th century American way.

We needed to say these things because we want now to consider the generosity of our Father's plans for our first parents. We know there was a first pair, though we need not feel confident that their names were Adam and Eve. We know God put them into a happy state, of His special favor, that He imposed some command on them—precisely what we do not know—that they transgressed, and that they lost much of what He had given them. They lost it also for us, for they could not transmit to us what they no longer had. And so we receive from them just the essentials of human nature, without His grace, without other added gifts. To be born without the grace that should have been there, according to God's plan, is what we mean by original sin. We can say original sin is transmitted to us by heredity inasmuch as we should have inherited grace, but do not.

---

[2]*DS* 3898.

[3]*DS* 3896. On the rib episode, see the words of Pope John Paul II, Audience of Nov.7, 1979: "The man (adam) falls into 'sleep' in order to wake up 'male' and 'female'.... Perhaps ... the analogy of sleep indicates here not so much a passing from consciousness to subconsciousness as a specific return to non-being (sleep contains an element of annihilation of man's conscious existence), that is, to the moment preceding the creation, in order that, through God's creative initiative, solitary 'man' may emerge from it again in his double unity as male and female." This is said within the framework of the special genre of Genesis. In *Original Unity of Man and Woman*, St. Paul Editions, Boston, 1981, p. 64. For further data on evolution *cf.* W. Most, *Free From All Error*, Prow Press, Libertyville, IL, 1985. chapter 11.

A comparison will help. If someone commits a mortal sin, his soul is without grace. So we say he is in the state of sin. But when we say a newborn child is also in a state of original sin, we mean something that is partly the same—his soul lacks grace—but also partly different: for that lack in the baby is not his own fault, whereas if an adult sins mortally, his lack of grace is his own fault.

The Genesis account brings out in a clever psychological way some other important facts. We know that if one has human nature without any added gifts, he will experience difficulties. For within human nature there are many different drives and desires, each basically legitimate and good in itself. But the problem comes from lack of coordination. Each drive goes after the things it likes and needs without any thought of the other drives and their reasonable needs and wishes. The most disorderly of these drives is that for sex. It can not only start up without any provocation, but can become very imperious and demanding. Now the Genesis account seems to want to tell us something on that score, by way of the writing pattern used. After Adam had sinned, God is pictured as calling to him: "Adam, where are you." Of course God knew, but this is a way of making a point. Adam replied that he had hid himself because he was naked. Now before the sin, Adam was also naked, but did not seem to notice it. Afterwards he did, and felt the need of just anything he could find—Genesis mentions fig leaves—to cover the critical spots that were rebelling, and making him feel shame.

The message is clear. Before the fall, Adam must have had some sort of coordinating gift, that kept the various drives under control of reason. He did have the power of sex, but it was subject to his wishes. If he wanted it to operate, it surely would; but if he did not want it, it could not rebel.[4] However, as St. Augustine puts it, "Because man had deserted his higher Master [God] by his own will, he was not able to hold his lower servant [his body] to his own will."[5] So the penalty of disobedience was disobedience, disobedience of man's lower nature to man's higher nature, plus disobedience of the animal and plant kingdom to man. For formerly Genesis pictures man as master of all creation. But now the animals run from him, and he must laboriously extract a living from the soil by the sweat of his brow; formerly the earth had brought forth an abundance without the need of tilling.

So our first parents lost this splendid integrating gift, and also the gift of immortality; for death, both spiritual and physical, was threatened against them as a penalty if they sinned. Spiritual death means, of

---

[4]Adam had not used the gift of sex before the fall. If he had, there would have been some children, part of his race, without original sin.

[5]St. Augustine, *City of God*. 13.13. PL 41.386.

course, the loss of grace, the life of the soul, that makes man like God, as we saw in the last chapter.

What irony! Genesis pictures the tempter as telling Adam and Eve they would be like gods if they disobeyed. But they were already like God, by grace. In seeking to get what they already had, they threw away a share in divinity, which they had really possessed.[6]

In this narrative we see also a most clever presentation by Genesis of the fact that all sin consists basically in pride. To see it, let us fill in a bit and retell the story in our own words. Eve is in the garden one day, and along comes the tempter: "My, what a fine garden. Does God let you eat from all these trees?" Eve replies: "Yes—O, just a minute—that one over there—He says that if we eat from it we will die." "He said that!" replies the tempter, in a tone of surprise. "Why don't you see what is really true? If you eat from that you will be like gods. God is really selfish; He doesn't want anyone else to be divine. He just wants to keep it all for Himself." So Eve looked at the forbidden fruit. She could just see that it was good. She thought to herself: "God may know what is right in general, but right now I can just see that this is good. So I will eat." She did, and asked her husband to do the same. So both, in seeking what they already had, lost a share in the divine nature, lost all the extra gifts God had lavished on them. For they believed God could be selfish, could hold out on them!

This is, as we said, an image of every sin. The sinner in effect says: God may know in general, but I can just see that this forbidden thing here and now is good. So I will take it. This is, of course, simply pride, to think one knows better than God. His commands, as we saw earlier are really means to make us open to receive what He so generously wants to give. Our obedience does Him no good whatsoever. So St. Thomas Aquinas wrote well: "God is not offended by us except because we act against what is good for us."[7] Sin does not touch Him; He is displeased that we, whom He loves, harm ourselves. (And He is also displeased that we act against what is good in itself—as we shall see in the next chapter.)

On that sad day on which our race first began to throw away His precious gifts, and to resist His generosity, our Father had several courses of action open to Him. First of all, He could simply have inflicted the threatened punishment of death at once on the guilty pair. Then our race would have come to an end, for as yet they had no descendants. Again, He could have delayed the punishment of death, but reduced them, with all their descendants, to the merely natural level.

[6] *Cf.* the explanation and the Patristic quotations at the end of chapter 2.
[7] St. Thomas, *Contra Gentiles* 3.122.

Then all hope of the marvelous divine vision would have been cut off, although those descendants who would not sin further might eventually reach a merely natural sort of happiness, such as that which most theologians think is the lot in limbo of unbaptized infants.

But if He willed to keep our race on the supernatural plane—and He did so—there were again several possibilities.

First, our Father could have forgiven sin without any reparation at all. This option was not too great for His generosity, but his loving wisdom preferred a still better way, one richer for mankind. And, as we shall see, He willed also to satisfy His love of what is right in itself, by rebalancing the disrupted moral order.

Another possibility was to provide for an imperfect reparation for sin. To accomplish this, He could have chosen some mere human, and could have sanctified him for the task, and then directed him to perform some specified act of religion, perhaps the offering of an animal in sacrifice.

Thirdly, He could have sent a Divine Person, His Son, to become man, but in a far different way from what actually happened. He could have had that Son born in a palace, equipped with every luxury that the technology of the last age of the world could dream of. He could have had that Son perform any small act of religion—no need for Him to die. For any act of this God-man would by its very nature have had infinite worth, and be more than enough to outweigh the sins of countless worlds. He might have had Him redeem us by saying a three word prayer, "Father forgive them." Then He could have ascended in a blaze of glory, before the eyes of admiring representatives of all the tribes of men.

This third option would have been strictly infinite in worth. Yet, our Father wanted to go beyond infinity. This is no mere rhetorical exaggeration. It is true that in mathematics infinity plus any addition does not increase. But this is not the terrain of mathematics, but the realm of Infinite Generosity. So our Father willed to go beyond the palace to the stable, beyond a three word prayer to the cross.

Why? We can see part of the reason by the help of a pattern in the life of St. Vincent de Paul. He told his associates who dispensed charity to the poor that they must use great care, even tact, in handing out their goods and help, so that the poor would be willing to accept their charity. The reason: people feel inferior when they are ever on the receiving end, never making a return.

Strange as it may seem, our Father knew well He would find a similar lack of openness to His favors in His children. We recall the words of St. John of the Cross and St. Teresa that, "God would never want to do other than give, if He found souls to whom He could give."[8] For we are so often not open to His gifts. Hence in His determined love, He planned a restoration beyond the wildest dreams of any creature, so that by it He might move as many as possible to refrain from resisting His generosity. So His Son said (Jn 13:32): "I, if I be lifted up, will draw all things to myself."

So He spared not His only begotten Son, but sent Him as an eternal priest, not to perform some easy, even if infinitely valuable, act of religion, but rather to be obedient unto death, even to the death of the cross, so that He might thus soften the resisting hearts of His brothers.

But there is even more. For it seems that our Father can never rest content with anything lesser—even if it be already beyond infinity—if anything can be added to make it still richer in some way. In the fall, in which man had become disobedient even to death, two had been involved. Adam, the Head of our race, had been joined by a helper like to himself, Eve, who should have been the mother of the living, but who instead shared in throwing away the life of the soul for all their children to come.

Hence, so that the restoration might be even more superabundant (*cf.* Rom 5:15-21), there were to be two, Christ, the New Adam, the eternal priest, together with her whom the Fathers of the Church with unanimous voice call the New Eve, the Virgin Mary, the true Mother of the living. Later we will see more fully how this took place. For now it is enough to say that, as Pius XII put it, "Our salvation flowed from the love and sufferings of Jesus Christ, intimately united with the love and sorrows of His Mother."[9] Or, as Vatican II wrote: "In suffering with Him as He died on the cross, she cooperated in the work of the Savior in an altogether singular way, by obedience, faith, hope and burning love, to restore supernatural life to souls."[10] Thus she reversed the ruin wrought by the first Eve, who became the mother of those destined for death. But the Virgin Mary instead, as Vatican II continued in the same text: "For this reason [her sharing in the great sacrifice] . . . is our Mother in the order of grace," the true Mother of those who live forever as partakers in the divine nature.

God is our Father. Yet His love has not only the strength of a Father's love, but also the persistence of the love of a Mother, that strives at all costs to avoid, if at all possible, the ruin or punishment of a child. He does not, of course, call Himself Mother, though He does, through the prophet Isaiah tell us (Is 49:15): "Can a woman forget her suckling

[8] *Cf.* Chapter 2, note 5.

[9] Pius XII, *Haurietis aquas*. AAS 48.352.

[10] Vatican II, *On the Church* #61.

child, be without feeling for the son of her womb? Even if she did, I will not forget you. Behold, I have carved you on the palms of my hands," by the marks of the nails. And by making Mary the Mother of all the brothers of her Son, He who made her so wonderful reveals the same Motherly persistence of love in Himself.

In Matthew 23:37 Jesus compares Himself to a mother hen: "O Jerusalem, Jerusalem, you that kill the prophets, and stone those who are sent to you! How often would I have gathered your children together as a hen gathers her brood under her wings, and you would not." St. Augustine comments beautifully on this verse:

> You see, brothers, how the hen is weak with her chicks. No other bird is [easily] recognized as a mother. We see various sparrows make nests before our eyes; every day we see swallows, storks, doves, making nests. But we do not know that these are parents except when they are in the nest. But the hen so makes herself weak with her chicks, that even if the chicks are not then following her, even though you do not see her offspring, yet you know she is a mother.[11]

[11] St. Augustine, Tract 15.7 on John's Gospel. PL 35.1512.

Chapter 4: Holy, Holy, Holy, Lord God of Power and Might

When He considered the various options or ways the redemption could be accomplished, our Father picked the one that was richest of all for us, one that quite literally went beyond infinity in worth. His love for us led Him to go so far. But, as we have already mentioned in passing, there is another dimension, one which has been forgotten today, or, more accurately, discarded by theologians. It is that of His concern for the objective order of goodness and holiness. If we overlook it, we will be lacking greatly in our understanding of the ways of our Father, for He pursues both goals—love of us and love of objective goodness—at the same time. There is no conflict between these, except where we humans deliberately resist His generous plans.

It is of great importance for us to understand this love of order/holiness correctly. We do not mean that He simply demanded reparation for the offence against Himself; He could rightly do that, and we note that the offense was even infinite, since the Person offended is infinite—not to forget the incalculable total of all sins of all ages. However, an objection is often raised against the thought of reparation: we humans do not always demand reparation for offenses against us. So, the objection says, could not God just let it go without reparation, as good people often do? The objection forgets the infinity of God, the immeasurable distance between creature and Creator, and, more importantly, His love of Holiness/goodness in itself.

When we speak of His concern for the objective order, we mean His concern for Holiness, for what is morally right in itself. Whereas some charge lack of generosity—falsely—in the fact that God might rightly ask reparation for the offense against His majesty, they cannot really object to His unselfish concern for what holiness calls for, for morality as such.

The Scriptural picture of God was a striking one to the contemporary world in which Scripture first appeared. For the gods of Greece and Rome were described in the literature of those nations as not so much immoral as amoral.[1] That is, they acted as if there were no such thing as morality at all. So in their own lives, they did what we rightly call sinful things: Zeus committed adultery many times with human women, and would have done it much more often had not his wife Hera been trailing him. But her objection was not based on morality—she knew nothing about a moral law—she was just a naturally jealous wife. Further, what the gods did in their own lives, they fully ignored in the lives of people: they cared not at all if men and women committed adultery, if they lied, if they stole, if they committed murder. Yes, there were some lesser beings, the Furies, who seemed to resent murder, and to try to drive the killer insane. But the great gods paid no attention to murder at all, or to most other sins. They would enforce honor for themselves, and were thought to care for a few isolated points of morality, chiefly, a dutiful attitude towards country, home, guests, and suppliants coming with the proper ritual in the name of Zeus. But other things meant nothing.

In sharp contrast, the God of the Old Testament is *sadiq*, morally righteous, and He loves what is morally right, as Psalm 10:7 sings: "God is morally right, and loves things that are morally right."

This attitude of His absolute Holiness shows all over Scripture. Already in Genesis 15:16 we meet with a remarkable statement. On that pivotal day in history when Abram believed God's promise of a progeny as numerous as the stars, and God counted his faith for him as righteousness (Gen 15:6), Abram was told to arrange a mysterious form of sacrifice. Then when the sun was setting and a deep sleep came upon Abram, God foretold that he and his descendants would possess the land of Canaan, but added that they would not get it at once: first, they must be in servitude in another land, Egypt, for four hundred years (Gen 15:16). "But in the fourth period they will return here, for not yet is the guilt of the Amorites complete."[2] Later, Deuteronomy 9:4-5 in-

---

[1]Yet, the literature is not fully consistent: some literary texts picture Zeus as guardian of justice. And Socrates surely held up and lived a most high moral ideal, so that in Plato's *Republic*, the conclusion is that one should observe justice even if he could get away with injustice. On the Mesopotamian gods, *cf.* Thorkild Jacobsen, "Mesopotamia. VII. The Good Life" pp. 202-19, in *The Intellectual Adventure of Ancient Man* edd. H. & H. A. Frankfort et al. University of Chicago, 1948.

[2]God's concern for the moral order shows especially also in Romans 3:

sisted that Israel was not getting the land because of its own righteousness; rather, because of the wickedness of the nations had the Lord driven them out.

Here is a remarkable concept indeed. Could not God at any time give any land whatsoever to whomsoever He willed? Of course, He is the absolute Master. What we call "rights" are in reality only claims that He wills to give us to have or to do things. But we see that His Holiness wills to observe right order in everything: hence He did not expel the Amorites until their wickedness had reached its fulness.

Here our Father was not only observing the moral order, He was showing the maximum tolerance in waiting, so that a people should not be despoiled without having most fully earned it.

That same concern for what is right in itself shows even more dramatically in a number of other Scriptural incidents. In chapter 12 of Genesis we read how Abram, after entering Canaan for the first time at God's command, continued on to Egypt, for there was a famine in Canaan. When he was near the border of Egypt, he told his wife Sarai that he feared the Egyptians might take her to the Pharaoh, but would kill him if they knew she was his wife. Therefore they agreed to say she was his sister, a name not technically untrue, since Hebrew *ahoth* could stand for even a fairly distant relative.

As anticipated, the Pharaoh's men did take Sarai to him. Abram was well treated, and even enriched by royal gifts. But then something happened. Genesis 12:17 tells us that, "The Lord struck Pharaoh and his house with great plagues because of Sarai, Abram's wife." We would say: Pharaoh was in good faith, he did not know he was doing something wrong in itself. Yet God's Holiness and love of the objective moral order wanted things rectified, and struck Pharaoh. As soon as the unhappy ruler learned the truth, he called Abram in and asked him why he had not told him she was his wife, and ordered him out of the land.

As a result, chapter 4 of Leviticus gives detailed rules for sacrifices to be offered in case a man violated any of the laws of God without knowing it. Of course, such violations were far less than sins committed knowingly. They were in a basically different class. Yet the con-

---

24-26: during the Old Testament period, God might have seemed to others not to be concerned about the full restoration of the moral order. He did punish sin, even openly, but that punishment was not a full restoration. So the Father sent His Son to fully rebalance. We get justification without earning it, yet, the moral order is preserved: Rom 3:31, since Jesus fully did make the restoration: "Do we then destroy law [concern for the moral order] through faith [the teaching of justification by faith, gratuitously]? Banish the thought: We establish law." For we have shown that the order is fully reestablished by Jesus.

cern of the Holiness of God for what is right insisted that even sins committed in good faith called for satisfaction: the moral order must be rebalanced.

Not surprisingly then, soon the concept of sin as debt that must be paid emerges. The Septuagint, the ancient Greek translation of the Old Testament, used the verb *aphiemi* to mean forgiving sin. But that word carried the connotation of remitting a debt. Still more clearly, the Hebrew *hobah*, debt (and Aramaic *hoba*) was often used in the intertestamental books of the Jews, written between the end of the Old and the start of the New Testament.[3]

This debt concept does not appear explicitly many times in the New Testament, yet the places it does appear are most significant. In the Our Father, Jesus Himself taught us to pray: "Forgive us our debts"—for that is the exact translation of the Greek *opheilemata*.

Similarly, St. Paul speaks of Jesus as paying "the price" of redemption (1 Cor 6:30 and 7:23), and tells the Colossians that the Father who raised Christ from the dead, made you (Col 2:13-14) "alive together with Him, forgiving you all your transgressions, wiping away the bill that was against us, with its claims . . . nailing it to the cross" as if marking it "paid" by the price of redemption. Similarly, Gal 3:13 says that "Christ bought us from the curse of the law" (*cf.* Gal 4:5).

The theology of the Rabbis, in which St. Paul was trained, expressed this idea with the image of a two pan scales. The sinner takes from one pan something he has no right to take: the scales is out of balance; the Holiness of God wants it rebalanced, so the sinner should put it back if he still has a stolen item. If he has stolen an illegitimate pleasure, he should in compensation give up something he could otherwise have properly had. Thus Rabbi Simeon ben Eleazar, quoting Rabbi Meir (a disciple of the great R. Akiba, and the most eminent of the Tannaim, born not far from 110 A. D.) wrote:

> A man has carried out one commandment. Blessings [on him]. He has tipped the scales to the side of merit for himself and for the world. A man has committed a transgression. Woe [to him]! He has tipped the scales to the side of debt for himself and for the world.[4]

---

[3]*Cf.* S. Lyonnet-L. Sabourin, *Sin, Redemption and Sacrifice*, Rome, Biblical Institute, 1970, pp. 25-26, 32. *Cf.* George F. Moore, *Judaism*, Harvard University Press, Cambridge, 1927, II, p. 95; M. Jastrow, *A Dictionary of the Targumim*, Pardes, N. Y. 1950, I. pp. 428-29. A similar attitude shows in Testament of Levi 3. 5; Psalms of Solomon 3. 7-8; Testament of Zebulon 1. 4-5 and Slavonic Enoch 30. 16; 31. 7.

[4]Tosephta, Kuddishin 1. 14.

We notice that Rabbi Meir teaches that we are all interdependent: a sin of one harms all. Even if it be a so-called "victimless crime" it does tip the scales unfavorably. In a parallel way, St. Paul expressed this same idea in his image of the Mystical Body of Christ, in which (1 Cor 12:26) "if one member suffers, all the members suffer with it; if one member is honored, all the members rejoice with it."

Christ, the Head of this Mystical Body, did the chief, the essential, really infinite work of balancing the scales.[5] Without Him it really could not have been done fully. For sin, under one aspect, has an infinity about it: the Person offended, God, is infinite. Hence there was an infinite imbalance, which could only be rectified by an Infinite Person. Given the fact that the Father decided, as we saw before, on a complete rebalance, only by the Incarnation of a Divine Person could it be done.

A major constitution of Pope Paul VI, *Indulgentiarum Doctrina*, explains this well:

> Every sin brings with it a disturbance of the universal order, which God arranged in His inexpressible wisdom and infinite love.... So it is necessary for the full remission and reparation of sins ... not only that friendship with God be restored by a sincere conversion of heart, and that the offence against His wisdom and goodness be expiated, but also that all the goods, both individual and social, and those that belong to the universal order, lessened or destroyed by sin, be fully reestablished, either through voluntary reparation ... or through the suffering of penalties.[6]

So again, there are no such things as victimless crimes. The sin of one harms others, just as the holiness of one helps others. Within this framework belong the expiation and the righting of the universal order accomplished by the death of Christ, who not only (Phil 2:7-9) "emptied Himself," giving up the honor and comforts that He could rightly have had as God, but even "humbled Himself becoming obedient, even to death, death on a cross." Sinners take what they have no right to from the scales; Jesus put it all back, most abundantly.

However, as St. Paul teaches, it would be strangely incongruous if Christ our Head were a suffering and atoning Head, while we, His

---

[5]A few of the Fathers had thought the "price" of redemption (*cf.* 1 Cor 6: 20) was paid to satan—thus Origen, On Matthew 20:28 and St. Ambrose, Epistle 72. But St. Gregory of Nazianzus rightly saw that it would be a "mockery" to say the price was paid to satan: Oration 45, on Easter 22. We solve the dilemma by showing that the price was paid to the objective order—for the word *price* is of course a metaphor.

[6]Paul VI, *Indulgentiarum doctrina*, Jan 9, 1967. AAS 59, 7.

members, would do nothing, would live lives of comfort. Hence we are called on to be like our Head in this. As St. Paul told the Romans, we are fellow heirs of the mansions of the Father with Christ (Rom 8:17) "if indeed we suffer with Him, so we may also be glorified with Him." For we are saved and made holy to the extent that we are not only members of Christ, but are like Him, especially in His reparation, in His obedience even to death.

This condition is stern indeed, but is also most comforting, for St. Paul continues in the next line (Rom 8:18): "I judge that the sufferings of the present time are not worthy to be compared to the glory that is to be revealed to us." For the more like Him we are in the first phase, His life of hardship culminating in death on the cross, the more shall we be like Him in the second and final phase, that of unending glory. We are to share in His glory in the measure in which we shared in His suffering. In fact, we are repaid with more than interest, for St. Paul assures us that even (2 Cor 4:17) "what is light and momentary in our troubles is producing us, beyond all measure, an eternal weight of glory for us."

Still further, St. Paul knew that if one member of Christ was remiss in doing his part in the work of rebalancing the objective order, someone else could make up for him. As a shepherd of souls, Paul felt that that was part of his assignment (Col 1:24): "Now I rejoice in my sufferings for you, and I fill up the things lacking of the sufferings of Christ, in my flesh for His body, which is the Church."

St. Paul knew too that he should not lightly dismiss even involuntary transgressions, committed in ignorance or "good faith." So he told the Corinthians (1 Cor 4:4): "I have nothing on my conscience, but not thereby am I justified." That is: I am not aware of committing any sin, but perhaps I did something unknowingly. In this spirit, a prominent Jewish scholar, A. Büchler, reports that "... the ancient pious men brought every day a doubtful guilt-offering, to clear themselves from any error of a grave religious nature possibly committed on the previous day."[7]

Even today in the Liturgy of St. John Chrysostom, there is a prayer before the Epistle: "Forgive us every offence, both voluntary and involuntary."

In his first Epistle, St. John wrote (1 Jn 4:8): "God is love." As we saw in our first chapter, it can be said that we finite creatures have love. That implies a duality: we and our love. But God is supremely one. So He does not just have love, He *is* love, is identified with it.

Now we can see a tremendous further truth: just as He does not

---

[7]A. Büchler, *Studies in Sin and Atonement in the Rabbinic Literature of the First Century*, Ktav, N. Y. 1967, p. 425.

have love, but is love, so also, He does not have justice, mercy, holiness and other attributes—He is justice; He is mercy; He is holiness. Being holiness itself and justice itself, we can understand how He insists on the observance of complete holiness, including balancing the objective order of morality.

A still further mystery appears; if He is justice, and is mercy—then justice and mercy must be somehow identified in Him, for they are identified with Him, and so must be the same. To our eyes, justice and mercy often seem not only different, but opposite. No wonder Dionysius wrote, as we saw, that God is best known by "unknowing."[8]

Though we cannot completely comprehend how He can be both mercy and justice, we can make a start. Suppose we think of a man who has never been drunk before, but Saturday night he gets very drunk. On the next day, among other effects, he will have guilt feelings. Why? As it were, there are two voices in him. One voice, that of his moral beliefs, says it is very wrong to get drunk; the other voice, that of his actions, says it is all right. This clash is upsetting. Our nature dislikes such tension, and so in time something must give: either he will bring his actions into line with his beliefs, or, gradually, over a period of time, his beliefs will line up with his actions. He will no longer be able to perceive clearly that there is anything wrong in getting drunk. If we call him on it, he will be apt to say: "A man has to have shum fun!" Further, over a longer time, his other moral beliefs may be strained. The total result is that his ability to register religious truths becomes dimmer.

This gradual blinding is a just punishment for his sins; but it is also a mercy from God. For the more clearly we see religious truths, the greater our sin if we still do sin. So in one and the same act God is showing both mercy and justice.

Conversely, if a man acts vigorously according to his faith, if he acts on what St. Paul tells us, that the things of this world, though good in themselves, are still only dung compared to the things of eternity—he will find his faith growing stronger. It is just that he should grow in spiritual vision, as a reward for his good life. Yet, in the most basic sense, everything we have from God is simply His gift, and so the man's gain is also a matter of mercy. Again, in one and the same act, God exercises both mercy and justice simultaneously.

Matthew, Mark and Luke[9] report that Jesus at first spoke openly to the crowds, but later He turned to parables (Lk 8:10) "so that seeing they might not see, and hearing they might not understand." We have

---

[8]Pseudo-Dionysius, *Mystical Theology* 1. 2. PG 3. 1025

[9]Mt 13:14; Mk 4:12; Lk 8:10. For the Hebrew pattern in which it is said God positively does things when He only permits, *cf.* 1 Sm 4:3 and Ex 9:12.

rendered the Greek construction as expressing His purpose; it would also stand a translation of mere result; "so that seeing, they did not see, and hearing they did not understand." In either case, we have another instance of mercy-justice. Many in the crowds were ill disposed. To speak to them in such a way that their lack of disposition would prevent understanding was an act of just blinding, earned by their perversity. Yet it was also an act of mercy, for thereby He refrained from increasing their responsibility for continuance in evil, which He foreknew. Even today, and in any century, similar conditions appear in those who read Scripture. Scripture in general is not easy to understand; even if we allow for the differences in language and culture, we still have a measure of unexplained difficulty. This is probably divinely intended to produce the same sort of effects we saw with the parables, namely, those well disposed would be more able to perceive spiritually: this is just reward, but yet, basically, all we receive is God's mercy. Again, those who are ill disposed by lack of faith or evil life will be less able to understand. Their dim eyesight is a just punishment, but also mercy, for then their responsibility is not increased by better understanding of the word of God.

So now we can begin to understand how in God Himself mercy and justice can be identified with each other, for in so many of His dealings with us, He exercises both virtues in one and the same action.

When one goes far enough on the evil spiral, there comes the "loss of the sense of sin" which was lamented repeatedly by Popes Pius XII and John Paul II.[10] People lose the ability to see that sin is an offense against God, against His Holiness. Yes, it is true that sin cannot touch or harm God, but it can harm those whom He so loves, His children. And it can upset the holiness of the objective order, which He likewise loves.

When the process goes on far enough there comes real spiritual blindness, even to the point of the sin against the Holy Spirit, which cannot be forgiven (*cf.* Mt 12:32 and parallels) precisely because the blindness makes repentance impossible. When one repents, he looks back on his sin and says to himself "I should not have done it; I wish I had not done it; I do not intend to do that anymore." But blindness from loss of the sense of sin prevents his seeing that, and so it prevents repentance. Hence the sin can never be forgiven, since there can never

---

[10]Pius XII in a Message to the National Catechetical Congress of the U. S. Oct 26, 1946 said: "The sin of the century is the loss of the sense of sin." Pope John Paul II said the same in his Post-Synodal Apostolic Exhortation, *Reconciliatio et paenitentia* Dec. 2, 1984. AAS 77 (1985) pp. 225ff and in his encyclical *Dominum et vivificantem* May 18, 1986, #47.

be repentance. (We will see further details on how this comes about in chapter 19.)[11]

We can understand something else better now. We said in the introduction that there are two poles in our relation to God: that of love, closeness, warmth, and the pole of a sense of awe, reverence, feeling of the presence of immense Majesty. The one corresponds to the fact that God is our good Father, who in planning our restoration went literally beyond infinity in His desire to make everything as rich as possible for us. The other reflects the absolute Holiness that He is, a Holiness which insists on fully balancing the scales of the objective moral order out of love of Holiness.

Yet there are not two Gods, but one, who simultaneously is Love, and is Holiness, in whom these are not different, but are fully identified.

---

[11]Can the merciful blinding mentioned above save one from all guilt? We note that degrees of guilt can be varied, and can diminish at varied points on the spiral. Yet the person can be responsible at an early point for what is done in blindness later. Cf. St. Paul Rom 1:31: "They, having known the justice of God, that they who do such things are worthy of death, not only do them, but approve of those who do them." We note two stages—formerly they knew, later they lost that knowledge and called sin good. We recall too such texts as Genesis 12:17 in which God punishes even involuntary sin—not as severely of course as voluntary sin. Cf. the whole concept of involuntary sin described earlier in this chapter.

Chapter 5: Covenant of Sinai

"What has he planned? What is in my father's heart? What is in Enlil's holy mind? What has he planned against me in his holy mind? A net he spread: that is the net of an enemy."[1] These words are part of a Mesopotamian hymn to Enlil, one of the most powerful gods of that land. It makes clear that that ancient people not only feared their gods, but actually mistrusted them: the gods might set a net or a snare for them.

The ancient Hebrews never expressed such a mistrust of God. But God did say through Isaiah the prophet (55:9): "As far as the skies are high above the earth, so are my ways high above your ways, and my thoughts above your thoughts." In context, God was encouraging His people to believe in His mercy. Yet in a broader view, they knew it was true that He was so far above them that they could not fully comprehend His ways. And the type of thought found in the Mesopotamian hymn has not been rare among men: Who can know the ways of God? Who can be sure of how He will act? True, the Hebrews did compare God to a Father (Is 63:16), "You are our Father. [Even if] Abraham would not know us, and Israel not acknowledge us: you, O God, are our Father; our redeemer is your name from everlasting."[2]

Still, God had not yet taken on a human heart, as He did in the incarnation, so that men would see fully—what was eternally true—that

---

[1]Quoted from T. Jacobsen, *op. cit.*, p. 144.

[2]The Hebrew for redeemer is *goel*, which stands for the next of kin who, in time of need, has both the right and the duty to rescue his family members who are in difficulty—so God by the covenant becomes as it were a member of the family. *Cf.* Roland de Vaux, *Ancient Israel*, tr. J. McHugh, McGraw-Hill, NY. 1961, pp. 21. 22.

He understood and loved them. But if their Father would as it were spell it out for them, if He would say, in effect: "If you do this, I will do that"—then they could be confident, could know how He would act.

This is precisely what His Holiness/Love did in making the Old Covenant; He provided a remedy for their tendency to mistrust.

After Moses had led the Hebrews through the Red Sea with mighty signs, and brought them to the foot of Mt. Sinai, with its thunder, lightning, and trumpet blasts, he heard God speak through the thick cloud (Ex 19:5): "If you really obey my voice, and keep my covenant, you shall be my special possession, more so than all people." In other words, He told them clearly in His covenant law what they must do: if they would do it, they would receive His special favor, as His specially dear people.

Some interpreters[3] have tried to see in these words just an imposition of commands by the Almighty on His slaves, who would have no claim to anything even if they carried out His will. But that is not the way God spoke: He really did say, in effect: "If you do this, I will do that; if you keep my law, you will be specially favored." These interpreters forgot that if God once gives His word, He owes it to Himself—even if not, technically, to His creatures—to do what He has pledged. So God did take upon Himself an obligation.

The inspired writers of the Old Testament clearly understood this situation. The prophets often compared God's relation to His people to that in marriage, in which both parties take on obligations, and receive claims. Speaking precisely of the covenant, God told His people through Hosea (2:18-25): "And it shall come to pass on that day, says the Lord, you shall call me 'my husband' and never more 'my Baal'.... I will betroth you to me forever." Similarly through Jeremiah (2:2): "Go and cry in the ears of Jerusalem: I remember the covenant-devotedness of your youth, the love of your espousal."[4] The language of Deuteronomy 26:17-18 is so bold that many modern versions do not dare to render it literally. But in the Hebrew it says: "You have caused the Lord today to say He will be a God to you ... and the Lord has caused you today to say you will be to Him a people, a special possession ... and to keep all His commandments." God seems really to have put Himself—we hesitate to say it clearly—on the same plane as His people as to the covenant, for the identical expressions are used of both sides. Obviously, He had bound Himself in the covenant.

St. Paul saw this fact clearly. In Galatians 3:16-18 he sees a diffi-

---

[3]*Cf.* W. Most, "A Biblical Theology of Redemption in a Covenant Framework," in *CBQ* 29 (1967) pp. 1-19.

[4]*Cf.* also Jer. 3:1; Ez 16:8; Is 50:1; 54:5; 62:5.

cult problem:

> . . . the promises were made to Abraham and to his offspring. It does not say "and to your offsprings," referring to many, but referring to one, "And to your offspring" which is Christ. This is what I mean: the law which came four hundred and thirty years afterward does not annul a covenant previously ratified by God, so as to make the promise void. For if the inheritance is by law, it is no longer by promise; but God gave it to Abraham by a promise.

To follow this difficult thought, we need to notice that Paul thinks he sees a conflict between two things: (1) God made a promise to Abraham, with no conditions involved. But then (2) 430 years later, God made a covenant, which Paul calls the law, and in it the same thing was held out which God had previously promised without any condition. So Paul asks: Did God go back on His promise in now asking for a condition, keeping the law? The answer need not detain us.[5] What we want to note is that Paul sees Sinai as a binding arrangement in which God's people must fulfill a condition, and then will get something. But, God had bound Himself to Abraham, without condition. Obviously, God still bound Himself 430 years later. If He had not, the two events would not seem parallel, and St. Paul would have seen no problem.[6]

At this point it is very helpful to delve more deeply into the reasons why God made a covenant—and afterwards to ask, secondly, the reasons why He gives favors under the covenant once it is made.

Why then did He make a covenant in the first place? The only answer is His own generous goodness, looking out for the welfare of humans, along with, as usual, His love of what right order calls for.

Once the covenant is made, we ask: Why does He gives His favors under it? Here we notice that there are two levels—a basic or fundamental level, a secondary, not basic level.

On the basic level, it is still out of sheer goodness on God's part that He gives His favors; no creature by his own power could possibly generate a claim on God.

---

[5]St. Paul says that since the Law could not give life, but the promise to Abraham (standing for salvation by faith) could do so—therefore, no conflict. This is a rabbinic type of solution. Really, both the promise and the law originally referred to temporal favors, which were extended at Sinai. Later as centuries went by there was a tendency to reinterpret in spiritual terms.

[6]Really, in Rom 2:6 St. Paul, speaking in a covenant framework, says that God "will repay each man according to his works." With the distinctions given in the following paragraphs above, this does not clash with Paul's theme of justification/salvation by faith.

But on the secondary level we find Him working out His usual two basic goals. By putting in a condition there can be titles for giving and receiving. His love of good order likes this fact. But, simultaneously, the condition, the law, also serves for the advantage of men, for the covenant law spells out what is needed to make us open, capable of receiving what our Father so generously wants to give. For His laws, as we saw earlier, are not for His benefit, but for ours.[7]

Ancient Hittite vassal treaties—on which some think the language of the covenant of Sinai was patterned[8]—did a surprising thing: they commanded love by the vassal. We ask: How can anyone command love? Yet Jesus does the same. When a doctor of the law from the Pharisees came to try to trap Jesus and asked Him (Mt 22:37-40): "Teacher, which command is greatest in the law?" Jesus replied in the words of the great Shema (Deut 6:5): "You shall love the Lord your God with all your heart and with all your soul and with all your mind." And, after adding the second commandment, love of neighbor, He went on to say : "On these two commandments depend the whole law [covenant law] and the prophets." So again, love is commanded. But again we ask: How is it possible to command love?

The root of the problem is the fact that so many people think love is a feeling. Some even equate "making love" with sex. But love had better be something more durable, more stable than a mere feeling. For love needs to be the basis of a lifelong commitment in marriage; but feelings are not dependable enough for that. Further, Christ commands us to love our neighbor—and then makes everyone our neighbor. Obviously I cannot at all moments have a warm feeling towards all men. Further, love of enemies would be impossible if love were a feeling.[9]

What love really is can be gathered from the words of John 3:16 "God so loved the world that He gave His only-begotten Son, so that

---

[7]Cf. 1 Cor 6:12: " 'All things are permitted'—but not all things are beneficial." Here Paul is quoting his own enemies who quote Paul's saying "You are free from the law" against Paul, to mean they are free to sin. Paul replies that sin brings harm even in this life. *Cf.* also St. Augustine, *Confessions* 1:12 PL 32. 670: "You have ordered it Lord, and it is true: every disordered soul is its own punishment."

[8]*Cf.* Dennis J. McCarthy, *Treaty and Covenant*, Rome, Pontifical Biblical Institute, 1963, and W. G. Most, *Covenant and Redemption*, St. Paul Publications, Althone, Ireland, 1975, especially chapter 3.

[9]Since love consists in willing or wishing good to another for the other's sake, we can wish the good of salvation, and even some goods in this life even to enemies, without much difficulty. Further, we must distinguish feelings of aversion from real enmity. More on these feelings in chapter 15.

everyone who believes in Him may not perish, but may have everlasting life." Now, if God's love led Him to go so far as to send His Son to a horrible death to bring us eternal happiness, then we must ask: What is that love in itself, so that its effect was to go so far for our happiness? Obviously, He must want, or desire, or will our eternal happiness. So it is clear: love is a desire, a will for the happiness and well-being of another, for the other's sake. (If I were to will good to another for my sake, not for his, then I would be using him, not loving him).

But a further problem arises. There is no difficulty in saying that love, when directed to any creature, is what we have said, willing good to the other for the other's sake. But can we really turn to God and as it were say: I hope you are happy, hope you are well off, that you get what you need? Of course not. He needs nothing, gains nothing from our "service."

So we must adjust our meaning somewhat when we apply the same word, *love*, to both God and to humans.[10] As we know, Scripture pictures God as pleased when we obey, displeased when we do not. As we have said several times, He cannot gain anything from our obedience, yet He wants it, just as a good father wants his children to obey because holiness and good order require that, and also because He wants to lavish his favors on the children: but if they are bad, he should punish, not reward.

So, since He is Generosity itself, it gives Him pleasure when we obey because then He can give to us effectively, when we are open to receive. Hence Jesus told His Apostles at the Last Supper (Jn 14:15-21): "If you love me, you will keep my commandments. . . . He who has my commandments and keeps them, he it is who loves me." Even more explicitly, St. John in his brief second Epistle tells us, in verse 6: "This is love [namely] that we walk according to His commands."

We can see now how wonderfully right is the saying of St. Irenaeus which we read in chapter 1: "God formed Adam, not because He stood in need of man, but that He might have someone to receive His benefits."

Interestingly, the Hittite vassal treaties we mentioned above, in commanding love were really commanding obedience. D. J. McCarthy, in an article in Catholic Biblical Quarterly, explained: "There is no question [in the treaties] of a tender, feeling love. It is simply a matter of reverence, loyalty, obedience, things subject to command and com-

---

[10]We are using the word love in an analogous sense, *i.e.*, in a sense that is partly the same, partly different, when applied to two different objects. In speaking of both divine and human things we constantly need to use analogous senses.

manded. It is the same attitude which Deuteronomy [6: 5]"—with its great commandment of love—"demands on the basis of the covenant relationship."[11] We mentioned briefly above that God wants us to obey so He can give favors, and so we can avoid the penalties built into the nature of things for sin. St. Augustine expressed this well in his *Confessions*, "You have ordered it, Lord, and it is true: every disordered soul is its own penalty."[12] The great Roman historian, Tacitus, in his *Annals* quotes from a letter sent by Emperor Tiberius to the Senate near the end of his life. Tiberius had holed up in the island of Capri, and was indulging himself in many horrid orgies of sex. But Tiberius wrote thus to the Roman senate: "May the gods cause me to perish, senators, even worse than I feel myself perishing now, if I know what to write to you or how to write it." Tacitus comments:

> His crimes and wickedness had turned into punishment for him. Rightly did the wisest of men say that if the souls of tyrants could be laid bare, one could see wounds and mutilations—swellings left on the spirit like lash marks on a body, by cruelty, lust, and ill-will. Neither the autocracy of Tiberius nor his isolation could save him from admitting the inner torments that were his retribution.[13]

The wisest of men to which Tacitus referred was Socrates, who in Plato's *Theatetus* said, "They [evil doers] do not know the penalty of wrong doing . . . it is not stripes and death . . . evil-doers often escape these, but a penalty that cannot be escaped . . . that they lead a life like the pattern into which they are growing."[14] To take a few more common examples: if a person becomes very drunk some night, the next day he will pay with a hangover. And if people indulge in premarital sex, they will seem to themselves to have love—chemistry makes a fine counterfeit—but not really have it. Later they will wake up and find themselves locked into a loveless marriage. So St. Paul was quite right, when he told the Corinthians—who had quoted his words about freedom from the law so as to permit licentiousness—(1 Cor 6:12): " 'All things are permitted to me'—but not all things are beneficial."

In passing, we can note the inescapable relation of the second commandment, love of neighbor, to love of God. If we really desire to please God, in loving Him, we will want not only to make ourselves

---

[11]Dennis J. McCarthy, "Notes on the Love of God in Deuteronomy and the Father-Son Relationship between Yahweh and Israel" in *CBQ* 27 (1965) p. 146.

[12]St. Augustine, *Confessions* 1:12. PL 32. 670.

[13]Tacitus, *Annals* 6. 6.

[14]Plato, *Theatetus* 176-77.

open to His favors, so He may have the pleasure of giving to us—we will want also to have everyone be open to Him, so He may have the pleasure of giving to them too. So we need not be concerned about finding a starter, as it were, for love of neighbor, trying to find good in him. It is enough to desire him to be good so God may have the pleasure of giving. And when we do see good in another, then of course, we have another motive, namely, wanting so good a person to be well off by being open to God's benefits. Further, in desiring the good of neighbor, for God's sake, and for neighbor's sake, we please God still more, and thereby become even more open to His benefits, which fact gives Him still more pleasure—and so on, in a spiral expansion.

Finally, when someone makes a vow with the right understanding of such an act, he as it were says to himself: "I want to embark on a path of pleasing God. But I know my instability, and I fear I may pull back after a while. So I will bind myself by vow, to try to prevent my failing God." In other words, intensity of love, of desire to please God, leads humans to bind themselves. Of course, God could not fear for His own perseverance in doing good, but yet, the very intensity of His love for us led Him to bind Himself by covenant, much as we bind ourselves by vows.

Thus does the covenant, in spite of its seemingly legal form, turn out to be a most wonderful invention of love.

Chapter 6: He Spoke Through the Prophets

Countless centuries before the Old Covenant, our Father planned to send His Son to us—actually, His plans are as eternal as His very being. For since He cannot change, He does not have one plan or decision now, another later. Nor does some plan arise today which had not been there before. Being utterly unchangeable, He is not in time; and so, He has no past, and no future. As we said before we think of creation as past, and the return of Christ at the end as future. But to the eyes of the Eternal Majesty, all is present, present all at once.

So it is most strictly true to say that He always planned to send His Son to become Man; and of course, then, He always planned for His Mother, Mary.[1]

But the manifestation and unfolding of these plans came and comes in the course of what we call time, and so we may trace the unfolding of what He always designs.

The great patriarch Jacob, son of Isaac, son of Abraham, was dying in Egypt. He called together his sons, and, moved by the Spirit, told them what things were to befall them and their descendants in the last days. His words about Judah are specially significant (Gen 49:10): "The scepter shall not depart from Judah, nor the ruler's staff from between his feet, until Shiloh comes, and his shall be the obedience of the peoples." Modern translators disagree much over the words which we have rendered "until Shiloh comes." But we are following the text as under-

---

[1]*Cf.* Vatican II, *On the Church* #61: "The Blessed Virgin, planned for from eternity along with the incarnation of the Divine Word, as the Mother of God, was the loving associate of the Divine Redeemer on earth, His associate in a singular way, more than others."

stood by the ancient Jewish commentators in the targums, and later Jewish tradition. The targums are ancient Jewish paraphrases, plus fill-ins, of the Old Testament. We have them for practically all the Old Testament, and in many places we have more than one. The date of composition of these targums is much debated, but one thing is sure: no matter when they were written, they reflect ancient Jewish understanding of the texts, without what is sometimes called "hindsight" through fulfillment in Christ, whom the Jews rejected. The Targum Neofiti confidently renders Genesis 49:10 thus: "Kings shall not be lacking from the house of Judah . . . until the time at which King Messiah will come."[2] A prominent modern Jewish scholar, Samson Levey, comments that this supposes the restoration of the dynasty of David, and he adds that other rabbinic sources, Midrashic and Talmudic, agree that the passage is Messianic.[3]

The sense is obvious: a Jewish ruler of some sort will not be lacking until the time of the Messiah. And so, historically, it was.[4] The Jewish state, reduced to the tribe of Judah, had its own rulers until 41 B. C., when Herod, the first non-Jewish king, began to rule. (He was half

---

[2]My translation, from Alejandro Diez Macho, Neofiti, *Targum Palestiniense*, Consejo Superior de Investigaciones Cientificas, Madrid, 1968. I. p. 331. Four Targums—Onkelos, Pseudo-Jonathan, Neofiti, and the Fragmentary Targum—all render, substantially, "until King Messiah comes." Onkelos omits the word king—perhaps a sign it was written in Macchabean times, when the word king would be considered treason. *Cf.* also W. Most, "Maria Conservabat Omnia Verba Haec" in *Miles Immaculatae*, Rome, 21 (1985), pp. 135-69, esp. pp. 141-42 (reprinted in *Faith & Reason* 11 (1985) pp. 51-76.

Jacob Neuser, a great Jewish scholar, gives us data that helps show the early date of the Targum on the prophets. (The same reasoning will apply to the Targum on Genesis, for Gen 3:15 and 49:10). In his *Messiah in Context* (Fortress, Philadelphia, 1984) he makes a great survey of Jewish literature from the Mishnah (around 200 A.D., the first great work after the fall of Jerusalem) to the Babylonian Talmud (closure 500-600 A.D.). In it we learn, step by step, that there was scant Jewish interest in the Messiah or prophecies about him until the Talmud. And even then, the only point of the major prophecies they mention is that the Messiah is to come from the line of David (Neusner, p. 175). So if the Targums were late—or at least, the portions dealing with these prophecies—it would be strange that they showed so much interest in the major prophecies of the OT on the Messiah at a time when Jewish theologians in general showed virtually no interest in them.

[3]Samson Levey, *The Messiah: An Aramaic Interpretation*, Hebrew Union College, Cincinnati, 1974, p. 8.

[4]If the Jews had not been so unfaithful to God, the actual line of David would have continued, instead of the tenuous rulers that actually came. *Cf.* 1 Kings 9:3-8.

Arab, half Idumean.) Then the time was ripe to hope for the Messiah, so that when Herod wanted to answer the Magi about Him, the King had no difficulty in learning from the Jewish theologians where the Messiah was born. They told him (Mt. 2:5-6): "In Bethlehem of Judah, for so it is written through the prophet: And you, Bethlehem, land of Judah, by no means are the least among the leaders of Judah. For from you there will come forth a leader who will shepherd my people Israel." The High Priests and scribes were quoting the prophecy of Micah 5:1. Levey comments that the Hebrew of Micah itself tends to support the idea of a pre-existent Messiah, even though that idea is not found in rabbinic texts.[5] The Targum Jonathan on this line reads: "From you will come forth before me the Messiah . . . whose name was spoken from days of old, from the days of eternity."[6] It is quite possible that the Targum meant the same as the Hebrew, for in Hebrew usage, the name is sometimes almost identified with the person.

Right after the sin of our first parents, God gave a prophecy of the Messiah to come in Genesis 3:15: "I will put enmity between you and the woman, between your seed and her seed. He will strike at your head and you will strike at his heel." It is fashionable among many modern commentators to refuse to see any mention of the Messiah in Genesis 3:15. There is only one woman on the scene, they say, and that is Eve, who was not the mother of the Messiah. Further, they continue, the very same Hebrew word *shuf* is used of both the seed of the woman and the serpent. So there is no hint of any victory, just a draw.

But again, there is help fom the Targums. Targums Neofiti, Pseudo-Jonathan, and the Fragmentary Targum all interpret Genesis 3:15 as Messianic. Their interpretation is, in part, allegorical. They say that the sons of the woman will observe the commandments of the Torah, and will fight the sons of the serpent, who are disobedient. But the Targums see a victory for the son or sons of the woman. So Targum Neofiti reads: "There will be a remedy [for the wound] for the son of the woman, but for you, serpent, no remedy."[7]

Besides, it takes quite a stretch of the imagination to suppose that the descendants of Eve (all humans, or just all women) are special enemies of evil, and are going to conquer evil. This is simply unrealistic, if we contemplate the human race today, or in the past. So we are led to see at least an opening to understand this text as meaning the Messiah.

---

[5] *Cf.* Levey, p. 93.

[6] My translation from the Aramaic in Brian Walton, *Biblia Sacra Polyglotta*, Academische Druck, Graz, Austria, 1964, III.

[7] My translation from Neofiti. *Cf.* also Genesis Rabbah 20.5, which also sees this verse as Messianic.

We, by our own mere human powers and knowledge, cannot strictly prove that the Messiah and His Mother were meant. But the providentially guided teaching authority of the Church can see things which weak human ability might not see. That is what Vatican II teaches in its *Constitution on the Church*. Speaking of the Old Testament, in which the history of salvation in Christ is gradually prepared, it says:

> These primeval documents, as they are read in the Church, and are understood in the light of later and full revelation, gradually bring more clearly to light the figure of the woman, the Mother of the Redeemer. She, in this light, is already prophetically foreshadowed in the promise, given to our first parents, who had fallen into sin, of victory over the serpent (*cf.* Gen 3:15).[8]

Earlier documents of the Magisterium of the Church prepared the way for this declaration of Vatican II. In the Bull defining the Immaculate Conception in 1854, Pius IX wrote that,

> The Fathers and ecclesiastical writers ... in commenting on the words [of Gen 3:15] taught that by this utterance there was clearly and openly foretold the merciful Redeemer of the human race ... and that His most Blessed Mother, the Virgin Mary, was designated, and, at the same time, that the enmity of both against the devil was remarkably expressed.

Pius XII, in the Constitution defining the Assumption in 1950, said that,

> Since the second century, the Virgin Mary has been presented by the Holy Fathers as the New Eve, who ... was most closely associated with Him in that struggle against the infernal enemy which, as foretold in the Protoevangelium [Gen 3:15] was to result in that most complete victory over sin and death.[9]

Pope John Paul II, in a general audience of December 17, 1986, said: "These words of Genesis are called the Protoevangelium, or the first announcement of the Messiah Redeemer. They reveal God's salvific plan in regard to the human race which after original sin is found in the fallen state which we know."

The passage of Vatican II which we cited above continues, saying: "Similarly, she is the Virgin who will conceive and bear a Son, whose

---

[8]Vatican II, *On the Church* #55.

[9]Pius XII, *Munificentissimus Deus*, Nov.1, 1950. AAS 42.768.

name will be called Emmanuel (*cf.* Is 7:14; Mich 5:2-3; Mt 1:22-23)."[10]

The Council was referring to Isaiah 7:14: "Behold the virgin shall conceive and bear a Son, and shall call His name Emmanuel." The Targums do not see a Messianic sense in this passage. However the Septuagint, the ancient Greek translation of the Old Testament, which is usually less inclined than the Targums to see a Messianic sense, translates Isaiah's word *almah* by Greek *parthenos*, virgin.[11] The Hebrew word *almah* means a young woman of marriageable age, who would be assumed to be a virgin. There was a more definite word in Hebrew *betulah*, for virgin. But the Septuagint definitely took *almah* to stand for a virgin here. This is important, because if we take the word for just a young woman, then an ordinary child could be meant. Jewish interpreters commonly thought it was Hezekiah, son of King Ahaz, to whom this prophecy was first spoken. If we read *virgin* then of course, the prophecy must refer to Christ. St. Matthew (1:23) definitely does take it that way, and quotes this prophecy to refer to the conception of Christ. So we must ask: Did not St. Matthew,[12] himself a Jew, know that Jews did not see it that way? Of course he did, and yet, guided by the the Holy Spirit, he did not hesitate to see the prophecy fulfilled in Jesus. St. Matthew did a similar thing in 2:15, where he saw the prophecy of Hosea 11:1 fulfilled: "And He was there [in Egypt] till the death of Herod, and so the word of the Lord through the prophet was fulfilled saying: Out of Egypt I called my Son." Again, St. Matthew surely knew that, in context, Hosea meant the whole people of Israel by "my son,"

---

[10]Vatican II, *On the Church* #55.

[11]R. Laurentin, in *The Truth of Christmas Beyond the Myths*, tr. M. Wrenn et al. St. Bede's, Petersham, 1986, p. 412 is in error in saying the Septuagint sometimes uses *parthenos* loosely. A check of every instance of its usage shows it is always precise, sometimes more so than the Hebrew (the context shows the sense intended). Laurentin appeals to Genesis 34:3, saying Dinah was called *parthenos* after being violated, but most probably this is the well-known Hebrew pattern of concentric narration. In the original French, Laurentin had tried to use Gen 34:4. Then, seeing that was a clear error—the Greek there did not have parthenos at all—he went back a step to verse 3, where one would have to suppose without proof that the Septuagint broke its consistent pattern.

Actually, there are only two places in the Old Testament where the Septuagint translates *almah* by *parthenos*. One of them is in Genesis 24:43, where the context clearly shows the girl is a virgin. The other is in Is 7:14. There are several other places where the *almah* is at least likely to be a virgin. But the Septuagint was so careful it used unstead a more general word *neanis*, which means simply "young woman."

[12]On the Matthean authorship of Matthew, see W. Most, *Catholic Apologetics Today*, Tan Books, Rockford, IL, 1986, pp. 48-58.

who were rescued from Egypt in the Exodus.

The key seems to be this: St. Matthew probably considered that prophecies, as divine words, could have multiple fulfillments.[13] In chapter 24 of Matthew, when the Apostles had asked Jesus what were the signs of the fall of Jerusalem, and also the signs of His return at the end, St. Matthew gives a long discourse by Jesus. In it practically everything can refer to both events. Similarly, St. Paul in 2 Timothy 3:1-5 says that, "In the last days, there will be difficult times. Men will be lovers of self. . . ." And he goes on to give a dismal litany of evil qualities.[14] And in 2 Timothy 4:3-4 he again says: "There will be a time when they will not tolerate sound doctrine. . . ." Commentators commonly say[15] that both passages refer both to all the time from the ascension to the return of Jesus, and to the time just before the end, a double reference.

In this perspective of multiple fulfillment, we could say that the prophecy of Isaiah refers both to Hezekiah and to Jesus.

We should add: There is a very solemn tone and setting to the prophecy, hard to understand if it foretells merely the birth of an ordinary heir to the throne. Further, the Hebrew has the word *ha* (the) with *almah—the* virgin. This seems to point to someone special. Also, the Hebrew says, "She will call him Emmanuel."[16] Normally, though not invariably, it was the father, not the mother, who gave a child his name.[17] So there could be an implication here that she was indeed a virgin, that the child had no human father.

Still futher, the wonderful child foretold in Isaiah 9:5-6 seems to be the same as the child foretold in 7:14, since it is generally agreed that both passages belong to the Book of the Messiah.[18] But the glorious description of 9:5-6 hardly fits Hezekiah. Isaiah 9:5-6 reads: "For a child is

---

[13]On multiple fulfillment, *cf.* W. Most, *Free From All Error*, pp. 25-30.

[14]The prophecies of 2 Timothy, and similar other texts, such as Luke 18:8 definitely rule out the unfortunate speculations of Teilhard de Chardin that just before the return of Christ at the end most of the world will be united in a glorious bond of love. Teilhard seems to have gotten a mental framework in his mind, into which these prophecies would not fit: therefore he did not see them. This phenomenon also accounts for how the Apostles could hear the several prophecies of Jesus about His death and resurrection and yet be surprised when it happened.

[15]*Cf. Jerome Biblical Commentary* on these passages.

[16]The Isaiah scroll from Qumran reads: "One will call." The Septuagint reads: "He will call," referring it seems to Ahaz. However, the text of the Hebrew was not fully settled at the time the Septuagint was translated.

[17]Sometimes the mother did give the name, e.g., Gen 4:1 & 25; 19:36; 32:1.

[18]The Book of Emmanuel runs 7:1-12:6.

born to us, a son is given to us, and the government shall be on his shoulder, and they will call his name wonderful counsellor, mighty God, everlasting Father, prince of Peace." The Targums have no doubt that the Messiah is meant in 9:5-6.[19] So if it is the same child as in 7:14, then the child of 7:14 must also be the Messiah. Why did not the Targums say so at 7:14? Some good modern Jewish scholars admit that the Jews, when they saw the use Christians could make of some prophecies, deliberately doctored the texts of Targums.[20]

The New American Bible is unwilling to render "mighty God" for Hebrew *el gibbor*. But *el gibbor* always elsewhere in the Old Testament means mighty God, never God-hero as NAB renders it. The Jerusalem Bible and the Revised Standard Version readily translate by *mighty God*.[21]

The Targum Jonathan also has no hesitation. It simply translates by *mighty God*. But the meaning of the Targum is disputed in another way. J. F. Stenning of Oxford renders: "And his name has been called from of old, wonderful counsellor, mighty God, He who lives forever, Messiah, in whose days peace shall increase upon us."[22] S. Levey, on the contrary, avoids calling the Messiah God by turning around the structure so as to say that "his name has been called Messiah by . . . the mighty God."[23] Levey claims he is just following the Targumic sentence structure. Stenning does not agree. Really, the Aramaic will stand either translation.

Obviously, the ancient Jews would have had trouble thinking the

---

[19]*Cf.* Levey, p. 46.

[20]*Cf.* Levey, p. 152 n. 10 and H. J. Schoeps, Paul, Westminster, Philadelphia, 1961, p. 129.

Jacob Neusner, probably the greatest of modern Jewish scholars, in his *Messiah in Context* tells us that the Jews once thought Hezekiah was the Messiah of Isaiah 7:14. Such was the opinion of the great Hillel, cited by Neusner on p. 173. But Neusner adds, on p. 190: "Since Christian critics of Judaism claimed that the prophetic promises . . . had all been kept in the times of ancient Israel, so that Israel now awaited nothing at all, it was important to reject the claim that Hezekiah had been the Messiah." Hence, the Talmud (*cf.* Neusner, p. 173) cites Rabbi Joseph as denying that Hezekiah had been the Messiah.

So we can now see how it is that the Targum sees Isaiah 9:5-6 as messianic, but does not see it for 7:14, when it is clear that the child in both passages is the same.

[21]A scholarly Jewish version, I. W. Slotki, *Soncino Books of the Bible*, Isaiah Soncino Press, London, 1957, p. 44 also renders "Mighty God," but manages by another device to avoid calling the Messiah God.

[22]J. F. Stenning, *The Targum of Isaiah*, Oxford, 1949, p. 32.

[23]Levey, p. 153, n. 31.

Messiah to be God. But at least, the Targums knew clearly that the child Isaiah foretold would be the Messiah.

The prophecy of Isaiah 53 has sometimes been called the Passion of Our Lord Jesus Christ according to Isaiah. It is truly remarkable. There is no doubt that St. Matthew's Gospel identifies Jesus as the Suffering Servant described in Isaiah, for Mt 8:16-18 says, "He cast out the spirits by a word, and healed all the sick, and so was fulfilled what was said through Isaiah the prophet saying [53:4] 'He took our infirmities and bore our diseases'."

Isaiah tells of the atoning, suffering and death of the Servant, who will have "no form or comeliness" who will be "despised and rejected by men," who has borne our griefs "... [and] was wounded for our transgressions ... was oppressed and afflicted, yet did not open his mouth ... like a lamb being led to the slaughter."

There is a clear indication that this is the Messiah in 53:2, which says the Servant grows up like a young plant. This plainly alludes to Is 11:1, which speaks of a shoot coming forth from the stump of Jesse. The Targum knows that 11:1 refers to the Messiah.[24] It also says explicitly, in its rendering of 52:13, that the servant is the Messiah.[25]

But then a strange thing happens. This passage, which beyond any possible doubt speaks of a meek and suffering servant, who opens not his mouth, like a lamb led to the slaughter, is made in the Targum into a proud aggressive person who subjugates mighty kings, and rebuilds the ruined sanctuary.

For example, the Scripture says in verse 3: "He was despised and rejected by men." But in the Targum we find: "Then the glory of all kingdoms will be despised and cease." Scripture has in verse 5: "He was wounded for our transgressions, he was bruised for our iniquities." In the Targum that becomes: "He will [re]build the sanctuary, polluted because of our sins, [and] handed over because of our iniquities." Where Scripture says in verse 7 that he was "like a lamb being led to the slaughter," the Targum says: "He will hand over the mighty ones of the peoples, like a lamb to the slaughter."

This of course is deliberate distortion. It is likely that the Jews were becoming unhappy with the use Christians were making of this passage, and so tried to stop them with such doctoring of the Targum. But, like Shakespeare's lady "who doth protest too much," they gave themselves away with their incredible distortion.

Still, we can gather this. The Targum does assure us that the Suffering Servant is the Messiah, and St. Matthew's Gospel tell us that the

---

[24]Levey, p. 49.

[25]Levey, pp. 63 & 67.

he is indeed Jesus. So this prophecy becomes astounding reading, for it tells that he was marred beyond human semblance, with no form, was despised and rejected by all, wounded for our sins. But His chastisement made us whole, and his stripes healed us. We needed that, for we had gone astray like sheep. Then God laid upon His Servant the iniquity of us all.[26] He was slain, and cut off from the land of the living.

But then, abruptly, verse 10 begins to speak of the Servant as alive again: He is to see the fruit of His labor, and be satisfied. He will be counted among the great. Strangely, John McKenzie finds the shift in verse 10 odd: "There is an obvious inconsistency between the death of the Servant (vss. 7-9) and what is said in these verses" (10-12).[27] The matter is strange only if one does not see in these lines a prediction of the resurrection.

If it is fundamentalism to read the Scriptures as if written by 20th century Americans, then it is at least close to fundamentalism to ignore the way the Scriptures were understood by the ancient peoples of the same language and same culture. Hence the Targums are an important aid to us, even though at times they may indulge in allegory.

If, then, we read the prophecies with the help of the Targums, we will see that they tell us that the words of the dying Jacob in Genesis 49 are to be taken as a prediction that the Messiah would come when self-rule finally departed from Judah, and that He would be born at Bethlehem. With the help of the ancient Septuagint, we can see that Isaiah 7:14 really did foretell the virgin birth of the Messiah. Turning again to the Targums, we can learn that the child of Isaiah 9:5-6, who really is the same as the child of 7:14, is again the Messiah, and if we put aside the fears that insistent Jewish monotheism generated, we can even see that the Messiah is the mighty God Himself. We can also learn that the Suffering Servant of Isaiah 53 is the Messiah, and, thanks to the fact that there the Targum "doth protest too much", in turning the meek servant into an arrogant conquerer, we can learn of the passion of the Messiah, and even, in verses 10-12, get at least a highly probable forecast of His resurrection.

Finally, we can get at least some help in seeing that the promise recorded in Genesis 3:15 does refer to the Messiah, and to His Mother, and the victory of both over the infernal serpent.

---

[26]Verse 6 has *all*; verses 11 & 12, referring to the same persons, has *many*. The reason is that Hebrew *rabbim* has the odd sense of "the all who are many." Hence a fluctuation is possible.

[27]John L. McKenzie, in *Second Isaiah*, Anchor Bible 20, Doubleday, N.Y. 1968, p. 132. *Cf.* p. 135 where McKenzie sees, but rejects, the presence of the idea of resurrection in the text.

What we see with some difficulty with the help of the Septuagint and the Targums, we can see in full clarity with the help of the providentially protected Magisterium of the Church, thanks to which, "These primeval documents, as they are read in the Church and are understood in the light of later and full revelation, gradually bring more clearly to light the figure of the woman, the Mother of the Redeemer," and of Her Divine Son, the Messiah, for both of whom the Father planned from all eternity, and both of whom He revealed gradually but sufficiently over the course of long ages, until the fulness of time should come.

Chapter 7: The Word was Made Flesh

"God who in many and varied ways spoke to us through the prophets, at the last, in these days, spoke to us through His Son, whom He made the heir of all things, through whom He made the ages." When the fulness of time came, according to His eternal plans and temporal prophecies, He sent a great prince of the heavenly court, Gabriel the Archangel, to the young virgin who was to bear a Son and call His name Jesus.

The angel's greeting was something never before heard: "Hail, completely graced." St. Jerome rightly translated it as "full of grace." Vatican II did not hesitate to adopt St. Jerome's translation.[1] We agree that that is the true sense of the word. But without the providentially guided teaching office of the Church, we might not have arrived at that complete sense. The Greek word in Luke 1:28 is *kecharitomene*. It is a rare form of an infrequent word. The word *charitoo* in general means to cause one to be in the state indicated by the root, favor or grace. It is a perfect participle, which expresses completion. The angel not only uses this perfect participle of *charitoo*, but uses it instead of a personal name. This use might be compared to our colloquial expression in which we say, for example, someone is "Mr. Tennis," which means he is the most outstanding of all for it. So instead of calling her by her name, Mary, the angel calls her "completely graced." (Therefore a translation that adds a noun, such as daughter is, strictly speaking, incorrect, and hides much of the force of the expression.)

Pope Pius IX, in the solemn document defining the Immaculate Conception, wrote:

---

[1]Vatican II, *On the Church* #56.

> He [the Father] chose and planned a Mother for His only-begotten Son . . . and attended her with such great love, more than all other creatures, that in her alone He took singular pleasure. Wherefore He so wonderfully filled her, more than all angelic spirits and all the Saints, with an abundance of all heavenly gifts . . . that she, always free from absolutely every stain of sin, and completely beautiful and perfect, presented such a fulness of innocence and holiness, that none greater under God can be thought of, and no one, except God, can comprehend it.

This sweeping statement definitely assures us that she was indeed "full of grace." Vatican II concurs: "Endowed with absolutely singular splendors of sanctity from the first instant of her conception, the Virgin of Nazareth is greeted by the messenger angel, by God's command, as full of grace."[2]

Did she, at that time, understand what she was being asked to do? Some have thouught she merely consented to be, if we may put it crudely, a body to produce a baby. But that is far from the truth. What the writers of the Targums saw in a limited way, she, full of grace, enriched "with an abundance of all heavenly gifts,"[3] would surely see clearly and fully.[4] Vatican II speaks strongly: "The Father of Mercies willed that the acceptance of the predestined Mother should precede the incarnation."[5] So what she accepted and consented to was not just to have a child, but to the incarnation. The Council continued: "so that thus, just as a woman contributed to death, so also a woman might contribute to life." The Council is alluding to the New Eve theme, found in virtually all the Fathers of the Church, especially in their comments on this scene, the annunciation. Vatican II explains further:

> Mary the daughter of Adam, consenting to the divine word, became the Mother of Jesus, and embracing the saving will of God with full heart, held back by no sin, she totally dedicated herself . . . to the person and work of her Son. . . . Rightly then do the Holy Fathers teach that Mary was employed by God not just in a passive way [as if not knowing what she was doing] but in free faith and obedience cooperating in human salvation. For she, as St. Irenaeus says, "by obeying, became a cause of salvation for herself and for the whole human race." Hence not a few ancient Fathers in their preaching gladly assert with him [St. Irenaeus] : "The knot of the disobedience of Eve was loosed through the obedience of Mary. That which the virgin Eve bound by disbelief, this the Virgin

---

[2]*Ibid.*

[3]Pius IX, *Ineffabilis Deus*, Dec. 8, 1854.

[4]*Cf.* W. Most, article cited in note 2 on chapter 6.

[5]Vatican II, *On the Church* #56.

Mary loosed by belief."

Clearly, she could not make the kind of acceptance of which Vatican II speaks if she did not know what she was doing.

Briefly, the fathers, with practically one voice—not often are they so unanimous—teach that just as Christ was the New Adam, who undid the damage wrought by the first Adam, so Mary was the New Eve. Just as the old Eve by her lack of faith in God's word contributed to bringing the disaster of original sin upon our race, so did Mary, the New Eve, by faith and obedience, contribute to reversing that harm: "She became a cause of salvation for herself and the whole human race," as St. Irenaeus said.[6]

To return to the fact that she knew, more than one Pope has taught she did indeed know that to which she was asked to consent. Pope St. Leo the Great, in his Homily on the Nativity, says,

> The royal virgin of the line of David was chosen who, since she was to become pregnant with sacred offspring, would conceive this divine and human child in mind before she did so in body. And so that she might not be frightened, in ignorance of the heavenly plan she learned from the conversation with the angel what was to be accomplished in her by the Holy Spirit.[7]

Pope Leo XIII in an Apostolic Letter, wrote: "O how sweetly, then, how pleasingly did the greeting of the angel come to the Blessed Virgin who then, when Gabriel saluted her, felt that she conceived the Word of God by the Holy Spirit."[8]

Really, the reason why some say she did not know what she was doing on the day of the annunciation is that the same misguided persons have convinced themselves that even He, her Divine Son, did not know who He was, although as we shall see later,[9] such a view not only lacks Scriptural or other proof, but flatly contradicts the reiterated, express teaching of the Church. But these persons in error continue their thought: If He did not know who He was, she must not have known, or she would have told Him. Actually, sometimes it is even hinted that perhaps there was no virginal conception—for then she would have known much, and would have told Him. But He was ignorant, so there may not have been any virginal conception.

---

[6]*Cf.* W. Most, "Coredemption: Theological Premises, Biblical Bases" in *Miles Immaculatae* 22 (1986) pp. 59-92.

[7]In PL 54.190.

[8]Leo XIII, EpiSt. , *Parta humano generi*, Sept 8, 1901. ASS 34, p. 194.

[9]In chapter 8.

Vatican II treats the annunciation account as fully factual,[10] so let us see for ourselves the implications of the account in St. Luke.

Before the day of the annunciation she, of course, like so many devout Jews, had been preparing for the coming of the Messiah, and, as Pope Leo XIII wrote, "The prayer of the Virgin surely had great force in [bringing] the mystery of the incarnation."[11]

Mary was at first frightened, as anyone might be at a supernatural appearance. The angel hastened to reassure her (Lk 1:30-32): "Do not be afraid, Mary, you have found grace with God. And behold, you will conceive in your womb and bear a Son, and you shall call His name Jesus. He will be great and will be called the Son of the Most High." Thus far she might not have gathered much of the nature of her Son, for the term "Son of the Most High" could be applied to any devout Jew—we think of Hosea 11:1, quoted by Matthew 2:15: "Out of Egypt I have called my son." The son meant the whole people of Israel, rescued from Egypt at the Exodus.

But things became clearer, for the angel continued (Lk 1:32): "The Lord God will give to Him the throne of David His Father." Many prophecies in Scripture—we have noted just one, Is 11:1[12]—had spoken of the Messiah as a son of David. So now she would readily grasp that her Son was to be the Messiah. But further (Lk 1:33): "He will reign over the house of Jacob forever, and there will be no end of His kingship." Most Jews believed[13] that the Messiah would live forever. That is why the Targum on Isaiah 53 could not see what was so obvious, that the Messiah (the Targum knew the Suffering Servant was the Messiah) would suffer and die, and the Targum reacted so vehemently as to make the Servant quite the opposite of what Isaiah foretold. But what most Jews could not see, that the Messiah of Isaiah 53 would suffer and die, Mary, full of grace, surely would see.

But now, those who wish to attribute ignorance to her must make a choice difficult for them: Since the angel said that her Son would reign forever, then either she would think of Him as the suffering Messiah of Isaiah 53 who was also to rise so as to reign forever, as we saw in chapter 6, or else, not thinking of Him as Messiah, she would have to reason: "Only God reigns forever, so my Son is to be God."

We insist that at least at this point in the angel's message she would think Him to be the Messiah. But there is more. For after her inquiry about how it should be carried out, since she "knew not

---

[10]*Cf.* W. Most, art. cit. in *Miles Immaculatae* 1985, pp. 161-66.

[11]Leo XIII, *Divinum illud*, May 9, 1879, ASS 29.658.

[12]*Cf.* W. Most, art. cit. in note 2 on chapter 6.

[13]*Cf.* Levey, p. 108.

man"—an implication of a vow or resolve of virginity[14]—the angel continued and explained (Lk 1:35): "The Holy Spirit will come upon you, and the power of the Most High will overshadow you. For this reason the Holy offspring will be called Son of God."

At this point Mary would readily grasp that her son was to be God, for the reason why He would be called Son of God was something unique: He would be called Son of God because the power of the Most High would overshadow her. That word had been used in the Old Testament to describe the Divine Presence filling the tabernacle in the desert (Ex 40:34) and similar language described the filling of the temple in Jerusalem with the Divine Presence at the time of its consecration.[15] The prophecy of Haggai 2:6-9 had said that the splendor of the Lord would fill the new temple with more glory than that of the old temple. But we need to note that precisely "for this reason," namely, because the Divine Presence would come upon her, her Son would be "Son of God."[16] This is obviously far different from the sense in which any devout Jew could be called a son of God. Her Son would be uniquely, naturally, the Son of God.

Further, since she, like any devout Jew, had often meditated on the ancient Scriptures, she knew the words of Isaiah 9:5-6 that the Messiah would be "Mighty God," as we saw in chapter 6. And although others, in the hardness of their hearts and stiff necks might not understand, certainly she, full of grace, could not fail to grasp the meaning. Really, when the angel came to Zachary to announce the birth of John the Baptist, it had already been indicated that the one whose forerunner John was to be would be God Himself. Using the words of Malachi 3:1, which in themselves foretold the coming of God personally, the angel said that John (Lk 1:16-17) "will turn many of the sons of Israel to the Lord their God. And he himself [John] will go before Him [God] in the spirit and power of Elijah."[17]

Mary at once acquiesced in what God asked through the angel. She, as Pope Leo XIII put it, consented "in the name of the whole human race," to be the Mother of the Messiah, the Mother of God.[18] "Behold the slave girl of the Lord," she said, "be it done to me accord-

---

[14] *Cf.* Neal M. Flanagan, "Our Lady's Vow of Virginity" in *Marian Studies* 7 (1956), pp. 103-21

[15] *Cf.* also 1 Kings 8:10.

[16] *Cf.* Manuel de Tuya, *Evangelio de San Lucas*, Biblia Comentada Biblioteca de Autores Cristianos, 3d ed. Madrid, 1977, pp. 26-27.

[17] *Cf.* R. Fuller, *The Foundations of New Testament Christology*, C. Scribner's Sons, NY, 1965, p. 48.

[18] Leo XIII, *Fidentem piumque*, Sept 20, 1896. ASS 29.206.

ing to your word." At the very moment at which she was raised to a "dignity second only to God," as Pope Pius XI said,[19] she called herself slave girl, for that is the precise meaning of the Greek *doule*.

Throughout the centuries since that day, many privileged souls have reached such a point of spiritual development—without yet being Saints—that they have been allowed to perceive[20] the presence of God to them, to feel it, not with the senses, yet in a way that seems as real as putting a hand on a table. Beginning with the Annunciation, that divine presence began to be even physically within her, as her Son. But she, as Pius IX told us, was from the start so far advanced in holiness that, "none greater under God can be thought of, and only God can comprehend it."[21] It is obvious that she must have registered, as it were, that presence within her, that presence which was her Son. Had she not learned from the angel's words of His divinity, obviously at least by this means she would have.

We speak of this Annunciation as a joyful mystery, and so it was. But the joys of this life are seldom without alloy. This great joy brought with it a double trial, and the beginning of the sword to Mary. For that day was a most severe trial of her faith, and a beginning of very painful adherence to the will of God.

Her faith was tried, for she, like all faithful Jews, had had it hammered into them incessantly that there is only one God. Yet, from Gabriel's message, she knew that there is God the Father, and then, that her Son was God also. How can that be? We today have sunk into a sort of comfortable rut: we can speak of the Most Holy Trinity saying there are Three Divine Persons, but only One God. We have, in other words, become accustomed to this staggering truth, we have, we might almost say, developed a callous, becoming used to it. We do not of course understand how there can be three such that of each one we say He is God—and yet one plus one plus one does not equal three Gods, but one God.

She did not have such a formula of words, but, as we said, the formula of words does not let us understand: it is just that we have gotten used to it. She had had no time to get used to it. She knew she had to retain the faith of her fathers that there is only one God, yet to know of two who are God. How to reconcile? She did not know; she had to

---

[19]Pius XI, *Lux veritatis*, Dec. 25, 1931, AAS 23.513, quoting St. Thomas, *Summa* I.25.6 ad 4.

[20]*Cf. Teofilo de La Virgen del Carmen*, "Experiencia de Dios y Vida Mistica" in *De Contemplatione in Schola Teresiana*, Ephemerides Carmeliticae, 13 (1962) pp. 136-223, esp. 205-220.

[21]Pius IX, *Ineffabilis Deus*.

merely hold on in the dark, as it were, without any possibility of understanding. And that she did: she believed the unbelievable.

Did she also gather from the archangel's words that there is a third Divine Person, the Holy Spirit? We do not know for certain. The mention of the Holy Spirit in this message could have brought a different thought to her mind. Many times in the Old Testament there was a mention of the spirit of God, for example, the spirit that moved over the waters at creation. But the Jews did not think of that spirit as a person, only as a power or force emanating from God. So we have no means of knowing what impression the words *Holy Spirit* made on her. It could have been either way.

We do know that her reverence for the Divine Presence within her was most profound. As we saw earlier, so many souls today suffer from a spiritual sickness because they think only of the love and goodness of God—which are infinitely real—but they forget in practice His Infinite Majesty. She had never forgotten. Good Jews in her day would never pronounce His sacred name, Yahweh, not even in prayer, not even in reading the Scriptures. So great was their respect. But now she had Him within her, for nine months, as her Son!

Secondly, the sword began to pierce her heart. For she knew in full light what the targumists knew less clearly, that He was the Messiah. And she understood what they missed, that that Messiah was to be "marred beyond human semblance . . . despised and rejected by men, a man of sorrows, and acquainted with grief." She knew He would bear our griefs, be smitten by God and afflicted, wounded for our transgressions because the Lord would lay on Him the iniquity of us all. He would be cut off out of the land of the living, stricken for the transgressions of His people. She knew too of course that He would see the fruits of His travail, and would be accounted great, by living again. But just as a woman about to give birth does not find her pain lessened by the anticipation of a future baby, so neither did the thought of the future make Mary's pain any easier to bear.

Rather, the fact that she would have to live with this painful knowledge for so many years would, as it were, wear the skin thin, and make it all the more painful. That happened even to Him, divine though He was. As we will see in the next chapter, His human soul even at the moment of conception, because it had the vision of God, knew fully all He would suffer. He at this instant accepted, as the Epistle to the Hebrews tells us (Heb. 10:7), saying: "Behold I come to do your will, O God." Thus He echoed her *fiat* at this very moment. So, years later He told His apostles (Lk 12:50) "I have a baptism in which to be baptized—and how am I straightened until it is accomplished!" And when His passion was only days away, in distress He broke into a discourse to a crowd (Jn 12:27): "Now my soul is troubled. And what should I say? Father save me from this hour!"

Yet her fidelity never wavered: she adhered without any hesitation to the acceptance of the will of the Father that she had made in saying "*Fiat*, be it done to me according to your word."

Now at last God had a human Heart. Men could confidently feel they could understand many things about His ways, even though those ways are as high above ours as the heavens are above the earth. God always was Infinite Goodness, Infinite Love. But we needed a help to understand Him.

The very existence of this humanity, the very fact of this Incarnation, would have been enough to redeem countless worlds. For if we recall (chapter 3) the various ways in which God could have effected our Redemption, we will see that the mere fact of God becoming man meant that humanity was offering God a worship, a reparation of infinite worth.

St. Athanasius, along with the Eastern Fathers in general, has a remarkable way of looking at this fact. In his Second Oration against the Arians he wrote that the Son assumed our nature, "So that He, the original Maker, might remake it [and] make it divine in Himself . . . that He might join what is man by nature to that which is divine by nature, so that man's salvation might be firm."[22] Similarly St. Gregory of Nyssa wrote that at the Incarnation, "He was mingled with our nature so that it [our nature] by mingling with the divine might become divine."[23] The thought is this: our humanity was sick or wounded by sin; but in the Incarnation, God joined divinity to that sick human nature by union with the humanity of His Son, which became part of humanity; that contact with the divinity healed our ills, and made us partly divine.

The frail edge of the mind of one of our greatest philosophers, Aristotle, thought, as we have seen, that even his god was so far above men that there could be no thought of friendship. What would he have thought had he learned that the Word became flesh, and dwelt among us, making Himself man, so He might make us gods by participation! What if Aristotle heard that this God-man would even die horribly and shamefully for us! No wonder St. Paul told the Corinthians (1 Cor 1:22): "We preach Christ crucified, a scandal to the Jews, foolishness to the gentiles!"

---

[22]St. Athanasius, Oration 2.70. PG 26.296.

[23]St. Gregory of Nyssa, *Oratio Catechetica* 25. PG 45.65-66. *Cf.* Also St. Thomas *Summa* III.48. 1 ad 2.

Chapter 8:
Offertory of the Great Sacrifice

The Incarnation alone, from the very start, would have been enough to redeem us abundantly, as St. Athanasius explained (chapter 7). Yet, as we saw in chapter 3, the Father wanted to choose the richest, most abundant means of redemption, out of love of the objective order (chapter 4) and out of love for us. Further, it was not enough just to provide a means by which we could be saved. Strangely, it was also necessary to move us to accept His favors. Hence He determined to leave nothing undone that could be done.

We may be sure that as soon as possible after the birth of Jesus in a stable, St. Joseph found more suitable lodging. St. Matthew (2:11) tells us that later, when the Magi came, they found the child in a house. But that must have been some months after His birth, perhaps even more than a year, for Herod thought it necessary to kill all boys up to the age of two years.

Long before the arrival of the Magi, forty days after the birth of Jesus, Mary and Joseph took the Child to the Temple in Jerusalem, which was about five miles north of Bethlehem. The law of Moses (Lev 12) commanded that the mother of a boy come to the Temple to be purified. The boy was not, strictly speaking "purified," though St. Luke uses the word purification broadly of both Mother and Son. The boy was redeemed at a price of five shekels (Ex 13:1, 12-15). This redemption could have been carried out by giving the ransom to any priest anywhere in Israel. But Mary and Joseph preferred to come to the Temple for it.

Mary could have rightly said that no purification was needed for the birth of the Holy One of Israel, and that He, her Son, did not need to be bought back, redeemed, from the service of God—He came precisely to do the will of the Father, to redeem the world.

Later, when John the Baptist was reluctant to baptize Him, Jesus said (Mt 3:15): "Let it be, for thus it is right for us to fulfill everything that is right."

But even more, in the Temple, He wanted to offer Himself for the great sacrifice to come later. And His Mother willingly joined in that offering, even though she knew all too well, as we saw in chapter 7, what she was consenting to: His death.

The Epistle to the Hebrews pictures the attitude of His heart at the first moment of His conception (Heb 10:5-7). It was impossible for the blood of bulls and goats to take away sins. For that reason, when entering into the world He said: "Sacrifice and offering you did not desire, but a body you prepared for me. Holocausts and sin offerings did not please you. Then I said: Behold, I come—at the head of the Book it is written about me—to do your will, O God."

The Epistle to the Hebrews seems to be in the literary pattern of preaching, sermons, in which there may be fanciful things. But according to the teaching of the Magisterium of the Church, there is nothing fanciful here. In his great Encyclical on the Mystical Body, Pope Pius XII wrote:

> But the most loving knowledge of this kind, with which the divine Redeemer pursued us from the first moment of the Incarnation surpasses the diligent grasp of any human mind. For, by that blessed vision which He enjoyed when just received in the womb of the Mother of God, He has[1] all the members of the Mystical Body continuously and perpetually present to Him, and embraces them with saving love. In the manger, on the cross, in the eternal glory of the Father, Christ has all the members of the Church before Him, and joined to Him far more clearly and far more lovingly than a mother has a son on her lap, or than each one knows and loves himself.[2]

---

[1]We note the Pope uses the present *has* to indicate the eternity of His mind inasmuch as He was a Divine Person.

[2]Pius XII, *On the Mystical Body*, June 29, 1943. DS 3812. On the teaching of the Magisterium on His human knowldge, *cf.* W. Most, *The Consciousness of Christ*, Christendom College, Front Royal, 1980, chapter 7.

The chief objections raised to His knowledge were answered already in the Patristic age (*cf.* chapter 6 of *Consciousness of Christ*). Lk 2:52 says that when young He advanced "in wisdom and age before God and men." St. Athanasius saw the answer: "Gradually, as the body grew and the Word manifested itself in it, He is acknowledged first by Peter, then by all." (Oration 3 *Against the Arians*. PG 26.436). St. Cyril of Alexandria wrote: "How then was He said to advance? [It happened] when the Word of God ... measured out the manifestation of the divine gifts which were in Him, according to the

The Pope said that He knew and knows us all, individually, by means of "the blessed vision." The Pope means that the human soul of Jesus, from the very first instant of its existence, had the direct vision of God, in which all knowledge is available.

We need to note that the Pope speaks of the human soul of Jesus as knowing. Those who attribute ignorance to Jesus, are really speaking loosely, and when questioned they readily admit it. They do not mean that He, a Divine Person, failed to know anything. They mean that a given thing did not, as it were, register on His human mind or soul. But Pope Pius XII assures us that it really did register, that His human soul knew us from the first instant of His conception.

From the teaching of the Church we know the fact of His knowledge. But it is something else to explain just how this happened and happens. Here the Church supplies us with some facts, but we have to work a bit further on our own. It is fascinating to try it.

We need to examine separately two sets of data, and then to put the two together.

First, we look at what is required for the beatific vision, the direct vision of God, in any soul, not just the human soul of Jesus. We already saw (chapter 2) that this vision is so direct that there is not even an image involved. In seeing persons or things in daily life, we do not take the person or thing within us, we take instead an image. That works well enough with creatures; for an image is finite but so are the creatures we want to know. But Pope Benedict XII defined[3] that there is no image involved in the beatific vision of God. It is really obvious: no image, since an image is finite, could show us Him who is infinite. So, St. Thomas Aquinas drew the inescapable inference that the divinity must join itself directly to the human mind or soul, with no image in between.[4] This, then, is one requirement. The second requisite for the vision follows readily: since this vision is so lofty, so far above the possibilities of any conceivable creature, then the power of the creature to know must be elevated. Of course, this is done by grace, which transforms the soul, and makes it, as we saw, partly divine.

The second set of data we look at concerns the structure, as it were, of Christ Himself. The Council of Chalcedon in 451 A. D. defined

---

growth and age of His body" (*Thesaurus* 28. PG 75.428). As to Mk 13:32 where He Himself said He did not know the day of the end: Pope St. Gregory the Great wrote that Jesus knew the day "in His humanity, but not from His humanity" (Epistle to Eulogius DS 475-76).

[3]DS 1000.

[4]St. Thomas *Summa* Suppl. 92.1.c. and Contra Gentiles 3.52.

that He has two natures divine and human, but that He is only one Person. A person is the center to whom we attribute things, e. g. we say that he this man, John Smith, knows these things, experiences these things, does these things etc. If there were two persons in Jesus, then we could not say that a Divine Person redeemed us: the passion would pertain only to the human person in Christ, and so would not be of infinite worth.

But a problem arises: Apollinaris was an early writer of the Church who defended the true teaching of the Council of Nicea, that Jesus is divine. Apollinaris did not intend to found a heresy, but yet he did, Apollinarism. Apollinaris saw something quite true: that if we take two natures and put them together, if each is complete, there will be no union. For a crude comparison, if I put steel balls and glass marbles into a bucket, no matter how much I shake them, there is no union of the two. So, reasoned Apollinaris, if two natures, divine and human, are each complete, they cannot form a union.

Apollinaris was correct so far. He was also correct in saying: therefore there must be something missing in one of the two natures to let them join. But he went wrong when he tried to find what was missing: he said Jesus had no human rational soul. That was error, and the Church condemned that error as heresy.

But, as we said, Apollinaris was right in seeing something had to be lacking. Of course it could not be lacking in the divinity, so it had to be lacking in the humanity. What was lacking? It is not too hard to find out: The Church tells us that in Jesus there is only one Person. Now, a human nature made up of body and soul would normally be a person, automatically as it were. In the case of Jesus, His humanity did not become a human person. So it is human person that is lacking. Why? Because that humanity was "assumed," that is, taken over by the Divine Person. The humanity did not exist separately, it existed only in the Divine Person. So it did not become a human person: personhood was supplied by the Second Person of the Blessed Trinity.

But this fact shows us a union so close that there is nothing really parallel to it anywhere: the two natures are united in the unity of one Person, a Divine Person. (We call this the hypostatic union.) The whole humanity was in most immediate contact with the divinity, since together there was but one Person.

Now at last we can find the answer we have been seeking. Let us recall the requirements for the beatific vision in any soul: (1) elevation of its power to know by grace, and (2) immediate contact of the human soul and the divinity, with no image in between. We apply this to the case of Jesus. (1) His human soul was, of course, full of grace, with an absolute fulness.[5] (2) His human soul was in contact with the divinity, not just in the way an ordinary soul could be, but because that human soul—in fact, not just the soul, but the whole humanity—was in most immediate contact, or rather union, with the divinity, in a most unique union, so close that the two natures, human and divine, made up just one Person, a Divine Person.

Now we can see that it is not just by a special grant from the Father, not just by a fitting favor, that the human soul of Jesus saw the vision of God from the first instant: it is something strictly inevitable, from the very nature of His structure, if we may use that word. His human soul and mind was incapable of not seeing the divine nature, directly, without any image in between. As a result, He had before the eyes of His soul the infinity of the knowledge of God Himself. Of course, even His human soul was finite, and as such could not contain infinite knowledge all at one instant. But it did possess knowledge far beyond our ability to grasp, and certainly included, among other things, everything conceivable that pertained to His saving mission.[6]

So we can see now how Pope Pius XII could teach that the human soul of Jesus knew each member of His mystical Body individually, from the first instant. It was strictly inevitable.

Similarly, on the day of His presentation in the Temple, His human soul or Heart offered itself most fully, in the offertory of the great sacrifice. His Heart renewed and continued its dedication, of which the Epistle to the Hebrews told us: "Behold I come to do your will, O God."

To His, "Behold I come," Mary's fiat at the annunciation corresponded: "Be it done to me according to your word." This day in the Temple she renewed and continued that dedication to Him, to the will of His Father, though that cost her dearly, for already on the day of the annunciation she knew He was to suffer and be rejected, "the man of sorrows and acquainted with grief."

She was most painfully reminded of this when the saintly old man Simeon approached. Some scholars think he was the son of the great teacher Hillel[7] who expected the Messiah to come imminently. Be that

---

[5]Mary had a relative fulness of grace, *i.e.*, her human soul contained, as it were, all grace it could hold at a given point. Yet she could and did grow, since her capacity could increase.

[6]Even though at conception His physical or bodily brain was not yet formed, yet His human soul, by contact with the divinity, could and did have this knowledge. *Cf.* St. Thomas, *Summa* III.10.2.c.

[7]On the view that Simeon may have been the son of Hillel, see Juan Leal, *Evangelio de San Lucas*, La Sagrada Escritura, Madrid, 1973, p. 92.

as it may, it had been revealed to Simeon by the Holy Spirit that he would not see death until he had seen the Messiah, the anointed one of the Lord. The same Spirit revealed at this moment to Simeon that indeed He was at hand. With tears of gratitude welling up, Simeon prayed (Lk 2:29-32):

> Now you can dismiss your servant, Lord, according to your word in peace, for my eyes have seen your salvation, which you prepared before the face of all peoples, a light to remove the veil from the gentiles, and the glory of your people Israel.[8]

Then Simeon blessed them, and spoke directly to Mary His Mother (Lk 2:34-35): "Behold, He is set for the fall and the rise of many in Israel, and for a sign that will be contradicted. And your own soul a sword will pierce, so that the thoughts of many hearts will be revealed."

Mary had known already about that sword, but this inspired reminder must have addded to the pain. Her pain was the greater, of course, in proportion to her love for her Son. As we saw above, Pius IX taught that even at the start of her life, her holiness was so great that, "none greater under God can be thought of, and only God can comprehend it."[9] Now of course, holiness and love of God are interchangeable expressions. So her love of God was so great that no creature could understand it—only God could. But that immense love was, if we may say it, increased by the natural love of a Mother for her Son. But her Son was and is God, so the natural intensified the supernatural and the supernatural greatly multiplied the natural: our ability to calculate, to picture it, is simply exhausted. So we say with Pope Pius IX, "Only God can comprehend it."

On that day there was fulfilled what God had promised through Haggai the prophet (2:7-9): "I will fill this house with glory. . . . Great will be the glory of this later house, more than that of the first." The material splendor of the Temple of the day of Haggai was far from surpassing that of Solomon's Temple—and so people should have been able to see that much more was to come in the future, as St. Augustine

---

[8]Lk 2:33 says His parents marvelled at this. This need not imply previous ignorance. To marvel is an emotional reaction, which one may have even at a sunset after seeing many of them. Similarly Jesus marvelled at the faith of the centurion. Lk 2:50 similarly says they did not understand His reply when found in the Temple: they could know His divinity, yet be surprised at this sudden shift in His pattern—He had never left without notice before.

[9]Pius IX, *Ineffabilis Deus*.

later observed.[10]

Then too began the fulfillment of the great prophecy of Malachi, the last of the Old Testament prophets (3:1): "Behold, I send my messenger,[11] and he will prepare the way before me; and the Lord whom you seek will suddenly come to his temple, the messenger of the covenant, whom you delight in." The first messenger spoken of was John the Baptist, who was to prepare the way for God Himself, Jesus, the "messenger of the covenant." On this day of the presentation, God did suddenly come to His own Temple in Jesus. Jesus came unexpectedly, unknown to all save His parents, Simeon and Anna. "He came into His own, and His own received Him not." And even later, when He came with the brilliance of miracles, He was to be not accepted, but instead, the man of sorrows, acquainted with grief. That prospect, and death, He now accepted in His tiny heart. The Immaculate Heart of His Mother was at one with His Heart in that offering. As Vatican II put it: "She endured her union with her Son even to the Cross." For to carry out her fiat, her union with the future Victim, was hard beyond all our ability to calculate, as we shall see in chapter 10.[12]

---

[10]St. Augustine, *City of God* 18.45. PL 41.606.

[11]*Cf.* note 17 on chapter 7.

[12]Vatican II, *On the Church* #58; "endured" in Latin is *sustinuit*.

Chapter 9:
Cenacle and Calvary

During the many long years of seclusion at Nazareth, He willed to give us the supreme example of the value of even a seemingly ordinary life, lived in accord with the will of the Father. But even more, He willed by this very obedience to begin to redress the imbalance caused by sin.[1]

But the Father had planned to go further. Centuries earlier He foretold through Jeremiah (31:31-33):

> Behold the days are coming, says the Lord, and I will make a new covenant with the house of Israel and the house of Judah. Not like the covenant I made with their fathers, on the day I took them by the hand to bring them out of the land of Egypt. My covenant they broke, and I was a master over them, says the Lord. But this is the covenant . . . I will place my law within them and write it upon their hearts. And I will be their God and they shall be my people.

We saw how our Father made a covenant with the people of Israel at Mount Sinai. He promised in it to act as their kinsman, even their Father. The regular Hebrew word for the covenant bond, *hesed*, makes clear that He really would act as their kinsman. The ceremony of ratification of the Sinai covenant underscored this. After Moses came down from the mountain, he had holocausts and other sacrifices offered, and then (Ex 24:3-8): "Moses took half of the blood and put it

[1]Even though His public ministry was intrinsically worth more, yet He wanted, by spending about 30 out of 33 years in a seemingly ordinary life, to show the most important thing is for each one to do what the Father wills for him—that is of much more weight than the intrinsic variation in worth of the things done.

into basins, and splashed half of the blood on the altar. . . . And Moses took the blood and sprinkled it on the people, and he said: 'Behold, the blood of the covenant which the Lord has made with you'." In Hebrew thought (Lev 17:11): "The life of a living body is in its blood." So this rite of mingled blood taught the people that God was their kinsman.

But now, through Jeremiah, He had to tell His people that because they broke His covenant, He could not act as their Father, but only as their master. Really, there had been a long series of breaks in the covenant. Their Father tried to bring them to their senses many times, by sending foreign nations to oppress them. Each time, when they repented, He would send a great leader to deliver them. But finally their infidelity became so great that He handed them over into captivity in Babylonia, when Nebuchadnezzar II, in 597 and 587 B.C., took Jerusalem, destroyed the Temple, and deported most of the people to a strange land, to break their national spirit.

Yet even at this time He did not desert His people, but planned for their restoration, which He announced in the beautiful prophecy of Jeremiah which we just saw.

He said that the new covenant would not be like the old, for the old was broken—but there was the clear implication that the new would be unbreakable.[2] Further, the old covenant was inscribed on tablets of stone, but as to the new He said: "I will place my law within them, and write it upon their hearts."

In spite of these differences, the new was to be parallel to the Sinai covenant on the really essential points. Sinai had brought into being a people of God; in the new: "I will be their God and they will be my people." The old people had been promised God's favor on condition of their obeying the covenant law; in the new, the law would not be on stone tablets, but would be written on hearts.

In the old covenant, He had pledged to act as though He was the kinsman of His people. But in the new covenant, He actually took on our flesh, and so became most literally our kinsman, our brother, who would even mingle His blood with ours in the Eucharist.

The great fulfillment of this prophecy of Jeremiah did not come in the period just after the end of the exile. Rather, the expectation of

---

[2]Vatican II, *On Divine Revelation* #4: "The Christian regime, as the new and definitive covenant, will never pass, and now no new [public] revelation is to be expected before the glorious manifestation of Our Lord Jesus ChriSt. " Therefore all other revelations are technically called private, even if addressed to the world, like Fatima. The Church does advance in its penetration into the content of public revelation, relying on the promise of Jesus in John 1:26 to send the Holy Spirit to lead the Church into all truth.

Jeremiah looked to the future. Vatican II, in its *Constitution on the Church*, quoted the chief part of this prophecy, and continued: "Christ instituted this new covenant, that is, the new testament in His blood, calling together a people from Jews and gentiles, which would be ... the new People of God."[3]

The obedience of the people in the old covenant had been poor. But even though the obedience of the people was still required in the new, at their Head would be Christ, the New Adam, whose obedience was perfect. For He (Phil 2:7-8) "emptied Himself, taking on the form of a slave ... being made obedient even to death, death on a cross."

He pledged that obedience in the Cenacle, on the first Holy Thursday night. He could have done it by signing a document, or by reciting equivalent words and accepting. But He actually chose to make a dramatized form of acceptance of the Father's will. So He took bread and wine and said over them: "This is my body.... This is my blood." Now if body is here and blood there, the man is dead. So in this way He wanted to indicate His acceptance of death on the cross.

We today are less accustomed to such forms of expression, so let us translate. It is as if He were saying to the Father: "Father, I know the command you have given me: I am to die tomorrow. I turn myself over to death. I accept, I obey."

He pledged His obedience that evening; the next day He carried out what He pledged.

But still further: Moses had sprinkled the blood of animals on the people to indicate that they were becoming God's blood relatives. Jesus did more. He instituted the Eucharist then to give us His blood to drink and His body to eat—a sort of transfusion, to make us His brothers.

What a time He chose to do it! The very time when our race was about to do its worst to Him, to make Him most fully the man of sorrows, acquainted with grief, and rejected by men! We, if someone mistreats us, find it hard to want to be close to that one again. He at this very time chose this strictly marvelous means of getting so close to us as to want to come inside us, as our food.

Right after this pledging of the new covenant, He took the eleven remaining Apostles—Judas was absent, busy betraying Him—and went down the southern slope of the hill on which Jerusalem stands, across the brook Kedron, and, by the light of the full moon—for it was Passover—ascended the side of the opposite hill, the Mount of Olives. Leaving all but three near the gate of the grove, He went in further with Peter, James and John. Then He dismissed even them, and went on a little way, and began to be "frightened and troubled." Yes, the original

---

[3]Vatican II, *On the Church* #9.

Greek of St. Mark (14:3) does have that incredible word, *ekthambeisthai*, "to be frightened."

We ask ourselves: How is it possible that the God-man, who knows all things, could be in fear? The answer is clear. He was truly man as well as truly God. When Satan after His 40 days fast in the desert suggested to Him to turn stones into bread, He treated it as a temptation. Why should it be a temptation? Was it unreasonable for Him to eat after the long fast? Or did He not have the power to turn stones into bread? But the reason was this: As St. Paul said, He had (Phil 2:7) "emptied Himself, taking on the form of a slave." He could not, of course, empty Himself of divinity, so as to no longer be God. But He could, and did, decide He would never use His divine power for His own comfort—for others, to heal their infirmities, yes. But not for Himself. And so, though His divinity could have rescued Him from this fear, in fact, from the entire ordeal, yet it was the will of the Father that He suffer it. And human nature, unsupported, will suffer the shrinking-back emotion of fear in the face of terrible suffering and death.

He even, according to the inspired physician, St. Luke (22:44), fell into a sweat of blood. Any good medical dictionary lists such a condition; it is hematidrosis. It occurs when the interior tension is so acute—if the victim does not lose consciousness—that the small blood vessels adjacent to the sweat glands rupture, and pour out their red fluid through those openings.

How could He suffer so terribly? Did not many other men in ancient times face execution, execution in the same form He was to suffer? Yes, but there were two special features to His suffering. First, He had alway known it was to come, had known every hideous detail in merciless, glaring clarity. His human soul, from the first moment of its existence, had the vision of God, as Pope Pius XII told us.[4] In that vision He could see all—and He saw even this moment. It must have been a nagging, wearing, eating thing, protracted through His entire lifetime. When we foresee something dreadful ahead, we can always take refuge in the thought: Maybe it will not happen, or maybe it will not be so bad. The clarity of His vision left Him no such help.

We saw already that one day during His public life He admitted to His disciples (Lk 12:50): "I have a baptism in which to be baptized; and how am I straitened until it is over!" In other words, He knew the waters of tribulation into which He was to be plunged. The thought would gnaw at Him interiorly until He could get it over. Again, only a few days before His passion, in front of a great crowd in Jerusalem, He suddenly interrupted His discourse and gave way to such feelings and exclaimed

[4]See notes 2 & 6 on chapter 8.

(Jn 12:27): "Now my soul is troubled. And what should I say? Father, save me from this hour!" Most persons at some time have suffered a nightmare during sleep: something frightful was chasing them, they were almost paralyzed, could not move, it was about to seize them—when suddenly, and gratefully, they woke up. But imagine Him, when the lifelong nightmare did finally catch up with Him, and He knew fully there was no escape.[5]

St. Margaret Mary, who received the great Sacred Heart revelations, tells of a vision:

> I saw this divine Heart as on a throne of flames, more brilliant than the sun and transparent as crystal. It had its adorable wound, and was encircled with a crown of thorns.... It was surmounted by a cross, which signified that from the first moment of His Incarnation, that is, from the time this Sacred Heart was formed, the cross was planted in it, that it was filled, from the very first moment, with all the bitterness, humiliations, poverty, sorrow, and contempt His sacred humanity would have to suffer during the whole course of His life and during His holy Passion.[6]

The second reason He could suffer so much in Gethsemani was the pain of rejection by the very ones whom He was dying to save. The pain of rejection is proportioned to two things: to the form the rejection takes, and to the love the rejected one has for the one who rejects.

How great was His love? If love is, as we saw, a desire, a will for

---

[5]Another very human reaction: Jesus was humanly distressed at the repeated dullness of His Apostles. In Lk 22:35-38 He had told them that he who did not have a sword should sell his coat and buy one. They replied: "Here are two swords." As so often, they missed what He meant. So He just replied, "Enough," as if to say: I have had enough of this dullness. And what were His feelings when they as it were failed their final exam, when just before His ascension they asked when He would restore kingship to Israel (Acts 1:6)—they still did not see His kingdom was spiritual, not temporal.

Also, He allowed Himself to weep at the tomb of Lazarus, just a friend, though He knew in seconds He would bring Lazarus out. He wanted to show us the true human feelings He had, and to teach us that Christianity is not Stoicism. So Pius XII, in *Haurietis aquas*, teaches that He had a threefold love for us: the love proper to His divine nature, the love of His human will (in willing us eternal happiness) and the human love of feeling, which, as we see in chapter 16, is the normal somatic resonance to love in the human will.

On Hebrews 5:8, which says Jesus "learned obedience," *cf.* chapter 16 at note 13. *Cf.* also articles by W. Most, "Jesus Christ, Yesterday, Today and Forever" in *Homiletic & Pastoral Review* June 1983, pp. 9-16 and *ibid.* Nov. 1985, pp. 31-32, 50-54, "Did Jesus Ever Worry?"

[6]St. Margaret Mary, *Letters*, tr. C. Herbst, Men of the Sacred Heart, Orlando, 1976. Letter 133, p. 216.

the well-being of another, then His love is immense in two ways. First, the well-being He wants us to have is not just a happy life for a hundred years: it is happiness forever. And He wants for us not just the happiness that is proper to a human being. For each animal, God has planned satisfaction proper to that kind of animal. But for us, He wills not just human satisfaction: He wants us to have the life of God Himself, for He has literally made us sharers in the divine nature. Secondly, His love was so strong that it could not be stopped even by so immense an obstacle as the Passion. We know that a small love can be blocked in its striving for the happiness of the beloved by a small obstacle. A great obstacle is needed to stop a great love. But what a love was this, that did not say, in the face of a sweat of blood, in the face of the cross: this is just too much; I would like them to be happy, but enough is enough. No, He went right ahead. His love for us was really measureless. We saw, with the help of the words of Pius IX, that Mary's love of God was so great that only God can comprehend it. What must the love of the God-man Himself for us be!

We said that love is measured by the love of the rejected one, and by the form the rejection takes. If someone just jostles me rudely in a crowd, I may feel slightly offended. If he beats me physically, it is far worse. But what if he wants to kill me, and is not satisfied with just death, but wants to kill me in the most horrid way he can think of!

So then, a strictly measureless love is rejected in the worst way conceivable. The pain of such a rejection is beyond our power to picture. Hence He is reported to have told St. Margaret Mary in a vision: "I feel this [the ingratitude and contempt of men] more than all I suffered during my Passion."[7] No wonder, the spiritual pain of rejection, being of a different, a deeper order, far surpasses mere physical pain, though that in Him was dreadful too.

There was not only rejection of His love. His very intelligence was outraged, insulted, when His Sacred Head was crowned in derision, and he was treated as a fool. Yet that Sacred Head was most literally the human physical organ of Divine Wisdom, the instrument of the Holy Spirit, who in the human order, moved Him in all things.[8] That human intellect, illumined by the vision of the divinity, saw each one of us even during the Passion. As Pius XII said, "In the manger, on the cross, in the eternal glory of the Father, Christ has all the members of the Church before Him, and joined to Him far more clearly, and far more

---

[7]St. Margaret Mary, *Autobiography*, Visitation, Roselands, Walmer, Kent, 1952, #55, p. 70.

[8]On this see chapter 23, especially the quotation from St. John of the Cross at note 6.

lovingly than a mother has a son on her lap."[9] Of course, no human heart can love someone it does not even know. But thanks to the unimaginable brilliance of His human intellect, which knew each of us individually, His Heart was enabled to love each of us individually, even when we rejected both His intelligence and His love.

To say that this "enabled" His Heart to love needs a certain qualification. When we ordinary humans love, we are stimulated to it by seeing some good in the one we love; but He, precisely at this point, saw in us not something lovable, but instead, sin, sin that was weighing down on Him at that very moment. Yet, as St. Paul tells us, He (Rom 5:8) "proved His love for us, because when we were still sinners, Christ died for us."

The divinely illumined wisdom of His human mind still directed His Heart to love us, not because of, but in spite of what it knew, in the only utterly disinterested, purely generous love the universe has ever seen.[10]

And, of course, His pain was compounded immeasurably by the nearly infinite weight of sin for which He was to atone. St. Paul puts it dramatically (2 Cor 5. 21): "Him who did not know sin, He made sin for our sakes, so we might become the righteousness of God in Him."[11]

The immeasurability of His love comes out even more clearly with the help of the covenant framework. A covenant is something like a contract: "I will do this, if you do that." Now anyone who makes a contract wants to at least think he is getting in return something of at least equal value to what he gives, else he will not make the contract. So in the contract of the new covenant, the Father obliged Himself to give something of the same worth as the (1 Cor 6:20) "price" of redemption, to use St. Paul's word. But that price of redemption was really beyond infinity—for if even the smallest act of an Infinite Person, the God-man, was of infinite worth, what was such suffering worth! So the Father obliged Himself to give an infinite treasury of grace, favor, forgiveness to the new People of God, who were to come into being, and receive

[9]See chapter 8 note 2.

[10]On the cost to His Mother on Calvary, see chapter 10. Her love for us too was without a starter: she saws no actual good in us at the time, but loved because He loved us and so willed.

[11]The same sort of expression appears in Gal 3:13, where St. Paul says He became a curse for us. Hebrew sometimes used a noun where we would expect an adjective, *e.g.*, *curse* where we would expect *cursed.* Further, St. Paul probably was using the mystery religion framework—not turning Christianity into a mystery religion, but using that mode of expression to help convey ideas to people so familiar with it then. In it, if one went through, at least ritually, the same things a god went through, he obtained the same result.

His benefits through this covenant. If we used legal language, we would say that an infinite objective title to grace and forgiveness for us was created by the new covenant.

But there is more. St. Paul wrote to the Galatians that (2:20) "He loved me and gave Himself for me."[12] Legal language will make this clearer: it means that the Passion, in the new covenant, not only created an infinite objective title in favor of mankind in general; it created an infinite objective title in favor of each individual man! This is the measure of measureless love!

We saw in chapter 4 that there are two great principles in God's ways: His love of us, and His love of the objective order or objective goodness. We saw too that Pope Paul summed up beautifully the conclusions we reached on the objective order when he taught that:

> Every sin brings with it a disturbance of the universal order, which God established in unspeakable wisdom and infinite love.... It is therefore necessary for the full remission of sins and reparation, not only that friendship with God be restored by sincere conversion of heart, and that the offense to His wisdom and goodness be expiated, but also that all the goods, both personal and social, and those that pertain to the universal order, diminished or destroyed by sin, be fully restored.[13]

Since sin, under one aspect, is infinite in that the Person offended, God, is infinite, only a God-man could fully restore the damage to that universal order. Hence the same document of Paul VI could speak of "the infinite and inexhaustible price that the expiation and merits of Christ have before God, offered that all humanity might be liberated from sin."[14]

Read in this light, we can see the marvelous depth of Romans 3:24-36. It refers to us

> being made righteous gratuitously [without our having earned it] by His grace, through the Redemption that is in Christ Jesus, whom God publicly set up as a means of expiation through faith in His blood, to manifest His righteousness [concern for the objective order][15] because of the

[12]Not only St. Paul, a special person, could speak thus. Vatican II explains (*Church in Modern World* #22): "Each one of us can say with the Apostle: 'the Son of God loved me, and gave Himself for me'."

[13]Paul VI, *Indulgentiarum doctrina*. AAS 59, p. 7.

[14]*Ibid*. pp. 11-12.

[15]This is the correct meaning of the words of St. Paul, "justice of God." *Cf.* chapter 4. Many commentators think the phrase means God's saving activity. This is not wrong, but shallow. His concern for righteousness or objective order leads Him to save when His people fill their condition. Otherwise, the

> passing over of sins committed in [the time of] the patience of God, to manifest His righteousness in the present time; so that He is righteous, and makes righteous the one who [depends on] faith in Jesus.

The sense is this: We are made just, instead of being sinners, without having earned it. But Jesus did earn it. He is the new propitiatory,[16] foreshadowed in the Old Testament propitiatory. That is, He is the means of expiation, of balancing the objective order. The benefit of this goes to those who have faith in His blood. In all of this, God shows He Himself is righteous, that is, concerned over balancing the objective order. During the time of His "passing over sins," the Old Testament period, that was not really clear. It is true, He did punish sins then, at times openly and dramatically. But the punishment could not at all really balance the scales, for as we saw, sin has an infinity about it. So God's intention to rebalance was not yet clear. But now with the infinite expiation accomplished by Jesus, it is fully evident that God is righteous, concerned over objective morality. And He makes righteous those sinners who depend for their righteousness on faith in Jesus.[17]

We said that now we can see the depth of this passage, because if we read it without this background of rebalancing the universal objective order, the death of Jesus would seem merely like a New Testament ceremony or liturgy, the new version of the Old Testament propitiatory. But then the thought would be shallow, and we would have to ask: Why such a painful death merely as a means of ceremony or liturgy?[18]

---

passage of Romans cited above leaves a puzzle: Why would the Father want His Son to endure such things, if it were merely to set up a new propiatory, a new liturgical ceremony? *Cf.* chapter 4, note 2, and chapter 5 note 6 (on Romans 2:6).

[16]In the old covenant, the propitiatory or mercy-seat was a flat, oblong plate of gold which was placed on the top of the ark of the covenant. At each end were fastened images of cherubim, each facing the other, with wings spread. Once a year on the Day of Atonement, the High Priest could enter the Holy of Holies, raise a cloud of incense, and sprinkle the propitiatory with the blood of a sacrificed bullock. *Cf.* Ex 25:17-20 and 37:6-9 for a description of the plate. For the ceremony: Lev 16:2 & 11-17.

[17]Paul uses the word *faith* to mean total adherence of a person to God, which requires: if God speaks a truth, we believe in our mind; if He makes a promise, we are sure He wll keep it; if He gives a command, we obey—all done in love. *Cf.* W. Most, *Catholic Apologetics Today*, Tan Books, Rockford, 1986, chapter 18, and Vatican II, *On Divine Revelation* # 5. Luther greatly misunderstood Paul's concept, as the Protestant reference work, *Interpreter's Dictionary of the Bible*, admits (Supplement volume, 1976, p. 333).

[18]Modern interpretations of Col 1:24 are commmonly shallow—they say it means merely that Paul had to endure hardships to preach the Gospel. True

There is another aspect to Calvary, that of sacrifice. A sacrifice consists of two elements: the external sign, and the invisible or interior dispositions which the sign expresses and promotes.[19] In the Cenacle, and in the Mass, the external sign is the seeming separation of body and blood, by having the two species, bread and wine, separated. On Calvary the external sign was actual physical death. But in the Cenacle, on Calvary, and in the Mass, the internal dispositions are the same, those of the Heart of Jesus. They include of course, adoration and love of the Father, and the intention to atone, to rebalance the universal order, "so that sins may be forgiven" as we hear in the consecration of the Mass. But most prominent, according to Vatican II, and as we could see from covenant theology alone, is His obedience. The constitution on the Church teaches that: "By His obedience He brought about redemption."[20] This is an echo of St. Paul's words in Romans 5:19: "Just as by the disobedience of the one man, the many[21] were constituted sinners, so also by the obedience of the one man, the many will be constituted righteous." St. Paul is bringing out the parallel between Christ and Adam. Adam, the first head of our race, plunged us into the ruin of original sin; Christ, the new Adam, the new Head of our race, reversed that damage by His sacrificial death. Similarly, St. Paul told the Philippians (2:7-8): "He emptied Himself . . . being made obedient even to death, to death on a cross." The first Adam became disobedient even to death,[22] for his sin brought death on himself and our whole race; the second Adam became obedient even to death. For mere physical suffering and death, without such interior dispositions, would have been only a dreadful miscarriage of justice: it would not have had any redemptive value. But when done as an act of obedience, then that death was a sacrifice, was able to redeem countless worlds.

Pope Paul VI brought this out beautifully in an Address of October 5, 1966. He said that the obedience of the members of Christ

> is first of all a penetration and acceptance of the mystery of Christ, who saved us by means of obedience. It is a continuation and imitation of this fundamental act of His: His acceptance of the will of the Father. It

---

but shallow. Really, Paul knew that he, as a pastor and member of Christ, could and should help to make up for the deficiencies of his flock in rebalancing the objective order. *Cf.* again chapter 4.

[19]*Cf.* St. Augustine, *City of God* 10. 19 & 20. PL 41. 297-98.

[20]Vatican II, *On the Church* #3.

[21]The word *many* stands for Hebrew *rabbim*, the *all* who are many. Whenever St. Paul uses Greek *polloi* as a noun, he means *all*, as we can see, for example, from several uses of the word in Romans 5:15-19.

[22]The fine phrase is in St. Augustine's, *City of God* 14. 15. PL 41. 423.

is an understanding of the principle which dominates the entire plan of Incarnation and Redemption.[23]

Nor are we neglecting love when we make obedience central. For as we saw in chapter 5, our love of God is in practice identified with obedience.

Thus this obedience-love of the Heart of our great High Priest won, through sacrifice and covenant, an infinite claim on the Father, a claim not just for our race in general, but for each individual person.

[23]Quoted from *Davenport Messenger,* November 17, 1966, p. 7.

Chapter 10: Infinitely Beyond Infinity

We have not yet seen an important aspect of the great sacrifice of Calvary. We saw in chapter 3 that our Father had many options open to Him when He decided to restore our race. First, He could have forgiven without any rebalancing of the objective order, but His Holiness wanted that rebalance; second, He could have arranged for an inadequate reparation, one offered by some mere human; third, He could have sent His Son to make a full restoration of the universal objective order by just being born in a palace and never dying at all. So He quite literally went beyond infinity in deciding to go from the palace to the stable and to the cross.

We noticed in all this that His policy seemed to be this: He would never be content with anything less, if more could be added. But something more, though finite, could be added to infinity beyond infinity. Just as He could have made the entire redemption consist in the second option, in having some mere human perform some act of religion, so, obviously, He could add Mary's contribution to the great sacrifice.

Did He actually do that? Vatican II, speaking of her on Calvary, wrote:

> . . . in suffering with her Son as He died on the cross, she cooperated in the work of the Savior, in an altogether singular way, by obedience, faith, hope and burning love, to restore supernatural life to souls. As a result, she is our Mother in the order of grace.[1]

This is an extremely rich statement. We need to look at it a bit at a time. First, we see that "she cooperated in the work of the Savior," which was "to restore supernatural life to souls." That clearly means

[1]Vatican II, *On the Church* # 61.

she shared in some way in the redemption.

In what way? Even without the help of Vatican II we would see that she contributed by the mere fact of being the Mother from whom He received a human nature, which made His death possible. But Vatican II, following several previous Popes, goes beyond that, and teaches that she shared on Calvary itself: "In suffering with her Son as He died on the cross." In what way did she share? "In an altogether singular way." This clause is needed to tell us that her sharing was entirely unique. For Pius XI in an address to young people engaged in Catholic Action had urged them to become "co-redeemers."[2] He meant this only in the broad sense that we can further the work of applying the fruits of the redemption. He was not speaking of the previous stage of the work of acquiring once for all, in the first place, that infinite treasury, on Calvary. But the Council, to prevent anyone from taking its words about her cooperation only in a loose sense, insisted that her sharing was "in an altogether singular way."

Now Jesus, as we saw in the last chapter, redeemed us precisely though His obedience: "By His obedience He brought about redemption," Vatican II had said.[3] Now the Council teaches that Mary shared in His work precisely by obedience, along with faith, hope and burning love, which are other aspects or parts of the interior disposition of His Heart in the great sacrifice.

The Council places special stress on this point of obedience. A few paragraphs earlier, it had written about her:

> Rightly then do the Holy Fathers teach that Mary was employed by God not just in a passive way [in the incarnation] but she cooperated in human salvation in free faith and obedience. For she, as St. Irenaeus said, "By obeying became a cause of salvation for herself and for the whole human race." Hence not a few ancient Fathers in their preaching assert with pleasure with him: "The knot of the disobedience of Eve was loosed through the obedience of Mary."[4]

We notice too that the Council is making use of the New Eve theme—that Mary, the New Eve, by her obedience undid the disobedience of the old Eve, just as Christ, the New Adam, by His obedience, undid the disobedience of the old Adam.[5]

The Council also expressed the idea of her obedience by saying:

---

[2]Cited in G. Roschini, *De Corredemptrice, Marianum* 17 (1939) p. 35.

[3]Vatican II, *On the Church* #3.

[4]*Ibid* #56.

[5]It does not mean that Jesus undid only the work of Adam: both Jesus and Mary shared in one work, undoing all sin.

> In faith she endured her union with her Son even to the cross, where she stood in accordance with the divine plan, greatly grieved with her Only-begotten, and joined herself to His sacrifice with a motherly heart, consenting to the immolation of the Victim that had been born of her.[6]

In saying she consented, the Council means that her will was in accord with the will of the Father, and of the Son—they willed that He die then, so horribly. So her union with the will of the Father and Son required that she not only refrain from protesting, but that she even will what they willed—will His death, in that dreadful way, at that time.

Benedict XV had taught the same thing:

> With her suffering and dying Son, Mary endured suffering and almost death. She gave up her Mother's rights over her Son to procure the salvation of mankind and . . . so much as she could, immolated her Son, so that one can truly affirm that together with Christ she has redeemed the human race.[7]

All these statements belong, of course, to the framework of the covenant, which Vatican II stresses so much. In the old covenant of Sinai, a people of God was created, to get favor on condition of obedience. Similarly, in the new covenant the people of God is to get favor on condition of obedience.

The basic, infinite obedience was that of Jesus. Yet as St. Paul makes clear so many times, we are to do everything *syn Christo*, with Christ—we suffer with Him, we die with Him, are buried with Him, rise with Him, ascend with Him (cf. Rom 6:1-5; Col. 3:1). In fact, we are saved precisely to the extent that we are not only members of His, but are like Him—and of course, like Him especially in this most essential feature of His work, obedience. For without it, His death would have been only a tragedy, not a redemption (*cf.* Rom 5:19). Vatican II underscored this when it also said, "By His obedience He brought about redemption."[8]

So she shared with Him precisely in the covenant condition, obedience, in that which gave the value to His redemptive death.

The Father had even made her especially fitted for this work, in advance, by the Immaculate Conception.

Now, could we imagine that the Father would make her apt for the role, call on her to do so difficult a thing as to will the death of her

---

[6]Vatican II, *On the Church* #58.

[7]Benedict XV, *Inter Sodalicia*, May 22, 1918. AAS 20.182. 8.

[8]Vatican II, *On Church* #3.

Son in so horrible a way, in obedience, the covenant condition, and then not accept it as part of the covenant, that is, of the redemption? Of course not. He had even, as we noted above, put her on Calvary not just as a private person, but as one officially appointed to cooperate; she was there, as the Council said, "in accordance with the plan of Divine Providence."[9]

Pope Pius XII, in the solemn Constitution defining the Assumption, gave us important added light on her cooperation as the New Eve. First he laid the groundwork:

> We must remember especially that, since the second century, the Virgin Mary has been presented by the Holy Fathers as the New Eve, who, although subject to the New Adam, was most closely associated with Him in that struggle against the infernal enemy which, as foretold in the Protoevangelium, was to result in that most complete victory over sin and death.[10]

The Protoevangelium is, of course, the prophecy of Genesis 3:15 of enmity between the serpent and the woman, whose Offspring is to overcome the serpent. So the Pope reminds us that the Fathers, virtually all of them, do speak of Mary as the New Eve, sharing the struggle against Satan.

Then Pius XII went on to show that just as she shared in the "struggle" of Calvary with Jesus, so also she would share in His glorification by her Assumption: "Wherefore, just as the glorious resurrection of Christ was an essential part and final sign of this victory, so also that struggle which was common to the Blessed Virgin and her Son had to be closed by the 'glorification' of her virginal body."

The force of the Pope's reasoning is remarkable: she shared with Him in the struggle of Calvary so fully that it could be called a work in common, common to both of them. And that word common is not taken in some loose sense. It is most strict, for it is precisely because Calvary was a work in common that a common cause had to have a common effect, namely, glorification.

The Pope was chiefly speaking of the Assumption. But in seeking a basis for it in the souces of revelation, he found it precisely in her cooperation in the redemption—and that cooperation had to be so strictly true that in the fullest sense the great sacrifice could be called a work in common, without, of course, denying her subordination to Him, which the Pope had expressed in the first part of this passage.

---

[9]*Ibid.* #58 and #61.

[10]Pius XII, *Munificentissimus Deus*, Nov. 1, 1950. AAS 42.786.

The very idea that any creature could join, in any way, in redeeming us is so striking, that we naturally want to see more fully just how this could be. Pius XII assured us it was true, in so strong a sense that there was a work in common. Vatican II used the same word "obedience" to describe both the heart of His redemptive work, and her cooperation with Him.

One way to examine the how is by way of the concept of sacrifice. As we know, a sacrifice includes an external sign, and the interior dispositions, which the sign expresses and even promotes, of obedience-love, and adoration. Now she obviously shared in the external sign, not indeed by putting Him to death—He Himself did not do that either—but in that she, as we said, furnished the very body which made that death possible. What of the interior element? the chief part of it was, of course, obedience-love, as we saw. She shared in it by obeying, that is, by accepting the will of the Father that He die.

How dearly did this cost her? The pain of a Mother at the death of her Son would be measured by two things: by how much He suffered, and by her love for Him. How much did He suffer? We already tried to fathom it, and found it measureless. Yet our realization of it is poor and weak compared to hers, for it was right in front of her very eyes, it was mercilessly vivid—the sword foretold by Simeon in its most pitiless thrust. That was multiplied by her love for Him, a love which was, as Pius IX already told us, so great that "none greater under God can be thought of, and no one but God can comprehend it."[11]

Yet, just as as He suffered for each one—for Vatican II tells us, "Each one of us can say with the Apostle: The Son of God loved me, and gave Himself for me,"[12]—so too did she willingly, though painfully, give Him for each one of us.

He, in the very midst of His pain, said: "Father forgive them, for they know not what they do." She was asked to "give up her Mother's rights over her Son," as Pope Benedict XV said, to "consent" as Vatican II said. And she too forgave us at the same time as He did, in the same way. Such was His will; such was her love for us, such her mercy.

We can also consider her cooperation with Him by looking further within the framework of the new covenant, in which, on Calvary, He carried out the obedience He had pledged in the Cenacle. Now Vatican II tells us that the Mass is the renewal of the new covenant.[13] A renewal, of course, presupposes a making of the covenant in the first place. But that making was done in the Cenacle, and on Calvary. But

[11]Pius IX, *Ineffabilis Deus*.

[12]Vatican II, *Church in Modern World* #22.

[13]Vatican II, *On Liturgy* #10.

we need to recall something about that renewal of the new covenant which is the Mass. The Church insists that we are to join in it especially by uniting our interior dispositions with those of the Divine Victim, who renews His offering of obedience to the Father, using the very same dramatized form of acceptance of the Father's will that He had used in the Cenacle, namely, the seeming separation of body and blood in the separate bread and wine.

So we can see that in the Mass, the renewal, there is a twofold offering of obedience that melts as it were into one—the obedience of Christ, and our obedience to the Father, which we bring to join with His, so that there is an offering of the obedience of the whole Christ, Head and Members.

But now we seem to make a remarkable discovery: if the Mass is, as the Council insists, the renewal, and if the renewal really renews or repeats, and does not instead change or modify the original, and if there is a twofold offering of obedience in the Mass, the renewal, there must have been a twofold offering of obedience in that which the renewal repeats, namely, Calvary. This obviously means that just as our obedience melts into one with His on the altar, so did her obedience fuse into one with His on Calvary. So we can see more fully the import of the words of Vatican II: "In suffering with her Son as He died on the cross, she cooperated in the work of the Savior . . . by obedience. . . ."[14]

Vatican II explicitly said it did not intend to settle existing controversies in Mariology.[15] Yet a Council is an instrument in the hands of Divine Providence. When St. Irenaeus wrote the words that Vatican II quoted about her becoming by obedience a cause of salvation for herself and the whole human race, he was, as the context shows, thinking of the day of the Annunciation rather than Calvary. But St. Irenaeus also, in a quote used by Vatican II, compared all sin to a knot. But a knot is untied only when we have taken the rope backwards through every twist and turn used in tying it. So, when St. Irenaeus said in the line quoted by the Council that Mary untied what Eve had tied, there was objectively—even though St. Irenaeus may not have seen it—an implication that Mary's cooperation in the redemption extended even to Calvary. In a similar way, Vatican II may not have realized all the richness of its words, but the Holy Spirit who guided it did not miss the full content. And it seems that the full content is what we have just gathered, namely, that her obedience formed with His one price of redemption, to use St. Paul's expression from 1 Cor. 6:20.[16]

---

[14]Vatican II, *On the Church* #61.

[15]*Ibid.* # 54.

[16]*Cf.* chapter 7, note 6, and 1 Cor 6:20; Col 2.14. Jeremiah in 31.31ff also

Some have suggested that Mary's cooperation on Calvary consisted only in receiving not in actively sharing in earning. But we notice the Council used the same word, *obedience*, to describe her role as it did for His role. There is nothing to indicate the Council meant a radically different sense of the word in the two cases, hers and His. So it would seem that her role should also be of the same general nature as His (with due subordination and dependence of course). He actively won salvation by obeying. So she did not merely receive—not even if we say "actively receiving," like one putting out a hand. No, obeying is a fully active response. It is not just receiving what someone else alone obtains; it was part of the very covenant condition, of that which gave the redemptive value to His death.

We recall of course also the text of Pius XII in the solemn document defining the Assumption, in which he spoke of Calvary as a work in "common" to Him and to her. Again, that would not leave room for a radical difference such as the objectors propose.

Let us also think of a parallel: When God sends us an actual grace, to lead and enable us to do a particular good thing here and now, there are two steps. First, He gives us an ability to do the thing; then, we are both moved by His grace, and simultaneously moving ourselves actively by the power currently coming from that grace. So the Council of Trent even defined[17] that we are not just passive under that grace. Similarly, in a greater sphere, Mary should not do less than we do: she did receive from her Son the very means of cooperating, but then, she actively joined with Him, actively obeyed, and so actively had a role in winning that which He was winning, salvation for us all.

Important added light can come from recalling that in looking at the old covenant, we found there were two levels. On the basic level, the reason God gave His favors was simply unmerited, unmeritable generosity; on the secondary level, the reason was that His people fulfilled the covenant condition or law (when they did so). We find the same situation with the new covenant. The basic reason why the Father grants grace and forgiveness is still simply His own generosity; even the work of Christ comes on the secondary level.

When we first think of this, it may seem strange. But we need to notice that the Father was not moved to lay aside anger and to love us again because Christ came—rather, Christ came because the Father always loved us. Hence His generosity-love is more basic than even the

hardly saw that the obedience of the new covenant would be that of ChriSt. But the principal author, the Holy Spirit, saw and intended that meaning. Jeremiah was His instrument.

[17]DS 1554. See also chapter 18.

coming of Christ. St. Augustine puts it well: "We were reconciled to the One who already loved us."[18] So the Father did not have to be moved—in fact, since He is unchangeable, He *cannot* be moved.

Now this helps us to understand how Mary could cooperate in the redemption. If the redemption had to move the Father, of course, she could not have done anything towards it. But when it was instead a matter of providing an objective title for redemption (we recall chapter 4) on a secondary level, that is within the power of a creature if God chooses to give such power and role.[19] The Father gave her the means that were apt by their very nature—obedience within covenant—to serve as a secondary title within the covenant. Why would He give a means naturally apt, and then not intend to accept it?

Of course all this does not mean she was on the same plane as her Divine Son—her very ability to cooperate came from Him. Hence Vatican II wrote:

> No creature can ever be counted [as if on the same plane] with the Incarnate Word and Redeemer ... [but] just as the one goodness of God is really poured forth in creatures in various manners, so also the one mediation of the Redeemer does not exclude, but [rather] produces among creatures a participated cooperation, from the one sole font.[20]

In fact, that Holiness and love of the objective order, which we saw in chapter 4 and in the old covenant, willed to add also the titles created by lesser Saints, besides Mary, to make everything as rich as possible. Their role has a part, of course, in the *distribution* of the fruits of Calvary, not in the once-for-all *acquisition* of those fruits. Hence the Church does teach the value and help to be found in invoking their intercession. Thus the title for granting favors is not only in Christ the Head and in Mary, but in the whole Mystical Christ. Further, the

---

[18]St. Augustine, On John 110.5. PL 35. 1924.

[19]The Father gave her the means apt in themselves—obedience, a part of the covenant condition, which He could have given as the whole of redemption to any mere creature, as we saw in Chapter 4—and He also gave her "a dignity second only to God ... a sort of infinite dignity," as Pius XI said (*Lux veritatis*. AAS 23.513, citing St. Thomas *Summa* I.25.6. ad 4) which made her intrinsically apt for such a role. Why would the Father give such means, apt in themselves, and then refuse to accept them?

Further, Vatican II says she was there in an official role, not as a private person: On the Church 58, "not without the divine plan" and 61, "by plan of Divine Providence ... she cooperated." And she was in the role of the New Eve.

[20]Vatican II, *On the Church* #62.

promise to hear prayer, "Ask and you shall receive" belongs also in this picture. The Father in His love of us, and in His love of objective order and goodness, willed even to bind Himself to grant prayers, made properly.

From the fact that she shared in acquiring or earning all graces on Calvary, it is obviously logical that she should share similarly in distributing all graces. In this role she is called Mediatrix of all graces.

We quoted Vatican II early in this chapter, and after describing her cooperation on Calvary, the Council added: "As a result, she is our Mother in the order of grace."[21] A mother in the natural order has two chief functions, to share in producing a new life, and to take care of that life so long as there is need, and so long as she is able. Mary shared in winning new life, the life of grace, divine life, for us on Calvary. And she takes care of us so long as we have need, which is until we arrive safely at our Father's house, for not before that will our need of grace and care cease. Earthly mothers are sometimes not willing to care—not so Mary. And earthly mothers are sometimes unable to help—not so Mary, whose every prayer to the Father through her Son is heard.

Vatican II, after noting that this role of hers really is a continuation of her fiat on the day of the Annunciation, added:

> After being assumed into heaven, she has not put aside this saving role, but by her manifold intercession she continues, in winning the gifts of eternal salvation for us. With motherly love she takes care of the brothers of her Son who are still in pilgrimage [cf. Heb 13:14] and involved in dangers and difficulties, until they are brought to the happy fatherland. For this reason, the Blessed Virgin is invoked in the Church under the titles of Advocate, Auxiliatrix, Adjutrix and Mediatrix.[22]

Some have noted that the Council simply said "Mediatrix", and did not add "of all graces." Yet the Council did teach that truth, in two ways. First, it added a footnote referring us to teachings of Leo XIII, St. Pius X, and Pius XII, who did teach she was Mediatrix of all graces.[23] Second, in section 25 of the same *Constitution on the Church*, it insisted

---

[21]Vatican II, *On the Church* #61.

[22]*Ibid.* #62.

[23]The reason the Council did not itself add the words "of all graces" was concern for Protestant observers. Father Balic, a chief drafter of the Marian chapter 8, tells us: "The protestants [observers at the Council] were waiting to see if there would be mention of Mary as Mediatrix or not. In case of an affirmative answer, the dialogue would be closed."—C. Balic, "El Capitulo VIII de la Constitucion 'Lumen gentium' comparado con el Primer Esquema de La B. Virgen Madre de la Iglesia" in *Estudios Marianos* 27 (1966), p. 174.

that all such papal teachings, even those that are not defined, require even our internal belief, and not just external compliance. Thereby it reaffirmed—not that it was necessary—all the teachings of such great Marian Popes as St. Pius X and Pius XII. Actually, there are twelve papal texts speaking of Mary as Mediatrix of all graces.

Indeed, the very fact that she shared in earning all graces means that absolutely every grace that is actually given comes in that way through her role. In addition, she actually intercedes, asks for each grace for us, and she knows all our needs. We her children are very numerous—but not too numerous for her to see in the infinite vision of God, with a soul illumined by such a light of grace, that is in proportion to her fulness of grace, so great, as we saw that, as Pius IX told us, "none greater under God can be thought of, and no one except God can comprehend it."

Actually, the sweep of the Marian teaching of Vatican II is magnificent. It tells us she was eternally united with Him in the decree for the Incarnation, and then goes through every one of the mysteries of His life and mission, and shows her association at each point, even on Calvary. After that, she "was taken up, body and soul, to heavenly glory, and was exalted as Queen of the universe . . . so that she might be more fully conformed to her Son, the Lord of Lords."[24]

So from eternity before time began, to eternity after the end of time, and in every mystery of His in between, she is His Mother and inseparable associate!

The Council rightly drew the logical conclusion from this breathtaking doctrinal picture of her constant union with Jesus. It admonished all "that they should cultivate devotion, especially liturgical devotion, towards the Blessed Virgin, and that they should consider of great importance the practices and devotions toward her that were recommended by the Magisterium over the course of centuries."[25] In fact, Vatican II went farther in teaching about her, and in urging devotion than all previous councils combined. So it could rightly be called the Marian Council.[26]

Yet all this greatness of hers is the Father's gift, in His love of us, and His love of the universal order, for He is Holiness-Love. He has gone infinitely beyond infinity: for the Incarnation in a palace, without death, would have been infinite. He went beyond that to the stable and the cross, and then even further, in adding the role of Mary.

---

[24]Vatican II, *On the Church* #59.

[25]*Ibid.* #67.

[26]*Cf.* W. Most, *Vatican II, Marian Council*, St. Paul Publications, Athlone (Ireland), 1972.

Chapter 11: Renewal of the New Covenant

Jesus made perfect atonement for our sins, and won for us, with an infinite title for each one, an infinite treasury of grace. His Blessed Mother shared in this work. Can we therefore conclude that we ourselves need not do anything except accept, for these merits are infinite, once for all?

The problem is compounded by the fact that the Epistle to the Hebrews speaks of the offering Jesus made as being once-for-all. For when Jesus entered this world He said, as we saw (Heb 10: 5): "Behold, I come to do your will O God." Then Hebrews adds: "In this [attitude of His] will we were sanctified through the offering of the body of Jesus Christ once for all."

This seems not only to leave no room for us to do anything, but it seems not even to leave room for the Mass, which Vatican II tells us is the renewal of the New Covenant.[1]

But the inspired writer of this Epistle was not ignorant of the fact that Jesus, when He instituted the Eucharist, ordered: "Do this in memory of me." How then could he write that we are sanctified thorough His offering "once for all?" The answer is not difficult.

There are two things to note. First, we distinguish between the acquisition of the treasury of grace and forgiveness for us, and the distribution of that treasury. The acquisition of the treasury is sometimes called the objective redemption; the distribution, which goes on throughout all ages, is called the subjective redemption. The acquisition was done once-for-all. It estabished an infinite treasury, that is, an infinite claim to grace and forgiveness for the whole human race, in fact,

---

[1]Vatican II, *On Liturgy* #10.

for each individual person, as we learn from Gal 2:20. Mary shared in that work of acquisition, as we have seen.

Secondly, He ordered His offering to be repeated, "Do this in memory of me," for two further reasons, namely, so that we His members, as St. Paul says,[2] might join in the offering, and so that an infinite objective title might be established by His offering in which we join. (As we shall see later in this chapter, His Mother also joins in every Mass.)

He wanted us to join, since as St. Paul tells us, we are saved and made holy if, and to the extent that, we are not only His members, but are like Him. It would be a strangely incongruous picture if our Head were a suffering, atoning, obedient Head, and we would not be like Him in these things.

Especially He wants our obedience joined to His. It is not that our obedience does Him any good—we have seen that before. It is that He knows our obedience makes us capable of receiving, open to receive. It is of no avail for Him to give, if we cannot receive.[3]

Secondly, the Holiness of the Father still loves the objective order, as we saw in chapter 4. We do not say He was obliged to provide an infinite title for forgiving us as He did, in the death of His Son. But just as He willed to do that, though He did not have to, so too, without any constraint, He wills to provide an objective title for the giving out of the gifts won once for all. Again, we notice that there are two phases, the objective redemption and the subjective redemption. The objective redemption is the once-for-all acquisition of the infinite treasury.[4] The subjective redemption is the work of giving out the riches of that infinite treasury, throughout all ages. The Father willed to have an infinite title in both phases. He willed that we join in that title, by our obedience, in union with His.

On the altar, Jesus renews His offering of obedience, even though the Father does not ask Him to die again—He did that once-for-all. But the dispositions of the Heart of Jesus today, in Heaven, are the very same dispositions with which He left this world in death. So Jesus on the altar renews, or, rather, continues His offering, an infinite title for the giving out of the fruits of Calvary in the Mass.

Further, just as the Father willed to have Mary's obedience joined with that of Jesus on Calvary, so, as we will see later in this chapter, He

---

[2]*E.g.*, 1 Cor 12:12-31; Col 1:18; 2:18-19; Eph 1:2-23.

[3]He also wanted us to avoid the penalties built into the nature of things for sinning. *Cf.* St. Augustine *Confessions* 1:12 (this thought is developed in the last part of chapter 5, especially near notes 11, 12, 13).

[4]By the "treasury" we mean an infinite claim generated by the redemption, to graces.

willed to have her obedience joined to His still in the Mass. Thus the title for the dispensation of all graces through the Mass is a twofold title, the offering of the obedience of Head and members.

This title for the giving out of the fruits of Calvary is, of course, like everything in both old and new covenants, on the secondary level. The generosity of Holiness-Love is the fundamental reason for these gifts.

We often hear it said that the Mass is a sacrifice. We do not mean that Jesus dies again, nor that He has to earn all over what He earned once-for-all. But yet it is a sacrifice. In the Cenacle He told the Apostles: "Do this in memory of me. " St. Paul therefore says (1 Cor 11:26): "Whenever you eat this bread and drink the cup, you announce the death of the Lord until He comes." In a sacrifice, as we saw in chapter 4, there are two elements: the external sign, and the interior dispositions which are expressed by that sign. The external sign of the Mass is different from that of Calvary. On Calvary it was His bloody death; on the altar, as in the Cenacle, the external sign is the seeming separation of body and blood. For when Jesus says through His priest, "This is my body," and over the wine, "this is my blood" so that the two, body and blood, seem separate, that is a sign of death. Hence as St. Paul wrote, we "announce the death of the Lord until He comes."

The interior dispositions of Jesus on the altar are not just a repetition of the dispositions He had on the cross: they are numerically one and the same! For death makes permanent the attitude of heart with which a soul leaves this world (hence both heaven and hell must be permanent). So on the altar Jesus does not repeat His attitude of obedience; it is still one and the same act of obedience with which He cried out: "It is finished. Father, into your hands I commend my spirit."

So the external sign of the Mass differs, but the Heart of the sacrifice, the Heart of Jesus, is not changed, is not repeated, for it is still in continuation with the act He made on the cross. Hence the Council of Trent could teach that the Mass is the same as Calvary, "only the mode of offering being changed" from the bloody to the unbloody.[5]

In saying to the Apostles, "Do this in commenoration of me," Jesus gave them both the command and the power[6] to do what He had done, to carry out the external sign of His interior offering in the Mass, in which He becomes present again. Whenever they or their successors, or a priest ordained by them, bring about this external sign, He, Christ, becomes present, in a remarkable act of obedience to their word,

---

[5]DS 1743.

[6]The Council of Trent defined that by these words, Jesus made His Apostles priests: DS 1752.

making Himself so lowly as to be present under the humble, lifeless appearances of bread and wine.

Vatican II speaks of two kinds of participation in the priesthood of Christ, that of the ordained or ministerial priest, and that of the laity.

Speaking of the laity, the Council said:

> Christ the Lord, the High Priest taken from among men, made the new People [of God] to be a kingdom and priests to God and His Father. For the baptized, by regeneration and the anointing of the Holy Spirit, are consecrated into a spiritual house and holy priesthood, so that they may offer spiritual sacrifices through all the works of a Christian man.[7]

A bit farther on the Council makes clear what it means by "spiritual sacrifices":

> For all their works, prayers, and apostolic endeavors, their married and family life, their daily work, their relaxation of mind and body, if they are carried out in the Spirit, even the hardships of life, if they are patiently borne, become spiritual sacrifices, acceptable to God through Jesus Christ which are offered devotedly to the Father in the celebration of the Eucharist, along with the offering of the Lord's Body.[8]

Since there are, as we saw, two aspects to a sacrifice, the external sign and the interior dispositions which it signifies, it is clear that we could speak of a participation in either or both of these elements. Since the external sign is there to express and even promote the interior dispositions, it is obvious that these interior dispositions are by far the more important of the two. In fact, on Calvary itself, the external sign, His death, would have been worth nothing, would have been just a miscarriage of justice, without His interior disposition of obedience to the Father. As Vatican II said, "by His obedience He brought about redemption."[9]

It is clear that the Council is speaking basically of the interior offering when it speaks of "spiritual sacrifices" which are "offered devotedly to the Father . . . along with the offering of the Lord's body." That is, the Council is telling us that, in our daily lives, we should live out the will of the Father in obedience to Him, and then bring that offering of our obedience to His will to be joined to the offering of the obedience of Jesus on the altar in the Mass. So before each Mass we would do well to look back on the period of time since the previous Mass, to see what

---

[7]Vatican II, *On the Church* # 10.
[8]*Ibid.* # 34.
[9]*Ibid.* # 3.

we have done in following the will of the Father since that time, to see what is fit to join with the obedience of Jesus. If we find some things not done well, these we may not join to His obedience; rather we will have to offer our sorrow, our regrets for not having done well enough in these points, and should ask for His grace to move us to do better in the future. We should also look forward to the days to come, to see if we can note any especially difficult thing coming up, in which it may be less easy to carry out the will of the Father. We should make a firm resolve not to fail Him at these junctures, and realize we cannot honestly join in the offering if we do not really mean to do our best to follow what He wants of us at all points.

The Mass really becomes the center, the focal point of life; if we unite in the one present moment of offering in the Mass both the past and the future, the Mass truly dominates all of life. Then no one could possibly say that to him the Mass does not mean anything. He may not have any special feelings, but they are not really important: it is the spiritual offering of will that is important and supremely valuable, with or without the presence of feelings.

In this vein St. Augustine wrote well: "The Church, since she is the body of the Head Himself, learns through Him to offer herself," in the "daily sacrifice of the Church."[10] We could say that by this interior union with our Divine Head, we get "straightened out" each day, that is, our wills are aligned with His.

It is important to distinguish the ordained or ministerial priesthood from the priesthood of the laity. Vatican II says on this matter that "they differ in essence not just in degree." That is, the priesthood of the ordained priest is not just a higher degree of basically the same thing as the priesthood of the laity—it is of a different essence or nature. Why? Vatican II says of the ordained priest that he "brings about the Eucharistic sacrifice in the person of Christ." For at the consecration he uses the very words of Christ, He acts as Christ, as another Christ.[11]

Pius XII, in his great liturgical Encyclical, *Mediator Dei*, on which the Council bases its presentation, wrote, "that unbloody immolation, by which . . . Christ is made present on the altar in the state of victim, is carried out by the priest himself alone, as he acts in the person of Christ."[12] He then went on to tell in more detail just how the people join in: "The faithful participate in the offering in this restricted sense, in their own manner, in a twofold way, namely, because they offer not

---

[10]St. Augustine, *City of God* 10. 20. PL 41. 298.

[11]Vatican II, *On the Church* #10.

[12]Pius XII, *Mediator Dei*, Nov. 20, 1947. AAS 39. 555.

only through the hands of the priest, but also along with him."[13]

Pius XII then goes on to clarify both ways still further: "It is clear that the faithful offer the sacrifice through the hands of the priest from the fact that the priest at the altar in offering a sacrifice in the name of all His members, does so in the person of Christ, the Head [of the Mystical Body]."[14] So the priest acts for Christ, and the people, being members of Christ, can therefore be said to offer through the priest. Secondly,

> The statement that the people offer the sacrifice with the priest does not mean that... they perform a visible liturgical rite ... instead, it is based on the fact that the people join their hearts in praise, petition, expiation, and thanksgiving with the prayers or intention of the priest, in fact, of the High Priest Himself, so that in the one and same offering of the Victim ... they may be presented to God the Father.[15]

That is, they join their "spiritual sacrifices" or their interior dispositions to those of the Divine Victim on the altar.

We need to take care to avoid a misunderstanding of this offering: it is not that the ordained priest makes Christ present, and then all, priest and people, offer him.[16] Pius XII made this clear in *Vous nous avez*: "When the consecration of the bread and wine is validly brought about the whole action of Christ is actually accomplished. Even if all that remains could not be completed, still, nothing essential would be lacking to the Lord's offering."[17]

Really, this is obvious when we recall that the Mass consists precisely in the fact that Jesus, through the ordained priest, uses exactly the same sign He used in the Cenacle to express His acceptance of the will of the Father, namely, He uses the seeming separation of body and blood in the separate species of bread and wine to stand for His acceptance of death. When that sign has once been produced, then the offering is complete, or rather, the offering consists precisely in His dispositions under that double sign. So "to offer" means that He makes this acceptance of the will of the Father, in which we all join. "To offer"

---

[13]*Ibid.*

[14]*Ibid.* p. 556.

[15]*Ibid.*

[16]There was a widespread error in the 1950s. *E.g.*, Clifford Howell, "What Happens at Mass" in *Orate Fratres* Sept. 1951, p. 439, said that the priest just makes Christ present: then all can offer Him, just as only a cook can make lemon pie, but then anyone can eat it.

[17]Pius XII, "Vous nous avez" To Liturgical Conference at Assisi, Sept. 22, 1956: AAS 48. 717. *Cf.* full text in *The Pope Speaks* Winter, 1956-57.

does not mean to lift up a host or chalice and say or sing: "Lord, we offer to thee," nor to sing Amen many times.[18]

What of the external forms of participation in the Mass—answering responses, taking part in offertory processions and similar things? Objectively it is better to take part in these than not to do so. We say "objectively" because the spiritual needs of different persons are different, and allowance should be made. Today we have guitar Masses to please teenagers, special Eucharistic prayers for children, and other adaptations. So the principle is surely valid. But yet the internal participation, the union of our obedience with that of Jesus, is the essential thing. Pius XII's great and fundamental liturgy Encyclical again helps us. After raising the question of how the people should participate, he begins:

> First of all, the more extrinsic explanations are these: It often happens that the people at Mass join their prayers alternately with the priest, and sometimes . . . they offer to the ministers of the altar bread and wine . . . and, finally, by their alms, they get the priest to offer the Divine Victim for their own intentions. But there is a more profound reason why all Christians . . . are said to offer the Sacrifice.[19]

Then he goes on to explain the interior participation, in the way we saw above.

At the time of the great prophet Isaiah, the people of Israel were quite good at external participation in their rites. They loved to clap their hands and shout to God with cries of joy. But it was all externalism, perhaps even fun, and so God complained (Is 29: 13): "This people comes near me with their mouth, and with their lips honor me, but their hearts are far from me." Similarly, through Hosea, God said (6:6) "Hesed is my pleasure, not sacrifice." *Hesed* we will recall, is obedience to the covenant condition: without it, sacrifice is worth nothing.[20]

We already explained (chapter 5) why our stress is on obedience, where one might expect to hear of love. The truth is that in loving God, obedience and love turn out to be identified in practice. Pope Paul VI,

---

[18]The Great Amen is not the heart of the Mass. It is as it were an extension: the real offering is in the double consecration, but since this goes through in a brief moment, it is helpful to have an extension. The Great Amen concludes the extension. To stress it at expense of the heart of the Mass or to think of it according to the error of Clifford Howell (note 16 above) is unfortunate.

[19]Pius XII, *Mediator Dei*. AAS 39. 555.

[20]In a word, because obedience is the covenant condition, and as we shall see in chapters 14-15, obedience and love of God are in practice identified.

in a text we have already seen, taught that obedience,

> is first of all a penetration and acceptance of the mystery of Christ, who saved us by means of obedience. It is a continuation and imitation of this fundamental act of His, His acceptance of the will of the Father. It is an understanding of the principle which dominates the entire plan of Incarnation and Redemption. Thus obedience becomes assimilation into Christ, who is the Divine Obedient One.[21]

And it is in the Mass that we are assimilated to Him in this.

In the light of this, we can see what to think of those who say that only by many illegitimate, that is, disobedient, changes in the Mass can they make Mass meaningful. No wonder they never find the meaning: they are running at full speed away from the real meaning! For the heart of the Mass is obedience, and they think disobedience is the way to join with Christ's obedience!

There are, of course, other dispositions of the Heart of Jesus on the cross and in the Mass, especially thanksgiving, petition for favors for us, and adoration of the Father. As we saw in our introduction, the spiritual lives of many today are sick for lack of realization of His majesty, which we recognize in adoration, for adoration is simply the attitude resulting from realizing who He is, and who we are. He is the Infinite; we are nothing at all without Him.[22]

Pope John XXIII in a radio message to the 16th Eucharistic Congress of Italy on September 13, 1959 expressed the hope that all the people of Italy would be strengthened in their fervor and veneration for the Blessed Virgin, "the Mother of the Mystical Body, of which the Eucharist is the symbol and vital center." And then he added: "We trust that they will imitate in her the most perfect model of union with Jesus, our Head; we trust that they will join Mary in the offering of the Divine Victim."[23]

---

[21]Cited from *Davenport Messenger* Nov. 17, 1966, p. 7.

[22]In a sense, the decline in reverence is planned. *Cf.* statment of Daniel Callahan, in *National Catholic Reporter*, March 1, 1967, p. 6: "Many find the notion of total dependence upon God somehow a very disturbing one.... So there is a desperate casting around to find a kind of liturgy which is not only intelligible ... but one which seems to express a different kind of relationship between God and man.... Many of the liturgical experiments seem to be trying to work in the direction of finding whether one can say and liturgically act out this kind of parallel relationship with God rather than just being a king-and-lowly-subject kind of relationship."A theortical basis for this was provided by Leslie Dewart, *The Future of Belief* (1966) pp. 200, 203-04.

[23]Radio message, Sept 13, 1959, AAS 51. 713.

This is a most remarkable statement. The people are asked to join Mary in the offering. They could hardly be urged to join her in what she did in the past, so there at least seems to be the implication that she is somehow involved in the Mass itself today.

Pope John Paul II brought out the same idea even more clearly in an address to the crowds in St. Peter's square on Sunday February 12, 1984:

> Today I wish to dwell with you on the Blessed Virgin's presence in the celebration of the Liturgy.... Every liturgical action ... is an occasion of communion ... and in a particular way with Mary.... Because the Liturgy is the action of Christ and of the Church ... she is inseparable from one and the other.... Mary is present in the memorial—the liturgical action—because she was present at the saving event.... She is at every altar where the memorial of the Passion and Resurrection is celebrated, because she was present, faithful with her whole being to the Father's plan, at the historic salvific occasion of Christ's death.[24]

Theological reasoning leads us inevitably to this conclusion that she takes part in the Mass. Vatican II, as we know, said that the Mass is the renewal of the new covenant.[25] The Council of Trent said that the Mass and Calvary are the same, "only the manner of offering being changed" from bloody to unbloody.[26] Now if the change in the mode is the only change then, since she was so intimately involved in the original sacrifice, she must be involved in the Mass too. Similarly, if the Mass renews the new covenant, and if in the making of that covenant she had the tremendous role we have seen—then if the renewal is faithful, and does not change that which it should renew, again, she must be involved in that renewal, in the Mass.

If we ask how this could be, we turn to the two aspects of sacrifice, the external sign and the internal dispositions. As we said before, she did not bring about His death, nor did He Himself do that, but she did supply, literally, the humanity in which He could die for us.

As to the interior dispositions: His dispositions are strictly a continuation of those He had on the cross, for He died in that attitude of Heart. She did not leave this world at once. But her union with His dispositions did not waver, did not diminish. Now in the glory of heaven, her dispositions of union with Him are as permanent as His. So she does really then join in every Mass.

---

[24]Angelus Homily on Feb. 12, 1984. From *Osservatore Romano* (English edition) Feb. 20, 1984, p. 10.

[25]Vatican II, *On Liturgy* #10.

[26]DS 1743.

So we reach a remarkable conclusion: though we may not realize it, yet, the more closely we are joined to Him in the Mass, the more closely we are joined to her. For these two Hearts are inseparable, and she is most closely united with Him in the Mass.

If this be true of all who join in the Mass, it is in a most special way true of the priest who acts "in the person of Christ," as Pius XII and Vatican tell us.[27] Precisely as another Christ, the priest is another son of Mary. On one occasion, when He was in the middle of a crowd, and it was announced that she was near, He decided to teach an important lesson forcefully. He asked (Mt 12: 48-50): "Who is my Mother, and who are my brothers?" And stretching out His hand to His disciples, He said: "Behold my Mother and my brothers. For whoever does the will of my Father in heaven, he is my brother, and sister and mother." He did not, of course, mean to disown His Mother. But He wanted to compare two greatnesses. One lies in one's position in the external order, that is, in dignity; the other in the interior order of doing the will of the Father. She was at the peak of all mere humans in both orders, for the dignity of the Mother of God, in the external order, is "second only to God," as Pope Pius XI told us.[28] But likewise in interior holiness, or love of God, or adherence to His will—they all amount to the same—her holiness is so great that "none greater under God can be thought of, and no one but God can comprehend it."[29]

So, though she is surpassingly great, at the very peak, in both orders, her Son wanted to make clear that the greater of the two is adherence to the will of the Father, hearing the word of God and keeping it.

In regard to the Mass, some are preoccuped with the dignity of the priesthood, whether that of the laity or of ordination. There is nothing wrong with this. But the lesson of her Son remains true: adherence to the will of the Father, with Jesus and Mary in the Mass, is far the greater of the two.

When Mass is over, some rush out at once, or stay to talk loudly even if others may be trying to pray (a lack of reverence to God and of courtesy to people). They seem not to realize that for some precious moments[30] they still carry within themselves the Divine Presence. Mary knew better. For the nine months before His birth, she had one long Communion. Who can picture its richness, its love! After His death, staying with St. John, she must have received Him often, and would

---

[27]Pius XII cited above in note 14, Vatican II, *On the Church* #10.

[28]*Cf.* Note 17 on chapter 10.

[29]Pius IX, *Ineffabilis Deus*.

[30]The time will vary. The principle is that as long as the Sacred Species remain in their basic form, Jesus is still present.

surely linger over the Presence within her.

Our thanksgiving should include both silent meditation and vocal prayers, for each has its own special kind of value for which the other will not substitute. Hence we should not just say: liturgical prayer or prayer in common is better than individual prayer. This is in general true. But just as in eating, we do not ask what is the most valuable of all food elements and then eat only that one thing—we would soon have deficiency diseases—so too it is with our thanksgiving, and other prayers, too.

We should ask Our Lady to come and join her perfect dispositions to our imperfection and weakness. One good way to do this and to extend our thanksgiving is to say the joyful mysteries of the Rosary, meditating on her welcome of Him in them, asking her to welcome Him now as she did at the annunciation, during the nine months, at Christmas, and to renew in us—and move us to do the same—her offering that she once made with Him when she presented Him in the Temple, or when she found Him again.

Pope John Paul II, in his very first Encyclical *Redemptor hominis*, gave some valuable advice on the need of working, as it were, at our reception of Him: "Without this constant ever-renewed endeavor for conversion, partaking of the Eucharist would lack its full redeeming effectiveness, and there would be a loss, or at least a weakening of the special readiness to offer God the spiritual sacrifice."[31] Indeed, frequent Communion without such effort can mean not only no spiritual gain, but even a spiritual loss.

---

[31]John Paul II, *Redemptor hominis*, March 4, 1979, #20. Vatican Press version.

Chapter 12: The Father Plans for Each One

"I know this is terribly displeasing to you, but I don't really mean to break with you. I will do it." This is a picture of the attitude of some very confused souls towards God. Many prominent U. S. moralists condone this. Some say that when they find a couple practicing contraception, they ask if they are good to people in general; and if they find out that in many things they are doing well, they conclude that they do not really mean to break with God by the sin of contraception. But the Church has condemned this theory[1]—called the "fundamental option"—which claims that to commit a mortal sin, one has to practically stand up and declare: "I hereby intend to break with God, to reject Christ, to be willing to see Him die again."

To say: "I don't really mean to offend you"—and then do what is actually very offensive, does not remove the offense. Really, it is all the more bold. So the fundamental option is not only an error, it is silly.

This reminds us of another question that seems similar, but is not foolish. To see it, we need to think of two sets of data, and then look at how they fit together.

First, people vary enormously in their response to God's grace. Some, at one extreme, are out of the state of grace and in the state of sin for most of their lifetimes. They may be in the clear for just one brief stretch. At the opposite extreme are those who are in the state of grace for all or nearly all their life. They might perhaps be out for just one brief period. And of course, there are all degrees in between.

For the second set of data, we recall that there are natural causes at work in this world of ours, operating according to their own laws,

[1] *Cf.* Sacred Congregation for the Doctrine of the Faith, *Declaration on Certain Questions Concerning Sexual Ethics,* Dec. 29, 1975. #10.

which God gave them. Some of these are capable of bringing sudden death to any person, at any age. Of course, some events are more likely at certain ages, *e.g.*, in the forties and fifties, death from a coronary is more of a possibility than it is for a teenager. On the other hand, a teenager is much more open to sudden death in an auto crash, as the insurance companies know so well.

So we need to ask some questions about how these two sets of things fit together. Namely: Will Divine Providence either order or permit sudden death to strike a man who is in that one brief period in which he is in the state of grace, so he will be saved? Conversely, will Providence either order or permit sudden death to hit one who is in the one brief period in which he is not in the state of grace, though normally he is?

It is obvious, that for these extreme cases, and for all points in between, there is a question to be answered, a decision to be made. Clearly it is Divine Providence, our Father, who makes the decision. If the decision is favorable, it is called predestination; if unfavorable, it is called reprobation.[2]

Some are frightened by the very word predestination. They have heard the foolish questions students sometimes ask in school: "Teacher, since God knows where I will go, how can I can help it; doesn't it have to be?" The question, as we said, is silly, for two reasons. First, the fact that God *knows* does not mean that He *causes*. Secondly, He really does not know the future. For there is no future for Him: since He is unchangeable, He cannot be subject to this constant succession of time in which a moment that was future, soon becomes present, then becomes past. No, for Him everything is present, eternally present. So, in the strict sense, He does not foresee, He just sees. And just as when we see something happening before our eyes, we need not be causing it, so He can know without causing it. Yes, to us the things seem future, but to the eye of His eternity, they are all simply present.

For centuries, practically since the beginning of the Church, theologians have tried to learn on what basis God makes these decisions about the intersection of death with the state of grace or sin. They have said that He must obviously decide to predestine or reprobate either before or after looking at human merits and demerits. Of course, those words before and after are metaphorical, for as we know, there is no time with God. What they really mean is to ask whether He decides these questions with or without considering how a person lives.

Throughout all centuries, all theologians have thought that both kinds of decisions—predestination (favorable) or reprobation

[2]Instead of reprobation, some theologians say: predestination to hell.

(unfavorable)—have to be made in the same way, *i.e.*, both must be decided with, or both without, looking at the person's life. For, they reasoned, if one is not predestined, he is reprobated—just two sides of the same coin, as it were.

As a result, theologians reached an impasse. Neither answer was acceptable or even possible, *i.e.*, neither to say God decides with, nor without, looking at merits. Why? Because God could not say that He wills all men to be saved, as He did in 1 Tim 2:4, and yet decide the ruin or reprobation of someone—who is included in the "all"—without even looking at his merits and/or demerits. So reprobation without looking cannot be the right answer. Turning to the other proposed answer, God could not decide to predestine because of or in consideration of merits—for we will not have any merits unless God gives them, since every bit of good we are or have or do, is simply His gift. As St. Paul put it (1 Cor 4:7): "What have you that you have not received?" It is only resistance to God's grace that God does not give us.[3]

In 1597 both major schools of thought (Dominicans and Jesuits) were ordered by Pope Clement VIII to send delegates to Rome, to hold a debate before a commission of Cardinals. In time, the Pope himself began to preside. Finally, Pope Paul V consulted St. Francis de Sales, who was a great theologian as well as a Saint. St. Francis advised the Pope not to approve either side. The Pope followed that advice, in 1607.[4] The time had not yet come when, by the will of our Father, the answer would finally become clear.

Part of the reason they failed to get the answer was that they were working in the wrong way, with the wrong method. The natural sciences give us a strong object lesson on method: for centuries scientists used the wrong method, and the results were poor, and often just erroneous. But in recent times they have shifted to the proper method, and so today we have a brilliant explosion of success in the sciences.

Now theology is the field of knowledge that tries to see what God has revealed. Clearly. we should first study the sources of revelation, Scripture and Tradition. Next, we need to decide what the sources mean. Scripture is not always clear, as we know, but God has given us a providentially protected teaching authority in the Church (Lk 10:16): "He who hears you, hears me."

The theologians who failed on predestination made two mistakes. First, as we said, they used the wrong method; they tried to solve the problems by metaphysics, a branch of philosophy. Now metaphysics is very good, and can do many splendid things. But it cannot solve all

---

[3]We are able to resist or to nonresist; *cf.* chapter 18.

[4]DS 1090.

these questions. Why? Because in part they depend on free decisions of God. Metaphysics can only find what must be in the nature of things. It gets no answers when the factor of free will is involved in deciding the outcome.

Secondly, when they turned to Scripture, they misinterpreted every text they touched. The reason was that they did not pay attention to the context, to the general thought of the passage. If one ignores that, he can do utterly wild things; for example, a line in Psalm 14 says: "There is no God." But the full text says: "the fool has said in his heart: There is no God." Now theologians dealing with predestination were not so blatantly foolish. Yet they did fall into serious errors. The chief trouble was this: there are only a few places in all of Scripture that even mention the word predestination. All are found in two Epistles of St. Paul: Romans 8:28 to 9:33, plus two lines in the first chapter of Ephesians. But—and here was the trouble—in both places St. Paul was talking not about a providential decision that resulted in someone reaching heaven or hell; he spoke of a decision on who would get the special favor of full membership in the Church, the people of God. Now a man can be saved[5] even if he does not have his name on some parish register. And he might be lost even if he does. Full membership in the Church is a great privilege and help, but whether one gets that membership or not does not settle the question of eternal salvation or ruin. So these passages really told us nothing at all about the question the theologians had in mind, predestination to heaven, or reprobation to hell. But theologians thought they did, and hence massive confusion.

Today, thanks to modern progress in Scripture studies, we see clearly what St. Paul was talking about, and hence we know that his assertion that God presdestines or rejects without regard to merits does not refer to our question. But we still want to find out what really is the answer.

If we approach Scripture without the old errors, and especially if we explore the Father analogy soundly and carefully—not just sentimentally saying, "A good Father would not condemn anyone to hell"—we can find the answer past centuries sought in vain.

In seeking the answer, we will have to find a way to pull apart the old dilemma that said that if God presdestines without looking at one's life, He also reprobates the same way. It must be possible, and it is, to have one kind of decision on predestination, another kind on reproba-

[5]The word *save* is used in three senses in Scripture: (1) rescue from temporal evils—found mostly in the Old Testament; (2) entry into the Church—*cf. e.g.* , Rom 11:25-26; (3) reaching heaven. Here we refer to final salvation.

tion. We will see presently how that can be done. But first, some preliminaries.

We already saw that in 1 Timothy 2:4 God said that He "wills all men to be saved." Some of the older theologians, whose ideas were not approved in the decision of Pope Paul V, had thought that God could reprobate someone without even looking at his demerits. But we already saw that if God did this, He could not also say: "I will *all* men to be saved." God would contradict Himself.

So we gather—and this is an important piece of the answer we will put together—that there is no reprobation without consideration of demerits.

This same fact is obvious when we consider so many other things we have already seen: God could not rationally provide in the New Covenant an infinite objective title or claim to an infinite treasury of grace for us—and then just reject us without any reason in sight (let us recall chapter 9). Further, we know that in Christ God has a really human Heart: but no human heart would act that way. And also we saw that Mary was made the Mother of all men, and the one who dispenses all graces: reprobation without even a look could never fit with her motherhood either.

Another major piece needed for our answer comes from the implication of the fact that God is our Father. St. Paul tells us in Romans 8:26-27: "We are Sons of God but if sons, also heirs, heirs of God, fellow heirs with Christ."[6] Now of course, when children inherit from their father, they do not earn their inheritance: that comes simply from the goodness of their father. Similarly, in Romans 3:24, St. Paul told us that we are "made righteous gratuitously by His grace." That is, we are made right with God, and hence able to inherit from Him, gratuitously, *i.e.*, without having earned it. Jesus earned it for us, but we did not earn it; we get it as a free gift.

So we reach the second piece of the answer: predestination, the decision to send us to our Father's house, comes without consideration of our merits. We simply do not earn it.[7]

Now if we put together the two things, we have the following re-

---

[6]*Cf.* also 1 Cor 6:10; Gal 5:21; Eph 5:5; Rom 6:23.

[7]The Council of Trent (DS 1582) defined that the good works of a person who has already been justified (has reached the state of grace without meriting it) do merit eternal life. This is true. We here insist that justification itself is without merits, is given out of the goodness of the Father, gratuitously (*cf.* Rom 3:24). That justification is as it were a ticket or title to eternal glory, and is a merit in that sense. This fits with the Father's love of objective order, and of titles within it, as we saw in chapter 4.

sult:

Predestination is without consideration of merits.

Reprobation is because of consideration of demerits.

Can we really hold both conclusions? We must, for as we saw, they are inevitable; each part flows inescapably from the Scripture passages we saw. So we must break wide open the old dilemma. Even if we could not see how to do it, we would still be logically driven to see the fact that our conclusions are true. For it is one thing to know a fact, another to know how it comes about.

But the same Father theme we have studied so much will also show us with surprising ease how to break open the dilemma. We begin by thinking of an ordinarily good father (and mother too) in an ordinary human family. His basic starting attitude to his children is that he wants them all to turn out well. That is obvious. But next: does a child say: "I know what I have to do. I must dry the dishes, cut the grass, and so on, and then I will get my father to love and care for me"? The thought would be outrageous, foolish. Even an ordinarily decent father takes care of his children not beause they are good, but because he is good. But there is something else: a child, even though he cannot and need not earn the basic love and care of his parents, yet can earn punishment if he is bad. And—though it is rare, it is real—if he is bad enough long enough, he can earn to be disinherited, to be put out of his father's house permanently and to lose his inheritance (*cf.* Rom 6:23).

The attitude of our Father in heaven is precisely parallel. His initial attitude is found, as we know, in 1 Timothy 2:4: He wants all to be saved, to turn out well. But then—if we may use a human way of visualizing—He looks ahead to see who will resist His grace. When He finds some who resist grace greatly enough, He knows they simply cannot be saved. For grace is the indispensable means of salvation: if someone throws it away so much, he throws away the only thing that could save him. So then, reluctantly, the Father decides He must reprobate that one—but He does it only with consideration of demerits flowing from the resistance to grace.

What about the others, those in whom the Father does not find such resistance? Those He predestines, decides to keep. Why? Not because He has seen merits in them—no question has been raised of merit. Nor is it because of the lack of a ruinous resistance. No, the reason is simply this: from the start, He really wanted to save *everyone* (1 Tim 2:4). *These* are not stopping Him.

So, the Father analogy shows us how to break wide open the ancient dilemma that caused the impasse. It shows us that predestination is without consideration of merits, while reprobation depends on demerits.[8]

We did not say clearly how much resistance is required to bring reprobation. We must now examine that. In dwelling on the new covenant, we found that Christ established for each individual an infinite title to an infinite treasury of grace and forgiveness. So, obviously, the resistance must be such as to cancel out all of that. That means the resistance must be both grave and persistent.

To see how grave and persistent it must be, we return to a problem we raised at the start of this discussion namely: Does God ever send someone to hell for his first mortal sin? With an infinite claim to grace going for him, it might seem that that would not be possible. The person might say: "I can afford a long life of sin, so long as I pull up just at the end." But that cannot be right, for Jesus warned us to watch and pray. So there must be something more to discover.

Now we said that God will reprobate in view of foreseen grave and persistent resistance to grace. (We know, as we said, that He does not foresee, for all is present to Him.) Therefore, suppose some man—we will call him Ike—has just committed his first mortal sin. But God knows that this is really the beginning of a long chain of sin that will add up to grave and persistent resistance, which will mean that Ike must be reprobated. Could or would God *ever*—we do not know if He does this *often* or *rarely*—decide: "It would be a kindness to take Ike out of this life right now, after one mortal sin. First, Ike is going to be lost anyway—to take him now means his ruin will be less. Second, by taking him early, he will have less chance to do harm to other souls." So God takes him, after one mortal sin, and he is lost. And the warnings of Christ retain their full value.

But we still must ask: Can even persistent resistance outbalance, as it were, the infinite title Ike has going for him? God wishes it would not, for certain. But yet Ike can make himself hardened, by repeated sins, so that he is unable to perceive or accept even the first thing grace tries to do for him, *i.e.*, the good thought. (How this can happen is described in chpater 19.) If grace cannot do even the first thing it needs to do, clearly, it cannot do the other things. So Ike is without grace. Yes, he has a title to it, and God wants to give it, but Ike is closed, hopelessly closed, so he cannot even begin to take in what God wants to give.[9]

Is there then no hope at all for Ike? Yes there might be. For just as in the natural order, there are miraculous things, things God does

[8]For a fuller treatment, *cf.* W. Most, *New Answers to Old Questions*.

[9]If a person decided to "live it up," relying on the infinite titles for him, and pull up at the last moment, it would be *presumption*, which normally causes hardening, which makes real repentance almost impossible.

beyond the realm of natural laws, so also in the supernatural order, God can give a grace comparable to a miracle. He cannot do this routinely—for then He would contradict Himself. Someone could rightly say: "Why did you establish those laws if you mean to bypass them most of the time?" But on special occasions He can do that.

When would He do that? It seems that if someone, by heroic virtue and penance, puts as it were an extraordinary weight into the scales of the objective order (*cf.* chapter 4), then God can and will grant a grace comparable to a miracle, and Ike could be saved.

Early in this chapter, we noted that St. Paul spoke of a different kind of predestination, *i.e.*, to full membership in the Church. He said that God does not consider merits in deciding who should get that special favor. But it is worthwhile for us to speculate a bit here. For St. Paul says only that on the negative side merits are not the reason for the grant of this favor. But, on the positive side, what reasons does God look at? There are some Scriptural indications.

First, St. Paul himself has some striking lines near the end of chapter 1 of First Corinthians. Earlier in that chapter, we learn that his Corinthians had become conceited, were boasting about which faction in the local church they belonged to. Probably they were also proud of themselves for becoming Christians at all.

St. Paul could not stand this pride. So, to deflate them, he wrote (1 Cor 1:26-27):

> Look at your call [into the Church] brothers. There are not many wise men in the worldly sense [in your community], not many powerful men, not many of noble birth. But God has chosen the foolish things of the world, to shame the wise, and the weak things of the world . . . to shame the strong.

In other words: You people are proud because of your call, but really the fact that God calls you into the Church implies the opposite. He has deliberately chosen the weak, the nobodies, to show that no human has anything to boast of before God, to show that the power is His.

Other Scripture passages give the same sort of picture. When God first appointed Ezechiel as a prophet, He said to him (Ez 3:5-7): "Not to a people of difficult language . . . are you sent, but to the house of Israel. . . . If I sent you to them, they would listen to you, but the house of Israel will not want to listen to you, for they do not want to listen to me." It begins to appear that the house of Israel was more resistant to God's grace than pagans.

This appears further in the book of Jonah. He was sent to preach to the pagan city of Nineveh, and at once they welcomed him, and did penance in sackcloth and ashes. But prophets sent to the holy people of God met with opposition if not death.

Further, in the parable of the Good Samaritan (Lk 10:30-37), a priest and a Levite of the people of God refuse to help the wounded man, but a Samaritan, not of the people of God, shows mercy.

Again, when Jesus healed ten lepers (Lk 27:11-19), nine out of the ten would not even come back to say thank you. They were of the people of God. The one who did thank Him was a Samaritan.

The implication in all these passages is that the members of the people or God are, in general, more resistant to grace than outsiders. Now this carries a strong implication and fits a predictable divine pattern, namely: We know that God wills all men to be saved. We know that this desire of His is extremely strong, so strong that He sent His only Son to the cross, going beyond infinity, as we saw, to save all.

On the other hand, we know that, given human conditions, especially our weakness, it is inevitable that there will be persons who, in good faith, will fail to find their way into full membership in the people of God.[10] First, some will simply be born before the Gospel is preached in their lands. Then, some who are born even in Catholic lands, will grow up in a Protestant family. Most naturally, they will think that what they have learned from childhood is right, and so in good faith will not come in.

We could dramatize this situation by imagining God looking over a giant checkerboard, before the course of history begins to run. He sees three classes of positions or squares on it: first are the squares in which a person will become a member of the Church in the full sense, and so will have all sacraments, the Mass, and all other external means of grace. Second are the places having some of the sacraments, but not all, and lacking the Mass: these are Protestant positions. Third are the places out in paganism where no form of Christianity has yet penetrated.

God sees, further, that some persons are more resistant to grace than others. In fact, some are so resistant that no matter what type of square He assigns them to, they will be lost. These, for the most part, we suppose He will put in the third class squares—that will leave the better squares open for those who may profit by them. This assignment will also avoid increasing the responsibilities (and so the ruin) of those who are so resistant. But He will see others who are resistant to grace, but not so severely that they could not be saved in any class of square.

[10]There are lesser degrees of membership, which still suffice to fill the requirement of membership in the Church for final salvation. On this *cf.* W. Most, *Catholic Apologetics Today,* chapter 23, and the appendix.

Some of these will need every help, all the external means of grace of the first class squares, otherwise they will be lost. Surely, He will assign such people to the first class squares. Still others are much less resistant to grace; they can be saved in the second class squares, or even in the third class squares. He will assign people accordingly.[11]

Not all those in the best squares are put there because of their greater resistance to grace: God picks some to put there for the sake of others. He intends to use them as His instruments to speak or to write, to do apostolic works, for the good of other souls. For although strictly He does not need any human, yet there is a sense in which He does, for while He could do these apostolic works directly Himself, that would be miraculous. He must not multiply miracles extensively, for it would be self-contradiction, frequently breaking through the normal laws He Himself has set in place. So to accomplish such works without miracles, He will use humans, who can do them without a miracle being involved—though without His interior graces to move those who work, and those who receive benefits from them, nothing would be accomplished.

Of course, there may be other types of cases too.

Obviously, He can make assignments in such a way that no one will be lost because of the type of square to which he is assigned. Since our Father so strongly desires that all be saved, we may be sure He will make such assignments—or, indeed, He may have a better way than the one we have pictured. But the point I wish to make is this: Our Father acts, again, like the father in a good family. If some children are sickly, they get the better care, for they need it. Those who are stronger get less, but still, all that they need.

We can see, then, that when His Son said that even the hairs on our heads are numbered (Mt 10:30), *i.e.*, that the Father takes individual care of each one, He meant it. We can see too that we who are given the first class squares have no reason to be proud. Rather, the implication is that, at least for the most part, we might not have been saved at all without such advantages, that we are the people most resistant to grace out of the entire human race.

There is still more. We have been speaking of full membership in the Church. This means, of course, that there can be lesser degrees of membership. We can gather this fact very definitely from comparing two kinds of statements of the Church. On the one hand, we have several texts, even a solemn definition from the Council of Florence

[11]It is quite possible that some will be saved more easily in the 2nd or 3rd class squares, where they have to face less strong explicitly taught requirements, *e.g.*, the teaching on contraception.

(1447), that there is no salvation outside the Church.[12] On the other hand, Pope Pius IX taught that "God . . . in His supreme goodness and clemency, by no means allows anyone to be punished with eternal punishments, who does not have the guilt of voluntary fault."[13] Vatican II agrees: "They who, though no fault of theirs, do not know of the Gospel and Christ and His Church, but yet seek God with a sincere heart, and try with the help of grace to carry out His will, known to them by the dictates of conscience, can attain eternal salvation."[14]

A full study of the Fathers of the Church on this point occupies the appendix to this book; it shows that sometimes they speak like the Council of Florence, and at other times, usually the very same Fathers, they show a very broad concept of membership in the Church. For example, St. Augustine wrote this:

> The very thing which is now called the Christian religion existed among the ancients, nor was it lacking from the begining of the human race, until Christ Himself came in the flesh, after which the true religion, that already existed, began to be called Christian.[15]

We know the fact that somehow this requirement of membership in the Church can be satisfied even by those who have never heard of the Church. What of the how? St. Paul in Romans 2:14-16 gives us a great help: "The Gentiles who do not have the law [revealed religion] do by nature the things of the law. They show the work of the law written on their hearts." And St. Paul adds that according as they do or do not follow that law in their hearts, they will or will not be saved at the judgment.

This law written on hearts really means the work of the Holy Spirit, or the Spirit of Christ, who makes known to them interiorly what morality calls for. Modern anthropology agrees: even primitive peoples show a remarkable knowledge of the moral law, even in some detail.

So a person may be following the Spirit of Christ without knowing that it is that which he is following. But then, in Romans 8:9 St. Paul tells us that "If anyone does not have the Spirit of Christ, he does not belong to Him." So, of course, if a person has and follows that Spirit, he does belong to Christ.[16] Now in Paul's language, to belong to Christ is

---

[12]DS 1351.

[13]DS 2866.

[14]Vatican II, *On the Church* #16.

[15]St. Augustine, *Retractations* 1. 13. 3. PL 32. 603. For many Patristic texts, see W. Most, *Catholic Apologetics Today*, chapter 23, and the appendix.

[16] Following the Spirit includes an implicit wish for full membership. *Cf.* Pius XII, *Mystici Corporis*. DS 3821. "A wish which they do not recognize" is

the same as being a member of Christ—but to be a member of Christ means to be a member of the Church. It may be in a lesser degree, something short of the full membership of which we spoke, so that the person may not have even heard of the Church. Yet this following of the Spirit of Christ brings that substantial membership which is needed and which suffices.

So our Father does make the needed provision even for these persons. St. Paul in Romans 3:29 asks: "Is God the God of the Jews alone?" He means this: if God did not make provision for the salvation of non-Jews, He would act as if He were not their God. Similarly here, if God did not make some provision for people to have a substantial membership in the Church even without hearing of the Church, He would act as if He were not their God. But He is their God. He has made excellent provision for all.

---

inscio voto.

Chapter 13: We are His Members

Chapter 12 leaves us with a problem: we saw that the true sense of membership in the Church is very broad, so that one can be, substantially, a member without even hearing of the Church or visibly adhering to it. Of course, this would not be full, but imperfect membership. If this is the case: Is there really any need of visibily joining the Church, of becoming a member in the full sense?

Clearly there is a need, even an obligation, because of the fact that the Father, and His Son, our Redeemer, the founder of the Church, so wills it. This is the full sense of 1 Tim 2:4: "God wills all men to be saved and to come to the knowledge of the truth." Coming to the knowledge of the truth of course includes explicit, visible adherence to His Church.

But there is more. Even though those who have not explicitly and visibly joined, if they fulfill the conditions we saw in chapter 12, can even be said to be members of the Mystical Body of Christ, since that Mystical Body is the same as the Church, yet we must add that Pope Pius XII in his great Encyclical on the Mystical Body[1] urged

> those who do not belong to the visible bond of the Church to . . . get themselves out of that state in which they cannot be secure of their salvation . . . [since] they lack such great and so many heavenly gifts and helps which can be enjoyed only within the Catholic Church.[2]

What are these gifts and helps of which the Pope spoke? He had

---

[1]Pius XII, *Mystici Corporis* AAS 35.1943. 242-43.

[2]The fact that we add to the teaching of Pius XII in saying there is a real membership, in addition to "pertaining to the Church" for some, does not contradict. To affirm more is not to deny the lesser.

in mind chiefly two things—the Sacraments, and the Teachings of the Church.

About the Sacraments: The Church itself is sometimes called the great sacrament.[3] This is true, provided we understand that we are using the word Sacrament broadly. In the first centuries that word was so broad that it took in literally hundreds of things—anything religious and mysterious. But finally, by about the 12th century theologians developed more precise ways of speaking, limiting the meaning of the word to a sacred sign instituted by Christ to give grace. Then the Council of Trent could define that there are, in that sense, seven and only seven Sacraments.[4] So we need to be careful not to lose the precision it took so many centuries to gain. Yet in a broad sense the Church is the great Sacrament, since it is the great channel of grace.

The security of which Pius XII spoke begins with Baptism. Yes, one can obtain remission of original and personal sins by an act of love based on the fact that the Father is good in Himself, not just good to us. But can one be certain one has achieved that? No, there is always a question. For forgiveness of original sin, and acquisition of sanctifying grace even in infancy, Baptism is the means.

Further, after receiving forgiveness of sin by such an act of love, there is commonly left over a debt of temporal punishment—a need to rebalance the scales of the objective order, of which we spoke in chapter 4. But Baptism provides a wonderful boon, a once in a lifetime gift of a complete payment of all such debts, so that one has an entirely clean slate.

Similarly, one can obtain remission of personal sins by such an act of loving contrition. But again, there is a problem of being certain. The Sacrament of Penance gives security, for even a lesser kind of contrition—attrition—suffices for certain forgiveness.

And it also is true that by the will of the Father and His Son, we are obliged to use the Sacraments of Baptism and Penance.

At the end of life there is the final anointing. If one is unconscious, but had the required minimum dispositions before receiving it, there comes the great gift of forgiveness, even when one is unconscious, by that wonderful Sacrament.

Interior participation in the Mass, as we described it in chapter 11, provides a stimulus and an opportunity to join our dispositions with those of the Divine Victim on the altar, and to join with His Mother's participation in that same renewal of Calvary.

---

[3]*Cf.* John Paul II, *Dominum et vivificantem* AAS 78 (1986) 892.

[4]The Council of Trent defined that there are only seven Sacraments: DS 1601.

There are other exterior means of grace to be had only with full membership in the Church. But what of those who through no fault of their own do not have these external means? They surely lack the security of which we spoke. But can they still have comparable graces? We do not entirely know. The Father wills that all come to the full knowledge of the truth, and to the use of these stupendous means. Yet His hands are not tied by these grants. He is still of course free to give His graces, even richly, outside of these external means. To what extent He does that, He has not revealed to us.

We cannot help thinking of the fact that there are remarkable souls such as Socrates. St. Justin the Martyr considered Socrates a Christian because, without realizing that fact, he was actually following the divine Logos, the Word of God made known to him interiorly[5]. Such was the dedication of Socrates to justice, that he would not take the opportunity offered him to escape from a clearly unjust condemnation; such was his zeal for truth that he asserted over and over again that the searcher for truth should have as little a possible to do with the things of the body![6] His attitude here follows the principles we will explain in chapter 19. Can we not suppose that God, who is more eager to give than we are to receive, would welcome so great an opening for His graces as He found in Socrates?

Vatican II, on this matter, tells us: "Beyond doubt, the Holy Spirit was at work in the world before Christ was glorified."[7]. Pope John Paul II, in his Encyclical on the Holy Spirit, quoted approvingly St. Basil who wrote: "The Spirit is present to each one who is capable of receiving, as if he were the only one, and gives complete grace to all."[8]

Nonetheless, there is still another kind of security that goes with full membership—the priceless help of the divinely protected Magisterium of the Church. Plato, in his dialogue called the *Phaedo*[9], describes Socrates, not long before his execution, discussing with friends the proofs for survival after death. Pathetically and bravely he tries to prove it to himself and to them. After many such efforts, Simmias says the effort to prove immortality is extremely difficult, and wishes some god would simply reveal the answer.

---

[5]St. Justin Martyr, *First Apology* 46.

[6]*Cf.* note 17 on chapter 16.

[7]Vatican II, *On Missions* 4.

[8]St. Basil, On Holy Spirit 9.22. PG 32.110. Cited in John Paul II, Encyclical on Holy Spirit. AAS 78 (1986) 886. The Latin text and the Vatican Press English are too weak in rendering Greek *holokleron* as "sufficient." It really means "complete, entire, perfect."

[9]Plato, *Phaedo* 85 D.

Yes, the history of philosophy shows so many great minds struggling to attain truth. Some of them did attain a large measure of it. But even the greatest of the pagan Greeks, Aristotle, at times made considerable mistakes. How much better and more secure if he could have had a divine revelation! The Church has such revelation,[10] along with a promise of her divine Founder that she will correctly interpret that revelation for us. She does this more abundantly than many persons realize: we are given not only solemn definitions, which are relatively infrequent, but also, as Vatican II assures us: "Although the individual bishops do not have the prerogative of infallibility, they can yet teach Christ's doctrine infallibly: this is true even when they are scattered around the world, provided that, while maintaining the bond of unity among themselves, and with the successor of Peter, they concur in one teaching as the one which must be definitively held."[11] That is, the day to day teaching of the Church throughout the world, giving us things as definitely part of the faith, is also infallible.

There is even more: Pius XII, in 1950, in *Humani generis*, pointed out that: "It must not be thought that the things contained in Encyclical Letters do not of themselves require assent [of the mind] on the plea that in them the Pontiffs do not exercise the supreme power of their Magisterium. For these things are taught with the ordinary Magisterium, about which it is also true to say: 'He who hears you, hears me'."(Lk 10:16)[12] Pius XII went on to say that such teachings are had when the Popes in their *acta* expressly pass judgment on a matter previously debated among theologians: then it can no longer be debated. We have the security that comes from the promise of Christ: "He who hears you hears me."

A less solid, but very valuable assurance can be had even below this level of teaching. Vatican II tell us that:

> Religious submission of will and of mind must be given to the authentic magisterium of the Roman Pontiff even when he is not defining, in such a way, namely, that the judgments made by him are sincerely adhered to according to his manifested mind and will, which is clear either from the

---

[10]After going through a process that does not depend on faith, namely, apologetics, we reach the conclusion that the Church has a commission from Christ, the Messenger from God, to teach, and a promise of divine protection. That Church can then determine which books are divinely inspired, so as to be Scripture. *Cf.* W. Most *Catholic Apologetics Today*. This is the only possible way to know which books are inspired. For vain Protestant attempts, *Cf.* W. Most, *Free From All Error* chapter 2.

[11]Vatican II, *On the Church* 25.

[12]Pius XII, *Humani generis*, DS 3885.

> nature of the documents, or from the repeated presentation of the same doctrine, or from the manner of speaking.[13]

This is a very broad declaration. Since it makes the level of teaching depend on the intention of the Magisterium, we can see that sometimes it belongs to the second level, especially when there is "repeated presentation" of the same teaching. Sometimes it will have the assurance of the third level, spoken of in the quotation we saw from Pius XII, which we know from the "manner of speaking". Sometimes the Popes do not intend to go so far: we still have a most valuable help, even if it be less than infallible.

A comparison will help. Suppose we are seated at a dinner table. Someone points to a certain dish, asks if it came from a can, wondering it it was sent to a lab for a check to be sure there is no Botulism (a specially deadly form of food poisoning, which routine opening of a can would not reveal). When he is told there was no lab check, he exclaims: Do you expect me to stake my life on a noninfallible assurance? Yet such are human affairs that we normally do ignore such a possibility for it is extremely infrequent, extremely rare. Now a teaching on a level below that of which Pius XII spoke in *Humani generis* is indeed not infallible. Yet the chances of error are far more remote than those of finding Botulism in canned food. So we do have an excellent help for securely finding the truth.

Really, without the Church, no one could know with certainty that there are such things as inspired books, *i.e.*, Holy Scripture. Other criteria for determining which books are inspired have all failed, *e.g.*, Luther's notion that if a book preaches strongly justification by faith, it is inspired. He had not proved that such was the criterion. And also, either he or I could write a book preaching that, and it would not be inspired.[14]

We need to realize too that we are not saved on, so to speak, a solo basis, each one working alone. This is the basic reason for the teaching that we saw in Chapter 12, that there is no salvation outside the Church. The Church is the extension of Christ throughout all time. On Calvary once for all He, with the cooperation of His Blessed Mother, earned for us all grace and forgiveness (the objective redemption). In the work of giving out the fruits of Calvary (the subjective redemption), we cannot dispense with Him and His Blessed Mother. No, we are saved precisely as His members, that is, members of the Church.

No, if we summed up the teaching of St. Paul (*cf. e.g.* Romans 6:3-

---

[13] *Cf.* note 11 above.

[14] *Cf.* note 10 above.

5; Col 3:1) we would find him telling us that we are saved and made holy if and to the extent that we are members of Christ, and like Him. Whatever "merits" we may have, that is, claims to divine help or reward, we have not as individuals. Rather, we share in the great claim Jesus established in the New Covenant. We are His members, we are part of the great People of God.

This teaching that the Church is the Mystical Body of Christ is exceedingly rich. We have it basically from St. Paul, and elaborated further in the Encyclical on the Mystical Body of Pope Pius XII, and further stressed in Vatican II. The word "mystical" does not occur in Scripture. But it is a useful, really, a necessary word. For our union with Christ is not that of a physical body—we are not physically parts of Him. Yet our union is more than that in a moral body, such as a corporation. In fact, there is no parallel anywhere to this kind of union. Hence the word mystical, to categorize it in a special way.

St. Paul begins to speak of it in 1 Corinthians. In 6: 15 he uses it as the basis for an argument against loose sex: "Do you not know that your bodies are members of Christ? So, taking the members of Christ [my body] should I make them members of a harlot?"(So as to be two in one flesh.) In 1 Cor 11:12-31 he goes into a long comparison: Just as the human body, though it is one, has various kinds of members, "so also is Christ. For by the one Spirit we all were baptized into [so as to form] one body." That is, the Church has, and needs, various kinds of members for diverse functions. The foot should not say that it does not belong to the body because it is not a hand. And similarly with other diverse members of the body. "But you are the body of Christ, and members (each in its own) part. God has placed in the Church: first, apostles, second, prophets, third, teachers. . . ."

Now of course, if we are members of Christ, it is implied that He is the Head. In the Epistles to the Colossians and Ephesians[15] that implication is confirmed beautifully, *e.g.*, in Col 1:18: "He Himself is the head of the body, the Church." A new term, the *pleroma*, the "fulnesss" appears. Col 2: 9: "For in Him lives permanently all the fulness of the divnity in a bodily way, and you have been made full in Him." So the

[15]Doubts on Pauline authorship of Colossians and Ephesians are weakly based. Reasons given: (1)language and style—but style is very inconclusive: *cf.* the style of Tacitus' *Dialogue*, compared to his other works. (2)similarity of the two Epistles—but a traveling speaker often repeats himself. (3)theological emphases and developments—but Paul, mentally alive, could develop. And emphasis would shift with the needs of the case. On other hand, ancient, external witnesses to authenticity are very strong. And it is generally admitted that at least the thought is Pauline.

Church receives from Him, and becomes His fulness (Eph 1:22-23): "And He subjected all things under His feet, and He made Him Head, over all things, for the Church, which is His Body, the fulness of Him who is filled in all things [or: Who fills all things]." The varied gifts He gives to His Church, mentioned already in First Corinthians, are aimed at the complete development of the pleroma (Eph 4:13) for God has given the varied gifts, "until we all come together into the unity of faith and the knowledge of the Son of God, to be a perfect man, to the measure of the stature of the fulness of Christ." Thus Christ becomes the center, or the new Head of all (Eph 1:10).

Even in heaven, we will be there as members of the Church, for Vatican II teaches: "The Church . . . will attain her full perfection only in the glory of Heaven."[16]

As we saw in chapter 12, one can be substantially a member of Christ, and so of His Church without external explicit adherence to the visible Church. In other words, one can have an imperfect membership. But the Father wills all to come to the knowledge of the truth (1 Tim 2:4), to have full membership and so to share completely in this rich fulness of the Body of Christ! The love of Jesus and His Mother invite us to this. Hence He prayed that there might be one flock and one shepherd (John 10:16). The Father's love of what is right in itself, what is part of good order (*cf.* chapter 4) wants all to have the fullest titles to grace and forgiveness through the fullest participation in the Body of Christ.

Without this full membership, and the full teaching of the Church, one is not likely to have the comfort of knowing fully the splendid truths about Mary which we have seen in the previous chapters. Nor would he understand her role as the Mother of the Church, the Mother of the Mystical Body.

Pope Paul VI, in an address at the close of the third session of Vatican II, explicitly gave her that title of Mother of the Church. But the doctrine was not entirely new. The Council itself had already said, quoting St. Augustine, that : "She cooperated in love that the faithful might be born in the Church."[17] Pope Pius XII, in a message to the Marian Congress of Ottawa, on June 9, 1947, implied she is Mother of the Church:

> When the little maid of Nazareth uttered her fiat to the message of the angel . . . she became not only the Mother of God in the physical order of nature, but also in the supernatural order of grace, she became the

[16]Vatican II, *On the Church* 48.

[17]*Ibid.* 53, citing. St. Augustine *De Virginitate* 6. PL 40.399.

> Mother of all who . . . would be made one under the Headship of her divine Son. The Mother of the Head would be the Mother of the members."[18]

It is sometimes objected: How could she be the Mother of the Church, when she is certainly a member of the Church? The reply is easy. In speaking of the Mystical Body we are making a comparison between physical and spiritual realities. It is not strange if physical terms do not fully work out. A different comparison will help: Mr. John Jones was the father of a corporation, for he started it, brought it into being. Yet after that, he was also a member of that corporation.

A few of the Fathers of the Church spoke of her as the type of the Church, *i.e.,* as the advance model of what the Church was to be at present, and in the glory of heaven. Vatican II made this teaching its own:

> The Mother of God is the type of the Church, as St. Ambrose had already taught, in the order of faith, love, and perfect union with Christ. For in the mystery of the Church, which is also rightly called a mother, the Blessed Virgin Mary went ahead, eminently and singularly giving the example of virgin and mother. . . . The Church, contemplating her hidden holiness and imitating her love, and faithfully fulfilling the will of the Father, by receiving the word of God faithfully, becomes a mother too; by her preaching and baptism she generates children, conceived by the Holy Spirit, and born of God, to new and immortal life. And she is a virgin, who completely and purely keeps the faith she gave to her Spouse, and, imitating the Mother of her Lord, by the power of the Holy Spirit, virginally keeps full faith, solid hope, sincere love.[19]

The Council goes on, saying that the Church "in the Most Blessed Virgin has already attained the perfection in which there is no spot or wrinkle."[20] This means that the Church at present has not yet attained the perfect holiness it will have in heaven, a holiness it admires and tries to imitate in Mary who already has such holiness. Now in this world, the Church is not always holy in all its members, though it can be called holy in that it posseses all the means of holiness, and that in itself, by its nature—though not in each member—it is holy.

The image of the woman clothed with the sun in Revelation/Apocalypse 12 is fascinating. On the one hand, it seems to refer to Mary, for her Son is clearly the Messiah, who will rule the nations with an iron rod—an echo of Psalm 2:9. On the other hand, she labors in

---

[18]English text from AAS 39 (1947) 271.

[19]Vatican II, *On the Church* 63-64.

[20]*Ibid.* 65 (alluding to Eph 5:27).

birth, which was not true of Mary. The result is that the image has some traits of Mary, some of the Church. St. Pius X puts these features together well:

> John saw the Most Holy Mother of God already enjoying eternal happiness, and yet laboring from some hidden birth. With what birth? Surely, our birth: we, still detained in exile, are still to be brought forth to the perfect love of God and eternal happiness.[21]

How can we explain the double reference? Quite easily. There is a well known pattern in Hebrew, in which an individual stands for a group, and in a sense is even identified with it; this is often the case with the Jewish king in the Old Testament. Therefore, we can say that the image represents both Mary and the Church.

A further conclusion is possible, even though not certain. In a dissertation for the Pontifical Biblical Institute in Rome, published in 1954, Bernard J. LeFrois suggests that since the image seems to refer to the last days of the world, then it could mean that then the Church is to take on a specially Marian character, in an age of Mary.[22] St. Louis de Montfort foretold an age of Mary before the end.[23]

If that age comes, will it also be the very time of the end? Definitely not. Jesus Himself tells us (Lk 18:8): "When the Son of Man comes [at the end] do you think He will find faith on the earth?" Yes, for the Church will endure to the end, but yet it will have declined greatly—so many will have fallen away. St. Paul in 2 Thes 2:3 foretells the great apostasy at the end. 2 Timothy 3:1-7 predicts dreadful times just before the end. 2 Timothy 4: 3-4 tells us that at that time men will not acccept sound doctrine, but will turn instead to fables. The reason, most probably, is that this will be the time of the great Antichrist.‡

These are fearful portents, yet those who are faithful to Jesus and His Mother will be enabled to persevere. Pope Pius XI assures us:

> Nor would he incur eternal death whom the Most Blessed Virgin assists, especially at his last hour. This opinion of the Doctors of the Church, in harmony with the thoughts of the Christian people, and supported by

---

[21]St. Pius X, *Ad diem illum* ASS 36 (1904) 458-59. *Cf.* Pius XII AAS 42 (1950). 762-63 and Paul VI, AAS 59 (1967) 465.

[22]Bernard J. Le Frois, *The Woman Clothed with the Sun*, Orbis Catholicus, Rome, 1954. Some commentators think Revelation is purely Apocalyptic genre, with no predictions. We believe there are probably some, such as the present passage.

[23]St. Louis de Montfort, *True Devotion* #49.

[24]There will also be lesser Antichrists: *cf.* Mt. 24:5.

> the experience of all times, depends especially on this reason: the fact that the Sorrowful Virgin shared in the work of the redemption with Jesus Christ.[25]

She shared in earning all graces; therefore no request she makes is ever denied by the Father. Hence Pope Benedict XV beautifully but precisely calls her "Suppliant Omnipotence."[26] Vatican II agrees, telling us that even in heaven: "She has not put aside this saving function, but continues by her manifold intercession to win the gifts of eternal salvation for us . . . the brothers of her Son, still in pilgrimage and involved in dangers and difficulties until they are led to the happy fatherland."[27]

As for her Son: He always knew and loved His Church from the first moment of His conception, as Pius XII tells us:

> The most loving knowledge of this kind, with which the divine Redeemer pursued us from the first moment of the Incarnation, surpasses the diligent grasp of any human mind; for by the blessed vision which He enjoyed when just received in the womb of the Mother of God, He has all the members of the Mystical Body continuously and perpetually present to Himself, and embraces them with salvific love. . . . In the manger, on the Cross, in the eternal glory of the Father, Christ has all the members of the Church before Him, and joined to Him far more clearly and loving than a mother has a son on her lap.[28]

---

[25]Pius XI, *Explorata res*, AAS 15 (1923) 104.

[26]Benedict XV, *Decessorem nostrum.* AAS 7 (1915) 202.

[27]Vatican II, *On the Church* 62.

[28]Pius XII, *Mystici Corporis*. AAS 35 (1943) 230.

Chapter 14:
Saved by Faith

For thirteen chapters now we have tried to see and understand somewhat the truths about the approach of our Father to our race, in marvelous goodness and generosity. We have seen that He pursues two goals simultaneously: love of us, and love of what is good in itself (objective goodness or objective order).

From neither of these pursuits does He gain anything at all. Even though we sometimes speak of Him as acting for His "glory," even that is no benefit to Him. He cannot gain anything at all. St. Augustine rightly remarks that honor from creatures is "smoke without substance".[1] How true! We gain nothing from such a thing as honor; neither does our Father. Yet He wants honor, simply because objective goodness requires that creatures honor their Creator, and so that He may be able to give to them in such a way that they can receive (for His commands are instructions on how to be open to His gifts). In one and the same act, as we said, He works for what is objectively good, which His Holiness wills, and for our good.

So, now, having come to realize to some slight extent His wondrous Love/Holiness/Generosity, we obviously should ask: What should our response to Him be? It will turn out to be a matter of emptying so as to be able to be filled: emptying of self, by humility, mortification, meditation, so as to be filled with His love and love for Him. Our chapters too thus far have shown the importance of getting the help of the

[1]St. Augustine, *City of God* 5.17.PL 41.161. Let us imagine ourselves walking in the ancient Roman Forum, on the Via Sacra, where Caesar rode in triumph, with crowds on both sides hailing him loudly. But: Where is Caesar now? Where are the crowds—all turned to duSt. We hope their eternal fate is good.

Mother of God, the Mother of Jesus. For although the Father did not need her at all—He needs no creature—yet He freely chose to put her everywhere in His approach to us. He gave her an all-pervading role in His plans.

Clearly, if we wish to imitate His ways—and nothing could be better or higher—ideally we would give her a correspondingly all-pervading place in our spiritual lives, taking into account in this, of course, individual spiritual differences among people.[2]

If we begin by asking what is the central, the most basic feature of our response to Him, we encounter a puzzle. He has chosen to deal with us by way of Covenant, Old and New. Within the covenants, as we have seen, we humans receive favor on condition of our obedience to the covenant conditions, that is, to His law.

But yet, Jesus Himself told us that the center of all is love. After replying that the first commandment is "To love the Lord your God with your whole heart, your whole soul, and your whole mind" and the second is like to it, "You shall love your neighbor as yourself," He added: (Mt 22:40): "On these two comandments depend the whole law and the prophets."

Yet St. Paul insists that we are free from the law, and the condition of salvation is faith. Over and over again Paul insists (Rom 3:28) "A man is made just by faith without the works of the law." Of course we know without looking that no statement in Holy Scripture will contradict another statement there, for all are written under inspiration, so that strictly, as Vatican I taught, "They have God as their author."[3]

The answer is not hard to find. We have already seen that love, when directed to God, amounts in practice to obedience to Him. For since He cannot gain anything, we cannot wish Him well, or wish that He may get what He needs; it is only love of creatures that consists in wishing well to them for their sakes. But Scripture shows He is pleased when we obey, because thereby we are made open to receive what His Generosity loves to give, and, at the same time, objective goodness is satisfied, which tells us that creatures should obey their Creator, children their Father. Hence Jesus Himself said explicitly at the Last Supper (Jn 14:21): "He who hears my commandments and keeps them, he is the one who loves me."

So, even though in theory there is a difference; in practice, love of God and obedience to Him are the same thing.

As to faith, if we understand the word the way St. Paul himself understands it, we find it is a very comprehensive virtue. It really means

[2]On the diversity of spiritual attractions *cf.* chapter 17.

[3]Vatican I DS 3009; Vatican II, *On Divine Revelation* #11.

total adherence of a person to God, so that if God speaks a truth, we believe it (*cf.* 1 Thes 2:13); if He makes a promise, we are confident He will keep it (*cf.* Rom 4:3); if He tells us to do something, we obey. Hence St. Paul can even speak of the "obedience of faith" (cf. Rom 1:5)—a phrase in which the word "of" is an "equals" sign: faith is obedience. All of which is to be done in love (*cf.* Gal 5:6).[4] Hence Vatican II rightly tells us that faith is the virtue "in which a person freely commits himself entirely to God, giving full adherence of mind and will to God who reveals; and freely assenting to the revelation given by Him."[5]

So whether we say that the basic condition of our response to God is love—or obedience—or faith—in practice, all come to the same thing, even though technically one could draw lines. Really, this equation is not strange—in God Himself, because of His absolute unity, all virtues—even justice and mercy, which seem opposed to each other—are identified with His divine nature, and therefore, identified with each other!

So we begin in this chapter to explore love/obedience/faith. After that we will look into the conditions mentioned above for carrying these out, a process of emptying of self to make room for being filled with love/obedience/faith.

We take up first the adherence to God in that aspect of faith in which we believe His words, and trust in them. There are many dramatic incidents in Scripture in which this is brought out forcefully. When Abraham was 99 and his wife Sarah was 90, and had been sterile all her life, God spoke to Abraham, and promised that he would have a son by Sarah. Abraham believed, and did have a son, Isaac. But later, when Isaac was still a little boy, Abraham showed even more remarkable faith. For God spoke again and ordered him to take Isaac to a certain mountain and there offer him in sacrifice. At this point Abraham could have very reasonably spoken to God and said: "My Lord, you told me I would be the father of a great nation through Isaac. So I must believe that, and I can believe. But now you tell me to kill him in sacrifice, preventing the fulfillment of that promise. So please tell me your holy will, and I will do whatever you wish."[6] But Abraham did nothing of the kind; he just went ahead, believing the impossible, until God told him to

---

[4]*Cf.* W. Most, *Catholic Apologetics Today*, chapter 18.

[5]Vatican II, *On Divine Revelation* # 5.

[6]Heb 11:19 speaks of Abraham as believing God would raise Isaac from the dead. However,the literary genre of Hebrews (on genre, *cf.* first part of chapter 3) is recognized by nearly all as homiletic, *i.e.*, a preaching style, in which the speaker often becomes rather free and even imaginative.

stop and not sacrifice Isaac. Here was a magnificent faith, a faith that held on in the dark, when it was impossible to see, when it seemed impossible to believe.

Not only Abraham, a great spiritual man, but the entire people of Israel was, it seems, put in a similar situation of having to believe the impossible.[7] For most scholars think that probably the people of Israel had no clear knowledge until about the middle of the second century B.C. that there was any reward or punishment in the future life. They did know there was survival, but reward and punishment would be something added to that. On the other hand, they knew it had been revealed that God does reward and punish justly. We, who know clearly that the future life makes everything right, have no problem. But imagine the plight of those who had to believe everything is made right in this present life—when their senses inescapably reported that many times the wicked prosper to the end, while the good are afflicted even until their deaths.[8] To have to believe God rewards and punishes justly, and not to know there is future retribution—this is to be asked to believe the unbelievable. Yet they were asked to hold on, in faith, in the dark.

We already saw the difficult demand on the faith of Mary on the day of the Annunciation. She is the greatest model of this aspect of faith, for her Son, being divine, never had to mentally hold to something He could not understand.[9] But she had to believe there is only one God—and yet that the Father is God, and her Son would be God.

After that day she had also to contend with a constant clash of what her senses told her, and what her faith said. Her faith knew He was the Son of God. Yet as she handled Him as an infant, fled into Egypt with Him, spent years of very ordinary life with Him at Nazareth—in all these, her faith and her senses did not agree, they clashed. So she had to believe. And that she did, most perfectly. She

---

[7]The problem is focused specially in the Book of Job. On this problem *cf.* W. Most, *Catholic Apologetics Today*, pp. 225-34.

[8]The problem was made especially acute by the martyrs under Antiochus Epiphanes of Syria in the 2nd century B.C. At the same time, Jews became acquainted with Greek thought on the two-part structure of man (body and soul)—which some think they did not know before. Thus they would be providentially guided to a clarification in their beliefs.

[9]One part of faith, holding on in the dark, was impossible for Jesus in view of the fact that His human soul always had the vision of God (*cf.* chapter 8 above). But He could and did, on His human side, obey the Father (obedience of faith) and trust in Him, with the absolute assurance the divine vision gave Him. Faith in general is the total adherence of a person to God: Jesus had this supremely.

might well have been tempted to wonder too, when He waited until He was 30 before beginning His mission—would it not have seemed, humanly speaking, that He was not going to do anything special at all?

We might be inclined to suppose that between the best of Sons and the best of Mothers everything would be sweetness and light. But what of His way of acting when He stayed behind in the Temple at the age of 12? St. Luke (2:50) reports that she and St. Joseph did not know what to make of it, or of His explanation. This need not mean that they did not know of His divinity. But, even knowing that, they could be puzzled over the strange departure from the ways they had seen in Him for so many years.

Still more difficult for her was the scene at the wedding at Cana. Seeing the wine running out, she, in a demure and quite feminine way, did not directly ask, but just hinted to Him to do something, saying: "They have no wine." But He replied in a line which causes much trouble to translators, as the variety of translations proposed testifies. The literal Greek reads (Jn 2:4): "What is it to me and to you, woman?" This expression occurs a few other times in Scripture,[10] and where it does, it always has a tone of rejection. Further, the word "woman," though it was an honorable title, yet it seems at least cold. The outcome, His working of His first miracle, shows it was not a rejection. And the word "woman" could even be the Evangelist's word, not that of Jesus, used to point out that Mary is the woman foretold in the prophecy of Genesis 3:15, of enmity between her and the serpent, and likewise the "woman" at the foot of the cross. For John has Jesus say to John (Jn. 19:26-27): "Son, behold your mother." But then, instead of the naturally matching expression, He says to her, "Woman, behold your son."

Further, Revelation (Apocalypse) 12:1 has a "woman clothed with the sun," who is probably both the Church and Mary under one image.[11] So the word *woman*, whether by John or by Jesus, could be meant to point out that she is the woman of these crucial Scriptural passages. But even so, would she know at the time? Surely it was a strain on her faith, but she held on in the dark, and confidently told the waiters at the wedding (Jn 2:5): "Whatever He says to you, do it."

St. Luke groups together three puzzling sayings of Jesus; we do not know if He gave them all on one occasion. First, someone said to Jesus (Lk 9:57-62): "I will follow you wherever you go." Jesus replied:

---

[10]The expression occurs only a few times in Scripture: Judges 11:12; 2 Chron 35:21; 1 Kings 17:18; 2 Kings 3.13; Hos 14:8.

[11]John Paul II, in *Redemptoris Mater*, March 25, 1987, makes this view of the "woman" his own in #24 and #47.

"The foxes have holes, and the birds of the sky have nests, but the Son of Man has nowhere to lay His head." This was not very encouraging, though realistic. The second saying is more of a problem. Jesus said to another one: "Follow me." That person replied: "Let me first go away to bury my father." Jesus told him: "Let the dead bury their dead, but you go off and announce the kingdom of God." This would of course seem shocking: respect for parents is commanded in the fourth commandment, and Jesus seems to ignore it. Of course, to omit attendance at a funeral would not, strictly, be a violation of the commandment. Some commentators think the man really meant he wanted to stay at home until his father died, at an indefinite future time. Next, another man said he would follow Jesus, but first he wanted to say goodbye to his people at home. Jesus replied: "No one who puts his hand to the plow and looks back is fit for the kingdom of God." Jesus is probably using a popular proverb. But again, it sounds almost harsh.

What goes on in these three incidents? It seems to be part of the same pattern we have been seeing, a pattern of calling on souls to believe without being able to understand, in the dark.

We recall too the occasion we have already seen, in chapter 13, in which His Mother was at the edge of a crowd, and it was announced to Jesus that she was there. Instead of giving her a warm welcome, He pointed to the disciples and said (Mt. 12:48-50): "Who is my Mother, and who are my brothers? . . . Behold, my Mother and my brothers. For whoever does the will of my Father in heaven, he is my brother and sister and Mother." He was, of course, teaching a profound lesson, that the dignity of adhering to the will of God is even greater than being physically the Mother of God.[12] Pope Pius XI taught that the divine motherhood is a "dignity second only to God" and he quotes St. Thomas Aquinas saying it is "a sort of infinite dignity, from the infinite good that God is."[13] She was at the peak in both categories, dignity of position, and adherence to the will of God. Yet His words must have been a trial for her, for they surely seemed strange.[14]

In chapter 6 of St. John's Gospel we have another striking incident. Jesus had announced (Jn 6:51) : "I am the living bread that came down from heaven. If anyone eats of this bread, he will live forever, and

[12]Vatican II, *On the Church* #58 says: "During the course of His preaching, she received His words in which He, her Son, praising the kingdom more than ties of flesh and blood, proclaimed blessed those who heard the Word of God and kept it, as she herself was faithfully doing."

[13]*Cf.* note 17, chapter 10.

[14]Even in Mary there could be a clash of what her senses reported and what her faith held.

the bread which I will give is my flesh for the life of the world." The Jews began to wrangle, and with reason. To eat someone's flesh could mean, in the language of the day, to slander him. That could not be it. Otherwise it would sound like proposing cannibalism. But Jesus did not explain, He merely repeated (Jn 6:53): "Amen, Amen I tell you, if you do not eat the flesh of the Son of Man and drink His blood, you will not have life in you." At this point many in the crowd began to leave Him. Far from explaining, He turned to the Twelve and said: "Are you going to leave too?" It would have been so easy for Him to say: "Hold on, please, do not leave. I mean no cannibalism. I will take bread and wine and say over them: 'This is my body . . . This is my blood' That is not so difficult iis it?" But instead, He demanded absolute faith, faith that would hold on in the dark, without being able to see.

We have noticed that He acted this way even to His own Mother, who on so many occasions had to show magnificent faith. At the cross, she had to believe that this wretched failure—for so it seemed to others, and even the Apostles except John had fallen away—was the salvation of the world. And when He gloriously appeared to many, first to the ex-sinner Mary Magdalene, Scripture does not report He came to show Himself to His Mother. Did He omit it? We simply do not know. What we do know is that this kind of treatment, insisting that people, even His Mother, hold on to faith in the dark, is the best way to cause them to grow spiritually.

Mary was, of course, full of grace, as the angel had said on the day of His conception. In fact, as Pius IX told us, from the first moment of her own conception, her holiness was so great that, "None greater under God can be thought of, and no one but God can comprehend it." Yet, even though full of grace, she could still grow. A crude comparison may help: we think of several glasses of different sizes. Each one may be filled with liquid. Yet some will hold more than others. Grace, of course, is not like a liquid—it is the radication of God's power in the soul. It is possible for a soul to grow in its capacity for that radiction, and hence, there can be a fulness of grace at each stage, yet that fulness can increase in this sense: this is a relative fulness, the fulness in Mary. Of course if one has the absolute fulness of the God-man himself, there is no room for growth. But in Mary, there was room for growth, room for greater enjoyment of eternal happiness. To will that greater happiness for someone, even if it costs some difficulties, holding on in the dark for a while—that is love, great love. For love means willing good to another for the other's sake. His love for her, then, led Him to act this way. His love for all of us means He will at various times put us into such straits. Then we must either grow greatly, or fall back. If we imitate His Mother, we will grow, grow greatly, and be capable of taking in more of that infinite vision and love that God offers forever.

We do not wish to give the impression that we can cause ourselves to grow in faith. That would be a mistake. Faith is God's gift to us, even though it is the condition on which we are saved or not saved. So St. Paul told the Ephesians (Eph 2:8): "By grace you are saved through faith and this [faith] is not from you [it is] the gift of God." (How it can be a condition of salvation, when it does not come from us, is a fascinating problem. We will explore it in chapter 18.)

Even though we cannot make ourselves grow in faith, since faith is a gift of God, we can do something in that direction, to make ourselves open—strictly, *non-resistant*[15]—to that gift in greater measure. Most obviously, we can pray for more faith. We can also welcome the difficulties of life, especially those in which we must hold on in the dark. For acting on faith makes us open to increase in faith. Faith tells us that, compared to the unending, unimaginable goods of the life to come, the things of this life are worse than worthless. We do not deny that they are good; God made them good. But we mean that when compared to eternal goods, things of this world seem to be no better than dung—that is St. Paul's word, in writing to the Philippians (Phil 3:7-9) "The things that were gain to me"—at first he refers to the privileges of being a Jew—"these I consider loss, on account of Christ. But I therefore consider all things"—not only Jewish privileges—"loss on account of the outstandingness of the knowledge of Christ Jesus my Lord, on account of whom I have taken the loss of all things, and I consider them dung, that I may gain Christ."

We called these things even worse than worthless in this sense: They can tempt us to forget the higher goods, and so put us in danger of losing them.

We need to realize—not just to know in a notional way—these great truths. One way to realize them is to meditate much, another is to act on them. How to act on them we may partly surmise already. We will see more fully later.

---

[15]This will be developed in chapter 18 in the material on Phil 2:13 and the philosophical explanation of the same.

Chapter 15:
The Obedience that is Faith

What is the basic reason why we should cultivate obedience/love? If we look at the aspect of obedience, the answer is obvious: He is our Father, and He is our Creator, to whom we owe even our very existence, and continuation of existence. Further, His Son has bought us back at a great price from the captivity of the evil one.

If we look at the aspect of love, the motive will be, clearly, His immeasurable, indescribable goodness, which we have tried to realize even a little in the previous chapters.

There are several types of this motivation. If we start at the lowest, we would find a servile obedience, resulting from even a fear of punishment. Now this motive is not wrong. Jesus Himself in the Gospels speaks strongly of it (Mt 10: 28): "Do not fear those who kill the body and cannot kill the soul. But rather fear the One who can bring to ruin both body and soul in hell."

But the very goodness of our Father urges us to rise higher, while not forgetting the wholesome warning of His Son. We should love/obey because our Father is good. We recall the dramatic teaching of His Son (Lk 18: 18-19): "Why do your call me good?" He said to an inquirer. "One is good: God." Jesus did not deny that He Himself was good—or that He was God. Rather, He wanted to bring out forcefully, as we saw earlier, that the word *good* when applied to creatures and when applied to God is partly the same, yet very different. God our Father simply is *Goodness*.

Yet even in this aspect of love/obedience there is a distinction to be made. We could look on our Father as good to us, or, better, as good in Himself. Both are true. The higher motive, the one He deserves, is the consideration that He is good in Himself. The most perfect love, which He deserves, comes from the higher motive.

Can a creature be capable of such lofty love? Yes, with a reservation. As we have already seen, when we love any other human person, our love has a starter: we see something good in the other person. This leads to the reaction: "So good a person. I hope he or she is well off, gets what he or she needs to be happy." But the love of our Father for us had no starter, for when He began—if we may use that word—to love us, we did not exist at all. And when we first existed, He found nothing lovable in us. Really, every bit of good that I am or have or do is simply His gift to me. St. Paul's comment is worth hearing again (1 Cor 4: 7): "What have you that you have not received? And if you have received, why brag as if you had not received." If I receive all the good I am and have and do—then it is God's gift. I did not generate a bit of that goodness myself. Really, if I could generate or produce any goodness myself that would be creation, making it out of nothing. Only God creates. So I must recognize my place, and not boast over what I did not produce.

The point here is that our Father's love is the only possible completely generous love. Only He can do utterly without a starter for love. Yet, even though we creatures need a starter, still, by His grace we can be elevated, made capable of reaching at times to such a level as to love Him simply becaue He is good in Himself. Of course it always remains true that we cannot avoid knowing at least in the depths of our consciousness that He will reward anything we do to please Him. So the motive of love because He is good *to me* is never completely gone, just pushed beneath the surface of consciousness at times.

However, we can and should try to reach such a level of pure love as much as possible. He surely deserves that, even if we are capable of it at all only by His grace. (How this works we will explore in chapter 18.) In this matter we need to strive always for more and more progress, more spiritual growth. For the goal is what His Son set for us (Mat 5:48): "Be you perfect, as your heavenly Father is perfect." It is only when we finally arrive at our Father's house, heaven, that we will have reached the maximum of which we are capable—not the absolute maximum. Then as St. Anselm wrote, the soul "... will love God incomparably more than self and all others with self; [and] so will rejoice immeasurably more over the blessednesss that God has than over its own blessedness and that of all others with it."[1] That is, the soul will will good to God—for that is what love means—will Him a good

---

[1]St. Anselm, *Proslogion* 25. Cf. also St. Thomas *Summa* II-II.26.13 and Suppl. 44.3.

infinitely greater than its own good, for His own sake, because He is Goodness.

Meanwhile, in this valley of tears, we can never say: "It is enough." For we never do reach the goal set for us by His Son, to be perfect as the Father is perfect.

In passing, let us note that this perfection is open to all persons, in every state of life. True, some states of life do offer added spiritual helps.[2] But the command of Jesus applies to all, as Pope Pius XI told us, in his Encyclical for the third centenary of St. Francis de Sales. Speaking of the command of Jesus, the Pope wrote: "Let no one think that this invitation is addressed to a small very select number and that all others are allowed to stay in a lower degree of virtue . . . this law obliges everyone, without exception."[3] It was highly suitable that Pius XI should write this on the anniversary of St. Francis de Sales, for St. Francis brilliantly explained in his *Introduction to the Devout Life* (1. 3) that although the practices of the spiritual life need to be adjusted to various states in life, yet all are called to be perfect. And if they are called, it must be possible in every state. That this is true is shown by the calendar of the Saints, which includes men and women from every walk in life.

In what does growth consist? Precisely in this love/obedience. It does not consist directly in multiplying various practices or spiritual exercises, even though these are needed as means to the goal He has set for us. But we must not confuse the means with the end.

St. Francis de Sales tells us that in general God does not let us know the degree of our spiritual progress at any one point, though we may gain some notion from our growth in a most basic virtue of humility—we say most basic, for though love is the greatest virtue, yet humility is needed as a precondition for love, as we shall see in chapter 18.[4]

Still, there is another scale on which we may make some attempt to gauge our growth in love. Perfect love will exclude all sin, and, so far as prudence advises, even imperfections. This means, in brief, that if love is perfect, one will never at all commit a mortal sin, or even a fully

---

[2]*Cf.* Vatican II, *On the Church* #46 says that the three evangelical counsels of poverty, chastity, and obedience "contribute not a little to purification of heart and spiritual freedom, they constantly stir up the fervor of love."

[3]Pius XI, *Rerum omnium perturbationem*, Jan 26,1923. AAS 15 (1923) p.50.

[4]*Cf.* St. Francis de Sales, *Spiritual Conferences* tr. under supervision of Gasquet & Mackey, Newman Westminster, 1945. VIII, pp. 135-36.

deliberate venial sin.

Here we do well to examine certain aspects of the spiritual life with respect to the nature of sin and imperfection. We spoke of fully deliberate venial sins, since there are also small sins that happen in a moment of frailty. Without a most special grace, no one could avoid all these sins of frailty. We think for example of cases in which a rather advanced, but not perfect, person might "blow off steam" a bit in anger. If one is hard on himself, allowing too few satisfactions, our weak lower nature becomes strained, and can slip on provocations that might not affect a person who is easy on himself. We do not mean we should avoid much mortification—chapter 20 will explore that matter. We mean a certain prudence is required. We need to be a bit patient with ourselves. St. John of the Cross warns us not to try to become Saints in a day.[5]

Of course, one can break with habits of mortal sin even at one stroke—as the Alcoholics Anonymous show us by their own experience. Many who come to them break with even a long habit of drunkeness in one moment, as it were. They propose many means. The most essential seem to be to realize the need of help—both divine and human—and to develop a powerful motive. That motive is developed in the same way advertisers try to work—by holding before ourselves, in much reflection, the reasons why we want something. Then our will is really strong. For a strong will seems to be one that has a strong motive. It is not that a will is like a muscle, that grows stronger with much exercise—though there is something resembling that to be seen in the growth of what psychologists call a favorable somatic resonance. (We will explore that in chapter 16, and will see that there are some conditions in which a large growth is possible in a short times, though in general, growth by nature must be gradual.)

However, in regard to venial sins, we need to beware of a special trap—what used to be called *affection* to venial sin. The word is not very clear. It means a gap in our resolve to do the will of God. For example, someone might have an attitude which if put into words would say: I do not intend to commit mortal sin, nor every venial sin that offers itself to me. But I have a reservation or two, *e.g.*, if it gets hard to sustain a conversation without some uncharitable remarks, I will join in on them. Or, given a strong reason, I will lie, etc. If one has such a reservation he cannot really grow much at all. For this is like a clamp on the heart, that lets it expand only to a certain point, and after that shuts everything off.

Something less than even venial sin is called an *imperfection*.

[5]St. John of the Cross, *Dark Night* 1.5.3.

What is an imperfection? There are many kinds and examples. Thus a remiss act, one in which we act as it were sluggishly, at a level below our normal level of love. Or an attachment to merely natural things (we will see more on this later), restless or useless desires, or omissions of good things that are not commanded, but which, considering everything, we could easily perform without excessive strain on ourselves. Are imperfections sinful? A few theologians have thought so.[6] That is not true, an imperfection by definition is still good, even though it is a lesser good. A generous soul will go far in avoiding imperfections. But can souls in general resolve to avoid absolutely all impefections? Surely, not all at once—it would put too much strain on our poor lower nature. So one needs to exercise much prudence, and pray for light in individual cases, as to what is the will of the Father. If one is close to our Blessed Mother, she will provide such guidance.

There is, however, such a thing as an attachment to imperfection. This is basically the same as the reservation we described above in regard to venial sin. Those reservations on venial sin are not likely to be fully conscious. Still less are the affections to imperfection likely to be fully conscious—the soul may not even be aware of them. So it is important, especially at a time of a retreat, to search for the presence of such things. Francis de Sales, a Saint noted for his unusually high degree of common sense and prudence, wrote :

> We can never attain to perfection while we have an affection for any imperfection, however small it may be, even nothing more than the harbouring of an idle thought ... and one fault, however small it may be, for which we keep an affection, is more contrary to perfection than a hundred others committed inadvertently and without affection.[7]

By affection the Saint means the sort of reservation we mentioned above.

St. John of the Cross, a sterner type, uses a dramatic image to bring out this truth: "It is the same thing if a bird is tied down by a slender or a thick cord ... as long as it does not break it to fly away."[8] The cord or thread lets the bird fly only so high, never higher, until it breaks it. However, later St. John admits that some whom he calls

---

[6]*E.g.* J. C. Osbourn, *The Morality of Imperfections* Newman, Westminster, 1950. But: the principles determining morality are three—object (nature of thing), purpose, circumstances. In imperfections all three are good. We should not call a lesser good a sin. *Cf.* R. Garrigou-Lagrange, *Christian Perfection and Contemplation*, Herder, St. Louis, 1946 pp. 428-34.

[7]St. Francis de Sales, *Spiritual Conferences* pp. 130, 131.

[8]St. John of the Cross, *Ascent of Mt.Carmel* 1.11.4. BAC edition p. 591.

"proficient", those who have made quite a bit of progress. may still retain, involuntarily, some of these affections to imperfection.[9] Precisely how this happens we will explain further in chapter 19.

In saying these things are we becoming mechanical in our explanations of love, or too meticulous? Not at all. We merely try to put before us what the absolute ideal consists in, so we may grow in self knowledge by comparing ourselves with it, and avoid becoming complacent. There is really a kind of cheapness about deliberate venial sin. We in effect say to our Father: "I do not intend to commit mortal sins; I might lose you, lose my soul. But venial sins? I can get away with them. I know you dislike them much. But that does not matter to me." The pagan Greeks had a valuable motto carved on the oracle of Delphi: "Get to know yourself." This is a precondition for us if we are to grow much spiritually—that is, if we are to try to return the immense love of our Father as fully as He deserves.

Modern psychology agrees with the oracle of Delphi. There are unsearched depths within each of us; we might even speak of submarine motives lurking beneath the surface of consciousness. We need to bring these to the surface, so we can deal with them. For example, suppose I heard an announcement that on an evening a week from now there would be a collection for some charity, and collectors would call at all places and pick up what people would give. I might think it over. And suppose I would decide to give $100—much more than most people would give. What could be my motive? I would like to think it would be 100% charity. Perhaps in a given case it might even be that. But it could easily be a mixture. Besides the motive of charity there could be another motive lurking in the depths, which I am not fully aware of. I might be anticipating with pleasure the big congratulations from the collector—or, alternatively, I might just want to pat myself on the back. There could be any proportion of these two motives, *e.g.*, 40% charity, 60% vanity.

How would this situation affect the worth of my action? Clearly an action done with such a mixed motive would be far less good than one done entirely out of charity. Similar mixtures can occur in things that are wrong—a student might decide suddenly to work really hard in a biology class—in which he had not done very much before—when he came to the chapter on sex. His study motive would be small; surely there would be at least an element of curiosity. And he might be kidding himself, for reasons that are obvious.

Some cynical person has said: Man is a rational animal because he can always find a good reason for anything he wants to do. We can

---

[9] St. John of the Cross, *Dark Night* 2.2.1.

deceive ourselves in this way: We begin by acting out of feeling, or following a course of least resistance, or a lower motive. Then if someone later asks why we did it, we think up a reason, which was not really present at the start. This is another of the many ways we can deceive ourselves.

Another very common way in which people fail to get complete self-knowledge and therefore deceive themselves, is by way of what we might call compartments in their life. We mean this: a person may have one pattern of behavior when he is at his place of work, and a quite different one at home. Yet, the person may be completely unaware that he is acting so differently, so inconsistently. Of course one ought to examine himself to look for these inconsistencies, so they can be corrected.

If we love our Father, something else inevitably goes with it. He wants to give most generously not only to me, but to all others—those whom His Son described as my neighbors. So if I love our Father, I will want, and work, so that He may have that pleasure. That is, I will want my neighbor to be open to these gifts of the Father. I will want this for a double reason: first, to let our Father have the pleasure of giving, as we said; second, out of willing good to my neighbor for his sake. These two things are inseparable in practice. Hence we see why our Lord spoke of a second commandment that is like to the first (the love of God). In practice these are really inseparable.

Can we love neighbor when our feelings go in the opposite direction? Certainly, for love consists in the attitude of will. How this relates to feeling we will explore later (chapter 17). But now we need to notice that we are not called on to have a warm feeling for all men at any time—still less to have such a feeling for enemies. Again, we recall what love is: it is to will or wish good to the other for the other's sake. This lies in our spiritual will, not in our feelings. So we can love even enemies by willing good to them, especially the good of eternal salvation, plus other things too. To this end, at a minimum we will include them in a general way in our prayers. Further, if our will for their well-being is strong as it should be, we will also act, will help others, especially the poor. (Acting on any attitude also strengthens it.) Hence the many exhortations in Scripture to help the poor. If we do so, it not only benefits the poor but helps us at the same time. In this vein, the great prophet Daniel gives the sound advice (4:24) "Expiate your sins by acts of mercy, and your iniquity by beneficence to the poor." And Tobit instructs his son (4:10): "Almsgiving delivers from death, and does not let one go into darkness."

This is a remarkable thought. Our Father has promised mercy to the merciful, in line with both His love of us, and His love of what is good in itself, objective goodness. When we do good to others, thanks to His promise, we establish a title on which He can more fully do good to us, which pleases Him greatly. We could actually say that by His kindness, there is a multiplier: one and the same action helps neighbor, as an act of love, and helps us, creating a title to receive favors from our Father. So there are two titles: the exercise of love of our Father, and the practice of love of neighbor. Both are found in one and the same action, thanks to His generosity. Hence His Son counts these things as done to Him, as the Gospel description of the Last Judgment scene shows.

If we relate this to the rebalancing of the scales of the objective order (recall chapter 4) we see that for us to give up good things we could have had makes up for the sin of taking from the scales things we had no right to take. Hence Daniel spoke of "expiating" sins.

A bit of a warning is in order at this point. Some today so exalt love of neighbor as to completely identify it with love of God, which they seem to say need not be exercised directly, by itself. In this vein a friend of mine once said: "If I were alone on a desert island, I could have no relation with God, for I have that only through people." Sad distortion! Wiping out the first commandment by thinking it the same as the second!

If we read passages in the Old Testament relating to the covenant, we could easily get yet another false impression. For example, in Exodus 19:5 we read: "If you really hearken to my voice and keep my covenant, you will be my special people." And again we read in many places: Do this and you will live. So the impression might be that by obeying we earn favors and graces. Is it true that we earn by obeying? St. Paul insists over and over again that we are free from the law, that we do not have to earn salvation. How can we reconcile these things?

St. Paul gives us the needed key when he says (*e.g.*, in 1 Cor 6:9-10) that great sinners will not inherit the kingdom of heaven. Our Lord Himself says (Mt 18:3): "Unless you become as little children, you wil not enter the kingdom of heaven." Now if we inherit from our parents, do we say that we have earned what we get? Not at all. They give us good things, both before and after their deaths (by inheritance) because they are good, not because we are good. But on the other hand, since St. Paul says great sinners will not inherit, we gather that while we need not and cannot earn our eternal reward, we could earn or merit being deprived of it, so that we would not inherit the kingdom.

This is a most basic central truth, and it parallels the truth we discussed concerning justification. We cannot earn the kingdom, but we can forfeit it by breaking the law of our Father, a law designed to make us open, capable of receiving what He so generously wants to give to us. Little children instinctively know they do not earn the care of their parents; they also know they can earn punishment by disobeying. There is no conflict between these two statements.

And yet there is a sense in which we *do* earn, for the covenant seems to say: "If you do this, I will do that." But this is a *secondary* sense. In the basic sense, no creature can by its own power establish any claim on God, so as to earn. But if God makes a promise or enters into a covenant, then He will owe it to Himself to give favor if the creature fulfills the conditions. In that sense St. Paul wrote in Romans 2:6 that God will "repay each one according to his works." This of course, is earning only in a secondary, not in a basic sense.

From what we have been saying, it is obvious that all perfection consists in aligning our wills with the will of the Father, by obedience/love. Really, there is in me only one free thing—my will. If I could make it completely in accord with His, there would be nothing more that could be done; that would be complete perfection.

But even this leads to a problem. If all perfection consists in being fully in accord with the will of the Father, then could I not go to a chapel, or to some quiet place, and say a prayer expressing complete acceptance of His will, *e.g.*, the beautiful prayer of St. Ignatius: "Take O Lord, and receive all my liberty, my memory, my understanding, and my will. . . ." *But* if I do this with all sincerity, trying to really mean it, am I then *instantly* perfect? We almost instinctively know that could not be true. But why? One reason is that I could not foresee at one point all that the will of the Father may call on me to accept before the end of my life. The other is that because of our very nature spiritual growth is tied to development in a thing we mentioned above: *somatic resonance*. Our next chapter will explore that.

Chapter 16: Help From Psychology

We already know that love is a desire, a will for the happiness of another for the other's sake. When directed to other human beings, this means we want them to get and have the things needed to be well-off. When directed to God it means that we please Him by making it possible for Him to have the generous pleasure of giving to us, since we make ourselves open to Him, by following His instructions for doing that, His commandments.

Both in love of God and in love of human beings, love in itself is clearly basically spiritual, centered in the spiritual will. Yet everyone is convinced that, at least in the love of other people, there must be feeling. Many identify love with feeling. In fact, intercourse is often called "making love."

We already saw that love cannot really consist in or even strictly require feelings. If it did, Christ's command to love all men, even enemies, and to love God above all would be impossible. For obviously, we cannot always, or even often, have warm feelings toward every human being, still less for enemies. Nor can we usually have a warmer feeling toward God than for our dear ones. (We will see later about feelings in love of God.)

Yet there really is a role for feelings to play. Feelings are the somatic resonance to love, that is, the counterpart on the physical side, to what lies essentially in our spiritual soul.

A great psychologist, who pioneered almost a revolution in

psychological thinking, in his last book[1] helps us to understand this matter. He tells us of a patient who came to him for treatment when he was practising in Washington, D.C. The poor man was suffering from manic-depressive psychosis, a mental illness in which the sufferer runs from high excitement and elation down to deep black depression, without ever leveling off on a normal plane. One day the man came for treatment when he was in the deep black cycle, and complained to Dr. Moore that he was losing his religious faith. Moore reports in his book that that was not true. When the man moved up from his blackness, he did not need to be re-converted to faith. Moore explained that the process of his disease (he seems to have meant unfortunate biochemistry) was interfering with the somatic resonance to his faith.

It is easy to see the picture. There are, of course, two parts to a human, the spiritual soul and the physical body. Because these two are so closely united as to form but one person, it follows that for *normal* running there should be a parallel condition on one side to match the condition on the other side. That parallel condition is called a *resonance*. When the resonance is on the side of the body—the more usual situation—it is called somatic (from the Greek *soma*, body).

In Moore's patient, faith was, of course, on the spiritual side. The resonance would be on the bodily side. Lack of the somatic resonance would not expel faith, and so the patient did not really lose his faith. But the lack of somatic resonance can prevent faith from functioning normally. Hence it seemed to the sufferer that he was losing his faith.[2]

This concept of somatic resonance gives us numerous very helpful insights into things in the realm of the spiritual life. We will be seeing more of them. Right now we are going to explore the role of this resonance in love, and its relation to sex and human maturing.

If love is basically on the side of the spirit, as we know, then for normal running in human affairs, there should be a resonance on the bodily side. What is it? It is a feeling. A broad spectrum of feelings can serve—anything from the nonsexual response of parents to their own children to the explicitly sexual feelings of marriage partners.

This insight makes it possible for us to see that sex is a most beautiful and helpful thing, if it is used according to the plan of our Father. To see that, we are going to follow the various stages of human development, from birth to true maturity.

We all have a start in life that is in a way very poor: we are totally enclosed in a shell of self. If we may dramatize it, the new baby looks on

---

[1] *Cf.* Thomas Verner Moore, *Heroic Sanctity and Insanity*, Grune & Stratton, NY, 1959, p. 102 n.

[2] *Cf.* Aristotle, *Psychology* 1. 1 & 4.

the giants around him as being there to give him what he wants, when he wants it, as he wants it—if not, he will cry.

How does one get from the self-enclosed shell up to real maturity, to the state in which one can really have the fulfillment God intends life to have, a stage in which one can be sincerely interested and concerned with the happiness of another, without seeking self thereby? Our Father has designed a splendid process, in which sex, a resonance to love, plays a tremendous role.

When baby has grown enough to play with other little ones, there comes a day when he makes a horrifying (to him) discovery: Why that little fellow thinks he has some rights! I am the only one who has rights! Thus babies quarrel over a toy or other thing, each thinking only he has real claims. Here a start is made, slowly and painfully, towards getting out of the shell of self.

Some years later comes another stage, which many psychologists call the flight of the sexes. That is the time when little boys are disgusted with the silly, gangly, giggly sissies. And little girls have equal disdain for uncouth, not-very-clean boys. If the boys watch a western movie, and the hero takes time out for a bit of romance, they are impatient: better he should be out shooting the bad guys!

One summer when I was teaching swimming to children, there was only one boy, aged 9, in the adjoining class. The others were all girls. He stuck it out for some weeks, then told his mother he wanted to quit: he could not stand to be with all those girls. A year or two later things changed. His mother told me he was beginning to comb his hair.

This flight of the sexes, running away from each other, is part of our Father's plan, so that each group will strengthen their own characteristics to prepare for the next phase.

That begins when physical changes, changes in resonance have begun, that is biochemical changes, including new hormones. Then little boy looks at little girl, perhaps even one he has long rejected, and behold, she is no longer a gangly sissy. She is wonderful! Similar things happen, of course, to the girls.

If a boy says a girl is a good conversationalist, plays tennis well, does well in school—nothing has happened inside him yet. But if he has to resort to such words as *wonderful*, then chemistry has been at work, bringing new somatic resonance, that causes the boys and girls to see each other in a different, probably a rosy, light.

At precisely this point there comes a great opening for real love, both spiritual and emotional, if only the young people play the game as the Creator designed it. If not, it will backfire, as we shall see. But now love tends to develop, in two independent but parallel ways.

The first way is easy to see: in the framework of somatic resonance, if a condition is present on either one of the two sides, there is a tendency for the parallel condition to develop on the other side. That is: if emotion of the right kind is present, then there will be a tendency for love to develop in the spiritual will. (We recall there is a broad range of possibilities for somatic resonance to love, but here it will be sexual, at first latently, then clearly so.)[3]

To see the second way, we recall that there are three stages in the formation of love. First, a person sees something fine in another. That leads to the reaction we have already seen: "So fine a person—I hope he/she is happy and well-off, gets what is needed to be happy." Then, thirdly, if this desire is strong, the person will not be content with a mere wish, but will go into action, will postively try to bring about the happiness of the other. The stronger the desire, of course, the harder the person will try.[4]

Now if merely seeing another as good or fine can be a starter to love—what will happen if the other is seen as "wonderful", thanks to the powerful resonance of hormones?

It is easy to see, then that there are two powerful channels that tend to develop love, thanks to our Father's invention of sex.

But we have been saying over and over, and underscoring it, that all this tends to produce love. Why? Because it is quite possible to "foul up the machinery" that our Father has designed.

There are two ways to do this. First if a boy or girl uses sex alone, for private stimulation, this is a means not of getting out of the shell of self, but of pulling more deeply inside the old shell. It is obvious that this is the opposite of preparation for marriage, in which each must really go outwards in care for the other.

The second way to derail the providential process comes when a boy and girl, especially if they have been dating steadily[5] over a long

---

[3]In cultures where marriages are arranged, not the result of romance, the partners can learn to develop love in the spiritual soul, with the help of the somatic resonance to that love in sex. Since its use is then legitimate, the providential arrangement normally does produce love.

[4]We know that love is the desire or will in the spiritual will for the well-being and happiness of another for the other's sake. If this desire is strong, it will want to act for that happiness. But if love is stopped in its course by a small obstacle, the love is small; if it takes a great obstacle to stop it, love is great; and so on. What must be the love of the Father for us, when even the tremendous obstacle of the horrible death of the God-man did not deter him. Hence St. Paul said (Rom 5:8) "God proved His love. . . ."

[5]Humans have a breaking point, different for each person of course: but no one can stand unremitting pressures. Beyond that point composure and

period, develop such an intensity of feeling that they lose control, and forget the plan of our Father, and then use each other for sensory stimulation. If one uses the other for sense pleasure, this is not the same as developing a sincere outgoing desire for the happiness and well-being of the other. It is closer to hate. For if they violate God's law gravely, and then—which is far from impossible—meet with an auto accident on the way back, each has put the other into such a spiritual state that the other will never be happy, will instead be miserable eternally. This, as we said, is closer to hate than to love, for it is using the other, thereby endangering the other's true eternal happiness.

Yet not a few couples, mistaking biochemistry, the resonance, for real love, fall into these things, and thereby fail to develop real love. Then they may marry, thinking and saying, "Never have two people been so deeply in love before!" But they really have no true love, just a biochemical jag. In a year to two years, that jag subsides. Each wakes up and finds him/herself yoked to someone he/she does not really love. Then trouble begins. This is a great reason for the frightening breakup rate for marriages today. (Later in chapter 20, we will see that a false modern spirituality is another great reason for marriage failures.)

But they will say: "We really do have tender feelings for each other, we want each other to be happy." We reply: Do not make the deadly, life-ruining mistake of confusing chemistry with love. An example may help. A friend of mine was once taking a prescription medicine. At the same time he ran into a touch of flu, and so took some aspirn—taking both within an hour of each other near evening meal time. Then something entirely unforeseen happened: He began to be frightened. Of what? Of nothing in particular, just frightened in general. Fortunately, he was able to keep his mind clear, and so said to himself: "I know what this is, this is some bad chemistry. I will have to put up with this for a few hours, and then I will be all right." This is the way it was: He lived on a split level for three or four hours, with one side of him in constant fright, but the other side, his mind, quite calm and understanding, "I know what this is." The fright did wear off in a few hours, as the chemistry dissipated itself.[6]

---

coping will break down. Repeated pleasurable experiences in steady dating tend to build up the pressure to go farther. Therefore, it is good judgment to avoid steady dating until reasonably close to the time of marriage.

[6]An infusion of lactate into the blood can trigger anxiety, especially in those prone to anxiety: *Science News*—hereafter SN—Oct. 9, 1971, p. 249. Biochemistry can explain anxiety: SN July 16, 1983, pp. 45-46. High or low levels of certain trace elements can predispose to violent behavior: SN August 20, 1983, pp. 122-25. (This does not mean that in most cases free will is taken

In a parallel way, a large dose of sex hormones can give feelings of warmth and tenderness—but it may be only a chemical counterfeit of love.

How can one know if it really is love? The only real protection lies in playing the game the way the Manufacturer, our Father, designed it. Then this process of sex tends powerfully, by a double channel to produce real love. Otherwise it generates fakes, counterfeits, and one may spend a lifetime—if not eternity—paying for it.

But if the young people do follow our Father's plans, they will develop real concern for each other, and so really get out of the shell of self in which they began life. As a commercial for insurance said: "Their goals become your goals." So a beautiful maturity has come, which lets the partners enjoy this life as our Father planned that they should, and prepares them for the real enjoyment forever.

We can see how right Pope Paul VI was when he said: "Christian marriage and the Christian family demand a moral commitment. They are not on an easy way of Christian life, even though the most common, the one which the majority of the children of God are called to travel. Rather, it is a long path toward sanctification."[7] For if the couple play the game the way our Father designed it, they are doing His will, becoming quite unselfish, and spiritually and psychologically mature, in the process.

Needless to say, the children in such a home are not going to be battered children. It is immature, childish parents who become indignant when babies are a chore: "Imagine the nerve of that little guy, interfering with my pleasure! Take that and that!"

It is also psychologically true that we tend to love those for whom we voluntarily accept hardship or even suffering—such as spouses and children. First, we accept it because we want to help the other, we feel for the other's needs. This is already love. Further if we took hardship for someone who did not deserve our efforts, we would have to think ourselves foolish. And since we do not want to think that, these efforts drive us to have a fine opinion of the other, which favors love. The

---

away, only that pressures can be great in the wrong direction, with a diminishing of responsibility—to a degree only God can judge.) *Scientific American*, February 1974, pp. 84-91 reports that low levels of the neurotransmitter Serotonin in the brain can greatly incline a person to sex and to insomnia. Raised levels have the opposite effect. (Interestingly, a pasta meal without meat tends to raise Serotonin.) There are countless other instances of the effect of biochemistry, as somatic resonance, to interior states of the soul.

[7]Paul VI, To 13th National Congress of the Italian Feminine Center, Feb. 12, 1966. *The Pope Speaks* 11, 1966, p. 10.

reverse pattern also happens: if we have done evil to another, we are driven in the direction of thinking that the other is evil, otherwise we should not have done it. Tacitus the pagan Roman historian said it well: "It is characteristic of human nature to hate the one whom you have offended."[8]

We can hint here at something we will see more fully later: many today, following a false spirituality, think there is no benefit in giving anything up for a religious reason—there is no good in "negative mortification." To follow that spirituality[9] is tragic. For marriage demands much give and take; male and female psychology are so different that each one can honestly say, even in a fine pairing: "I have to give in most of the time to make this work." But doing so pays off in this world as well as in the next. It is needed to make any marriage work.

All this spirit of generous self-sacrifice for the other is in itself objectively beautiful. It is a fulfillment of what is good in itself, the objective order, which the Holiness of our Father loves. He has therefore sugarcoated things, to get people to become generous—which will happen, again, only if they play the game the way He designed it. He loves goodness so much He is pleased to get it even if it takes what we called sugar-coating, the pleasure of sex. That pleasure is very strong, so strong that it can lead people into spiritual disaster. Yet it needs to be that strong to get the beautiful results we have described. Otherwise many people would not get started in the sanctifying process of sharing their lives completely with another.

Those who embrace a vow of celibacy/virginity do not have the help of the sugarcoating to get away from selfishness. Hence they will need to consciously work harder to make up for that lack. However, if they do reach an unselfish level they show a greater attachment to the will of our Father, precisely because it cost more effort. (We notice again, as we have noted many times before, that our Father's pursuit of what is good in itself runs parallel to our happiness, really brings about our happiness even in this life.)

If these feelings serve as a resonance to love, what would be the resonance to hatred? Obviously, feelings of aversion. Yet it is important to notice that these feelings are not in themselves hatred—they are only the resonance to hatred. Real hatred is the opposite of love, and lies in the spiritual will. To love means to will good to another for the other's sake. To hate means to will evil to the other, so it may be evil to him.[10]

---

[8]Tacitus, *Agricola* 42.

[9]*Cf.* chapter 20 for reasons why this modern spirituality is wrong.

[10]To will evil to another so it may be evil to him is the opposite of love;

We can see it is important to try to get rid of feelings of aversion, for they can tend to develop an attitude of hatred or something close to it, for somatic resonance already present tends to pull our spiritual side into line with it.

Sometimes we can put our finger on the reasons for an aversion. At other times we cannot. Then the aversion is irrational. It is as if someone said: "That person over there—I just don't like him." If another would ask why, the reply might be: "I don't know, I just don't like him." This reminds us of an old joke: "That person—I have only supernatural love for him." That is: I will pray for him, but I surely do not like him.

What do we do about such feelings? Obviously, we do not foster them or cultivate them. But most directly, we do well to pray extra for the object of our aversions—for that is real love. Love and hate cannot coexist, so this doing good to the other tends to remove the feelings of aversion. At least, it makes the feelings definitely involuntary. To work against these feelings it is a help to realize that no one does evil precisely as evil; he always does it because it registers on him as some kind of a good, even if the notion is perverse. Even terrorists think they have a good motive. And of course, we always have greatest difficulty in knowing the interior of another person—we do not even find it easy to know our own interior![11]

In some cases—not always—people report that if they deliberately go out of their way to cultivate, to be kind to the one for whom they have an irrational aversion, they find that person to be quite nice.

There are other cases, cases in which we can name the reason for an aversion, *e.g.*, we find that the other party always holds views opposite to our own. Not always, but sometimes, one can laugh about it and say to the other in a friendly way: "I always know what you are thinking. I just look inside to see my own view, find the opposite, and that is what you think!"

At the end of chapter 15 we raised the question: Could I, by

---

it is desire for revenge. This differs from desire that the objective order may be rebalanced—a thing God Himself wills.

[11]If quarrels develop, St. Paul's advice is excellent: 1 Cor 13:5 says: "Love does not keep a record of evils." (The Greek *logizetai* does permit this translation.) When two are in a quarrel and have used up the immediate reasons they have on hand, they will tend to escalate the conflict in two ways: (1) one will recite the whole list of past injuries by the other party, (2) one will generalize as if to say "You are mean in general, not just on this occasion." The hurt from these things is deep, and hard to heal unless there is a very sincere deep and explicit apology.

making an act of complete acceptance of the will of God, become perfect instantly? Now we see more clearly why the answer is *no*. Part of the reason, again, is that I cannot at one time foresee everything that His will may ask me to accept during the rest of my life. But now we see a more basic reason: somatic resonance. Precisely because somatic resonance lies in a condition on the side of the body, it must follow the laws of bodily things. Now all bodies grow in spurts. That is, if we were to make a graph of the growth of a plant of animal, it would not be a straight or curved line steadily rising. It would be a step graph—small rises, with long flat plateaus in between. Coaches of athletes know this well: the performance of their young people necessarily follows such a pattern. The coaches inform the athletes of this, else they might get discouraged and quit when they are on one of the long plateaus.

The result is this: Our spiritual perfection does indeed consist in the alignment of our will with the will of God, but to really carry that out requires a parallel development in somatic resonance, which has to grow according to the law of the growth of bodies.[12]

Are there times when we can make a large leap up, as it were, in the spiritual life? Not ordinarily, but yet, if we encounter something terribly difficult to accept as the will of God, and then do embrace it heartily, our somatic resonance can be so shaken by the very difficulty as to be close to being in a flux—this permits a large sharp rise at the moment. We can see a hint here relative to the importance of certain kinds of mortification. (More on that in chapter 20.)

We mentioned before that according to the best psychologists, our will is not like a muscle that grows strong with exercise, flabby without it. No, it is more comparable to an electric contact, which either makes or breaks. However, in view of what we now know of somatic resonance, we can see that even though the will is not precisely like a muscle, yet something similar to the growth of muscles can be found. In other words, we can and should develop our somatic resonance to hard things, for this confers a certain facility in accepting them. For example, let us think of a man who all his life has been very devoted to the will of God, but who yet has never experienced a difficult illness. But now he falls into a painful stretch in the hospital. His usual dedication to the will of God will still tend to persevere—but he will find he must fight hard to fully accept God's will. For his somatic resonance has never been much developed in this sector. Indeed, this is the probable way to explain the mysterious line in Hebrews 5:8 which says that Jesus

[12] *Cf.* A. Tanquerey, *The Spiritual Life*, tr. H. Brandeis, St. Mary's Seminary, Baltimore, 2nd ed. 1930 #1092.

"learned obedience from the things He suffered."[13] In any case, note that in time the man in the hospital may become more accustomed to his pain, and find it far easier to maintain his acceptance of the will of God.

Somatic resonance is part of the explanation of a crisis of faith that many experience starting around the last year of high school. This is a time when great bodily changes are starting, especially in the area of sex. These changes put somatic resonance into a flux, as it were. The result is that many previously held ideas will waver; young people tend to lose their belief that their parents know much of anything, and their religious faith comes into doubt. If only they can be brought to see what is the reason, while it will not cure their troubles, it will help them to stand outside themselves and look on themselves objectively.[14]

St. Francis of Assisi, in his genius for helpful expressions, liked to call things brother or sister. He called his body "brother ass."[15] (He meant the long-eared kind.) Such an ass never goes over to another ass and says: "Brother, you have lived longer than I, help me to understand." No, an ass learns not from others, but only from his own experience—preferably a hard experience, such as a swiftly moving boot at his south end. The brother ass pattern often shows in our lives. If someone gets a temptation to rob a bank, he might reason himself out of it—thinking of the danger from armed guards, and the fact he must give it back if the sin is ever to be forgiven. But imagine a young man viewing a pornographic magazine. He is looking at the centerfold, and getting, literally, worked up at it. Then brother mind speaks: "See here, brother ass, why get excited? That is just a piece of paper with ink on it. So why get excited?" Is brother ass likely to be calmed? Hardly. This is probably the reason that St. Paul told the Corinthians (1 Cor 6:18): "Flee from sexual looseness." He did not say: Talk yourself out of it. Brother ass just does not and really cannot listen to brother mind. Instead, brother ass, with his powerful somatic resonance in such a

---

[13]*Cf.* W. Most, "On Jesus Learning Obedience: Hebrews 5:8" in *Faith & Reason* 3 (1977) pp. 6-16.

[14]There is another reason for the crisis: When we are little, we merely believe things because older people said so—all that can be done at an early age. But we should reach the point at which we can, as 1 Pet 3:15 urges: "Be ready to give a defense to anyone who asks of you a reason for the hope that is in you." That is, we should learn the rational basis that precedes faith itself. When one has completed the passage, he can be stable and comfortable. Out in the middle, he is neither fish nor fowl, and wavers much. On the process itself, *cf.* W. Most, *Catholic Apologetics Today*.

[15]*Cf.* St. Bonaventure Legenda Maior S. Francisci 5. 6, In *Analecta Franciscana* X, Quaracchi, 1926-1941.

case, will try to pull brother mind into going along.

St. Paul too, after a great vision (2 Cor 12:7-8), was given "a thorn to the flesh", some kind of powerful temptation, to keep him humble.[16] St. Paul's mind knew well he should not be proud. It knew all the good he was and had and did was God's gift to him (cf. chapter 18 on Phil 2:13). But his bodily side, brother ass, had to learn it by hard experience—the only way it could learn. The trial caused St. Paul to realize his need of God: "Power is made perfect in weakness." (See 2 Cor 12:8-10: four times in these verses Paul speaks of weakness, glories in it.) The feeling of weakness he experienced was part of the somatic resonance to humility, which is essential to make one open to God. If one lacks humility, in effect he thinks or implies he creates the good he is or has or does. Only God creates. So when humility is present, our Father, finding a soul open, happily grants His richest graces.

Similarly, if we have difficulties or trials from creatures or from other people, it helps our somatic side to realize that the things of this world are not the final and essential goods. Hence, as even pagan Greeks and Romans knew, simplicity and even austerity in one's way of life makes it easier to see the great truths. (Chapter 18 will add another dimension to this point.) Conversely, material affluence makes a whole civilization lose interest in God and religion.[17]

We can use somatic resonance to help in other ways too: for example, if our outward behavior is reverent, that tends to pull our interior attitudes into accord. Or, if we are tempted to rush during prayer, forcing ourselves to go even more slowly than usual tames brother ass, and brings our interior into an attitude of greater

[16]Commentators differ on what the trial was: 1) Persecutions—but St. Paul welcomed them; 2) sickness—but would he pray so earnestly to be rid of it when the suffering could make him more like Christ? 3) violent sexual temptations—these do promote a humble opinion of self, for after a long and hard siege, even a good person may wonder: "Did I really hold out fully?" *Cf.* A. Poulain, *The Graces of Interior Prayer*, tr. L. Smith, Routledge & Kegan Paul, London, 1949, pp. 409, 447-48.

[17]Socrates over and over again insists that the true philosopher, to attain truth, and to become as much as possible like to God (*Republic* 613), should have as little as possible to do with things of the body: *Phaedo* 65, 66, 82-83, *Republic* 485-86, 519.

Pagan Romans up to about 200 B. C. actually lived the ideal of *frugalitas*, a sparing way of life, and thought themselves happier that way. Later they recognized the ideal, but did not on the whole live up to it. Livy attributes decline of Roman strength to luxury: 23. 45;30. 14;30. 44;38. 17;39. 6. The Greek Historian Polybius insists on the same: 6. 57; 18. 35; 32. 11. *Cf.* also Tacitus, *Agricola* 21. 3; *Histories*, 2. 69. *Cf.* also St. Augustine, *City of God* 1. 8.

reverence. To hurry amounts to feeling: "Let's get this over with, and get on with the real business of the day." But, prayer, especially Mass, is the most important part of any day—the part during which we are most open to our Father's gifts.

Chapter 17: Feelings in Love of God?

Emotion or feeling is normal in human love. Is it also normal when we love God? We can see at once that the two situations will not be entirely parallel. We often get sensory pleasure from the sight of another human being. But God is not the object of our senses in any way. Further, as we saw, love of God is in practice identified with obedience to Him, as we know, in aligning our will with His. Clearly, that can be done without any feelings at all. In fact, when we hold strongly to His will even when things are most difficult, when pain instead of pleasure is at hand, then it is that our attachment to Him must either be very strong, or fail for the moment.

Even in love for human beings, emotion is not always present. In love for all, even persons we have never seen, and in love of enemies, feeling is normally absent.

Yet there is such a thing as feeling in love of God. There are two greatly different levels in it: the lower level, for those not very far advanced in the spiritual life; and the higher level of infused contemplation. On the lower level, when we have any sort of feelings or satisfaction in religious things, theologians call that *consolation*; the opposite, the lack of any feeling, or even the presence of positive distaste, is called *dryness* or *aridity*.

At the end of this chapter we will see something that is a satisfaction given by God, but not precisely an emotion. This comes as an abiding peace to those who are very strongly devoted to His will, no matter what that will may call for at the time.

On the higher level of infused contemplation, feelings may or may not be present. When they are, they are only the result of a sort of overflow of a phenomenon that really takes place deep in the spiritual part of a person. Contemplation with such an overflow is called sweet, without it, it is arid. (We will see more about this in chapter 22.) In this chapter we will speak only of the lower level. On that lower level, both consolations and dryness can be spiritually helpful, but they can also be harmful. In themselves, they are neutral.

It is obvious that consolations can be a great help to a soul in breaking with attachments to things of sense. They can encourage one to make good resolutions, to pray more, to be more generous in self-denial.

On the other hand, there is a subtle danger in consolations. For there is a real problem, when a soul is engulfed in them, of knowing precisely what it is that moves the soul. Is the person doing well because of the pleasure, or solely to please God, or part each way? St. John of the Cross speaks strongly on this: "Every soul that seeks to go on in sweetness and ease, and flees from the imitation of Christ—I would not consider this good."[1]

By fleeing from the imitation of Christ who is the way, St. John meant largely omitting self-denial. St. Paul, if we gather up and make a synthesis of many of his statements, presents the whole Christian life in this way: A person is saved and is made holy, precisely if, and to the extent that, he is a member of Christ and like Him. Now in the life of Christ there are two phases: first, a hard life, poverty, suffering, death; second, glorification. Of course we are still in that first phase, and so the more we are like Him in these things, the more shall we be like Him in glory. St. Francis de Sales follows up on the thought of St. John of the Cross:

> From time to time we ought to make acts of renunciation of such feelings of sweetness, tenderness, and consolation, withdrawing our hearts from them, and insisting that, even though we accept them in humility, and love them because God sends them to us, and because they encourage us to love Him, yet it is not these things that we seek, but God and His holy love: we are not seeking the consolation, but the One who consoles.[2]

Really, we must add that not all consolations are from God. Satan himself sometimes produces pleasure in souls that pray. Why? Because he likes to "transfigure himself into an angel of light" (2 Cor 11:14). It means that Satan can well afford to give us a consolation, even to promote some short-term good, so long as in the end, he works more devil-

[1]St. John of the Cross, *Ascent* 2. 7. 8. BAC edition, p. 621.

[2]St. Francis de Sales, *Introduction to a Devout Life* 4. 13, Oeuvres, Annecy, 1893, 3. p. 324.

try. He can by consolations try to make us attached to the pleasure, not to God. He can make us think we have arrived, that we are already saints—and there is no more deadly vice than spiritual pride. St. Teresa of Avila wrote: "The chief aim of the devil here [in this world] is to make us proud . . . tears, though good, are not perfect. In humility, mortification and detchment and other virtues there is more security."[3] Satan can also try to lead a person to make good resolutions that go too far, more than the soul can really bear, more than are prudent for it at that stage. Then Satan knows that souls will not persevere in the good resolutions: they will soon give them up, and perhaps give up even more, so as to fall back to a point lower than that from which they thought they began to rise. A soul might even give up all serious attempts to grow spiritually.

Aridity too can be either helpful or harmful. It is obvious that Satan can promote aridity, to discourage us, to make us give up or slacken our attempts to please God. But God Himself commonly sends aridity at times. In fact, a quite normal pattern is this: when a person reaches what is sometimes called the "second conversion", that is, a point at which he resolves to be really in earnest and serious about pleasing God, then it is usual for God to send consolations to encourage that soul, to help it get into a pattern of breaking with attachments to things of sense. But if the consolations continued indefinitely, there would be the danger of which we spoke: one might serve God for pleasure, not for God's sake.

To guard against this danger God commonly sends aridity. St. John of the Cross aptly suggests[4] that if a child is holding a sharp knife in his hand, we must not try to take it away forcefully—the child would get cut. So we need instead to dangle a toy in front of the child, get him interested in it, so he will drop the knife. Similarly, consolations are like toys, useful to help disengage us from attachments to the world. But one should eventually grow up, and learn to turn from danger without the need of toys.

This very statement suggests another way in which Satan can turn aridity to his own ends: he can make a soul in aridity think, "I do not need consolations, I am too strong, too holy for that now."

Aridity especially promotes distractions—though they can come in the midst of consolations too. When distractions come, if we resist

---

[3]St. Teresa of Avila, *Way of Perfection* 17.3 & 4. BAC edition, p. 142. *cf.* St. Louis de Montfort, *True Devotion*, #214, saying the more one grows in Marian devotion and in her favor, "the more you act by pure faith . . . which will make you care hardly at all about sensible consolations."

[4]St. John of the Cross, *Ascent* 3. 39. 1.

them as soon as we notice them, they cannot harm the substantial value of our prayer. (We said "as soon as we notice them" for they can begin almost unnoticed, and unroll themselves like a movie until we wake up and see we should act to shake them off.) Really, prayer made at the expense of hard work in fighting temptations will please our Father more than one in which the soul is immersed in the pleasure of consolations.

We should not forget that consolation and aridity can be greatly affected by merely natural conditions, even by the state of our digestion, by how tired we are, how we feel in general, by preoccupation with our work or with our troubles. Suggestion too can bring on many things, including consolation leading to pride.

Of course sin and lack of meditation or lack of a spirit of recollection can bring on aridity too.

Bodily posture during prayer, as we indicated in chapter 16, can favor or hinder recollection, and thereby affect consolation and aridity. There is a strong tendency for our interior attitudes to follow our external conduct. So if one tries to pray in a slovenly posture, one that does not express reverence for God, it is not likely he will have much reverence. Conversely, if he adopts a respectful stance, especially kneeling or even prostration, humility is promoted. Muslims know this, and so make much use of bending low. Ancient Near Eastern Kings used to require *proskynesis*, that is, the subject was ordered to prostrate himself in front of the king as a sign of reverence—and it tended to produce interior respect at the same time.

Natural or national temperament can affect the presence or absence of consolations. St. Augustine, for example, seems to have often experienced various consolations in prayer, which reflects partly his individual temperament, partly the Latin temperament.[5] In contrast, St. Thérèse of Lisieux wrote to one of her sisters after a retreat:

> Do not think that I am swimming in consolations. No! My consolation is to have no consolations on this earth. Without showing Himself, without making His voice heard, Jesus instructs me in secret—not by means of books, for I do not understand what I read, but at times by a word such as that which I found at the end of a period of prayer (after resting in silence and in dryness): "Here is the master I have given you. He will teach you all that you should do. I want to cause you to read in the book of life, in which is contained the science of love."[6]

---

[5] *Cf.* the emotion told of by St. Augustine in his retreat before baptism: *Confessions* 9. 4-5.

[6] St. Thérèse de Lisieux, *Manuscrits Autobiographiques*, Carmel de Lisieux, 1957, p. 418.

She was a Saint who seems to have had rather little consolation. She was pleased with the fact, seems to have felt safer without the dangers of deception that can come from consolations.[7]

Differences in spiritual attractions can also greatly affect consolations and aridity.[8] To explain such differences, let us notice that there are two tiers or levels in the spiritual life. First, there is the level of the fundamental principles, which no one at all can ignore or violate without taking a spiritual loss. These fundamental rules are the same for absolutely all persons. But beyond them, on a secondary level, there is room for a marvelous variety. Here we find many differences in approach to spirituality.

A couple of examples will make this clear. We could compare St. Francis de Sales, refined enough to associate familiarly with the dandies of the French royal court, with St. Benedict Joseph Labré, living like a tramp in the ruins of ancient Rome, spending his days in the churches of Rome. One anecdote asserts that if one of the body lice he had would try to crawl out of his sleeve, he would push it back in again—for mortification.

Both of these Saints observed the same basic principles of the spiritual life—but what a difference on the secondary level!

Again let us think of St. Francis of Assisi, the outstanding specialist in following Lady Poverty. Many anecdotes are told about him, so that it is often hard to sift fact from fiction, but the total picture given fits that Saint very well indeed. It is clear, however,[9] that he was reluc-

---

[7]Her aridity seems not to have excluded some satisfaction, without feeling, probably of the sort we will discuss at the end of this chapter, on the fine point of the soul.

[8]Pius XII, *Mediator Dei*, #179: "As regards the different methods employed in these exercises, it is perfectly clear to all that in the Church on earth, no less than in the Church in heaven, there are many mansions; and that asceticism cannot be the monopoly of anyone. It is the same Spirit who breathes where He wills; and Who with differing gifts and in different ways enlightens and guides souls to sanctity. Let their freedom and the supernatural action of the Holy Spirit be so sacrosanct that no one presume to disturb or stifle them for any reason whatsoever." (Vatican Library Version). We add this: As a result of this diversity, what is best in itself is not always best for this particular soul. Further, there can be variations within the same soul at different stages in its spiritual development or progress.

St. Ignatius of Antioch wrote in his Letter to St. Polycarp 1. 1 & 2. 1: "Speak to each one individually after the manner of God . . . not all wounds are healed by the same remedy." *Cf.* also St. Francis de Sales, *Introduction* 1. 3.

[9]*Cf.* Thomas of Celano, *Vita Secunda S. Francisci* 32. 62, *Analecta Franciscana* X. p. 168.

tant to let his brothers have many books. In contrast, St. Thomas Aquinas spent his life immersed in books and in writing books. Both were great Saints—but how different in their approaches!

Again, St. Francis was a poetic type, and seems to have been prone to emotion—he loved to speak of various creatures as brothers and sisters. He found creatures helped lift his heart to God. The beauty of birds could lead him to give thanks to our Father, for the delicate kindness of giving us such charming creatures! In contrast, St. John of the Cross seems to have been little inclined to look at created things; what emotions he felt did not arise from that source. And St. Thomas Aquinas surely had some feelings in prayer, some emotions, but he does not show much of them, so that even his works on the Holy Eucharist seem to be a almost an intellectual exercise.

Failure to recognize differences like these can lead to great dangers. One of the worst is this: someone whose spiritual pattern involves much emotion may see another person whose dominant state is arid. The emotional perons may look down on the arid one, and call him a "dead Catholic." This could involve spiritual pride, the deadliest of all vices.

Some of these emotional people point to the Old Testament, *e.g.*, they appeal to Psalm 47:2: "All you peoples clap your hands! Shout to God with a loud sound!" Then some of these persons will say to the unemotional types: See, you are not opposing us, you are opposing Scripture itself! At the same time, of course, a non-emotional type might regard himself as superior in spirituality, as we indicated before, because "he does not need" such emotional aids.

A special comment is in order about emotion in relation to contrition. Contrition is basically a change in the attitude of our will toward God. The sinner looks back on what he has done and as it were says to himself: I see now I should not have done that. I wish I had not done that, I do not want to do that again. (The motive for this change of attitude may of course be either mere fear, or regret for offending God who is so good to me, or regret for offending God who is so good in Himself—we saw these possibilities in relation to love of God. The same apply in the matter of contrition.)

Whether or not feeling is present is not essential to contrition. A person may shed abundant tears and have no real contrition at all. Another may be completely dry-eyed, and have deep contrition. The same factors we already saw as affecting emotion in general apply here too.

We said earlier in this chapter that there are three possible sources for emotion or aridity in the spiritual life: God, ourselves, and Satan. It is not always important to determine from which source consolation comes, though that can be helpful. The chief thing is to know how to use both consolations and aridity, to recognize that neither one proves great sanctity or the lack thereof. The important thing is to use well whatever comes.

We mentioned earlier something that is really a form of consolation, but which in general does not involve emotion. To explain, let us think of a high mountain, 20,000 feet in elevation. It will often happen that the peak of the mountain projects above dark clouds and storms on the lower slopes, so that the peak is in calm. A plane rising above a storm gives the same effect.

Now we humans have in us, both in body and in soul, many different levels of operations. That is, we have many different drives and needs, each of them legitimate in itself. Yet each one operates automatically, blindly, seeking only the things it needs or likes, without any consideration for the other needs, or for the person as a whole. As a result of all these different levels, we can see that it is possible to have much distress on the lower slopes, and yet to have calm on the peak of the soul. St. Francis de Sales describes this well:

> The soul is sometimes so pressed by afflictions within that all its faculties and powers are weighed down by deprivation of all that could give relief and by taking on the impression of all that can cause sadness ... having nothing left but the fine point of the spirit, which, since it is attached to the heart and good pleasure of God, says in a very simple resignation: O Eternal Father, may always your will be done, not mine.[10]

St. Paul seems to have this great peace on the fine point of the soul in mind when he writes to the Philippians (4:4): "Rejoice in the Lord always. Again I say, rejoice." This deeper joy, as we saw, comes from God Himself. In deep trouble we can get some help towards it by meditating on two other lines of St. Paul (2 Cor. 4:17 and Rom. 8:18):

> That which is light and momentary in our tribulations is producing for us, beyond measure, an eternal wealth of glory for us, as we look not to the things that are seen, but to those that are not seen.... I judge that the sufferings of the present time are not worthy to be compared to the glory that is to be revealed to us.

If the light and momentary can do this—what of that which is not light but heavy, not momentary but long-lasting! Yes, the troubles on the lower slopes are not worthy to be compared to what is to come, from the inexpressible goodness of our Father.

---

[10]St. Francis de Sales, *Treatise on the Love of God* 9. 3. Oeuvres Nierat, Annecy, 1894, V. 117.

Chapter 18: Is it Good to Pray: "O God Help Me?"

The answer to our title for this chapter is: Of course. But the language is rather weak, as we shall see. For our dependence on God is much greater than such language suggests.

The problem we are to explore now is that of humility. And indeed it is a problem. For we say, rightly, that love is the greatest virtue. Yet humility occupies a unique position.

If we read the Gospels attentively, we will notice this: Jesus, of course, shows remarkable mercy to sinners. Some were even scandalized at His reception of the woman caught red-handed in adultery, to such an extent that some manuscripts of St. John's Gospel simply omit this incident. Even so, there was one kind of sinner that more than dried up the font of mercy: The Pharisees. Those who think of Jesus as always being "nice" to people, like a sort of Casper-Milk-Toast, may be surprised to hear the way He spoke to the Pharisees (Mt. 23:33): "Snakes, brood of vipers! How can you flee from the judgment of Gehenna?" And (Mt 23:27): "Woe to you, scribes and Pharisees, hypocrites, for you are like whitewashed tombs, which outside seem beautiful, but inwardly are full of dead bones and all filthiness!"

What was their crime, so great that it could turn Mercy Incarnate against them? It was simply pride, hypocritical pride. St. Peter, who heard these words, later echoed them strongly (1 Pet 5:5): "God resists the proud, but gives grace to the humble." These words are positively frightening. They do not say that God gives less grace to the proud, nor even that He gives no grace to the proud. What they say is that God actually *resists* the proud! If God Himself is against one—there is no rescue possible, except to stop the attitude that so disgusts Him.

How can this be? Is not love the great virtue? There are two answers, one of which we can see easily now; the other must wait until the last part of this chapter, when we will see that pride amounts to a claim to be God!

To turn to the first answer: Even though love is the greatest virtue, the relation of humility to love is such that without humility there can be no love at all. In fact, there is even a proportion: a great love is possible only if there is a correspondingly great humility. St. Augustine gives us a helpful comparison: "The greater the superstructure [of a building] will be, the deeper one digs the foundation."[1] So then love does remain the greatest virtue, for on it depends the law and the prophets. Yet humility is needed to make room for love : It is only in the measure in which we are empty of self that there is room for the selflessness of divine love.

Of course, one may seem to have great love even without humility—but pride is the great mimic. It can give the appearance of all virtues, yet the soul may in reality be void of them. St. Augustine brings out this fact brilliantly in his masterwork, *The City of God*. He explores why it could have been that the Romans were given so great an empire by Divine Providence. He finds the answer in the words of a pagan Roman historian, Sallust. Speaking of the early period of Roman history (up to 265 B. C. or even, to a large extent, up to 200 B. C.), Sallust says that the Romans practiced great virtues, to such an extent that people conquered as recently as ten years before would then be willing to fight with, not against Rome, in a new war. But, sadly, the mainspring of those virtues was that they were "eager for praise, generous with their money; they desired immense glory."[2] St. Augustine comments: "This [glory] they loved most ardently, for this they wished to live, for this they did not hesitate to die; they suppressed other desires out of their great desire for this one thing."[3]

If we stop to think about it, it is obviously true that pride can mimic all virtues. What virtuous act can we think of that a person might not do out of desire to be praised? In fact, pride can even imitate humility: a man can act humbly so as to be praised for his humility!

The Mother of Jesus surely imitated His humility. At the very moment when she had been raised to the highest honor of any mere creature, the divine motherhood, which as Pope Pius XI wrote, was "a dignity second only to God" and in fact, "a sort of infinite dignity, from

[1]St. Augustine, Sermon 69. 1. 2. PL 38. 441.

[2]Sallust, *Catiline* 7

[3]St. Augustine, *City of God* 5. 12. PL 41. 154.

the infinite good that God is"[4]—at that very moment her response was: "Behold the slave-girl of the Lord" (for St. Luke's Greek *doule* more commonly means slave-girl, not just handmaid). Nor did she tell others, to seek recognition from men. Rather, moved by the Holy Spirit (as we will see later in chapter 23), she remained silent to such an extent that even St. Joseph, her husand, needed a special visit of an angel to keep him from thinking her guilty of adultery.

But now a great problem arises: Many Saints, out of humility, spoke badly of themselves. Yet the Church has canonized them and praised them highly. Could it be that humility consists in self-deception, in this world, which can be dropped later, so that a person must tell himself now he is worthless, but later on will be able to admit he was spiritually great? In fact, how could Jesus Himself be "humble of heart"? How could His Mother speak of herself as a slave-girl?

We notice at once that no virtue could be a virtue if it required a person to lie, to say he was worthless when he really was very good, So then humility must be based on truth. But then: Could I say to myself: "I must face the truth. I of course admit I am not Saint. But neither am I an evil person. Really, I am a rather nice guy, somewhere in the middle." And soon my hand creeps around to pat myself on the back.

Not even that will solve the problem. For the Saints really did speak ill of themselves, and yet were spiritual heroes. Both points must be true. How? In any complex problem we must begin by making distinctions. Only then can we find the means to reconcile seeming opposites. So there must be two aspects to a holy person, such that when looking at one, he can speak badly of himself, but when looking at the other, he can admit he is very holy.

We start this exploration by noting that there are two very different levels on which I can speak of myself: the fundamental level, and the secondary level. On the fundamental level I ask: What good am I, have I, or do I accomplish that originates in me, and does not come from anywhere else, not even from God? On the secondary level I consider: What good is there that I am, or have, or do in virtue of God's gifts to me?

We turn first to the fundamental level, and at once St. Paul meets us and says (2 Cor 3:5): "Not that we are sufficient to think anything by ourselves, as from ourselves, but our sufficiency is from God." The Second Council of Orange in 529 A.D. taught,

> If anyone asserts that we can think any good that pertains to eternal sal-

---

[4]Pius XI, *Lux Veritatis*, Dec. 25, 1931. AAS 23. 513. Citing St. Thomas, *Summa* I. 26. 6. ad 4.

vation, as is needed, or choose [any good] or consent to the saving preaching, that is, the preaching of the Gospel, without the illumination and inspiration of the Holy Spirit . . . he is deceived by a heretical spirit and does not understand the word of God in the Gospel saying, "Without me you can do nothing" and that passage of the Apostle: "Not that we are sufficient to think anything by ourselves as from ourselves, but our sufficiency is from God."[5]

So it is defined doctrine that of ourselves, without the Holy Spirit, we cannot even get a good thought that leads towards salvation.

But: Could we say that after God gives us the good thought, we can think over what grace proposes, and then make the good decision (act of will)? Surely we are free? The answer is: Yes, we are free, but yet, St. Paul also tells us (Phil 2:13): "It is God who works in you both the will and the doing." If we study this statement carefully, we find that the word "works" must mean that God actually produces or causes in me even the good act of my will that comes before doing anything good. The New American Bible translation tries to soften the strength of these words by speaking not of will but of desire. Could we accept that, so as to say: "God gives me a good desire, but it is I who produce the goodness of a decision or act of will?"[6] No. The same St. Paul stops us again (1 Cor 4:7): "What have you that you have not received? And if you have received it, why boast as if you had not received?" That is: Whatever good you are or have or do is simply God's gift—you have received it . Had you not received it, but instead had originated it of yourself then you could "boast." But as it is, there is nothing to boast or brag of: You have received all the good you are or have or do from God.

In fact, to say God causes only the good desire, but we cause the good will, would be the heresy of Pelagius.

St. Augustine puts the matter with devastating impact: "When God crowns your merits, He crowns nothing other than His own gifts."[7]

---

[5]Canon 7, II Orange. DS 377. Special approval by Pope Boniface II made the canons like canons of a General Council. Can. 4 DS 374.

[6]There is a Semitic pattern in which something is attributed to direct action of God, when He really only permits it, *e.g.*, 1 Sam 4:3. That pattern could not be had here, for if it were, we would have Pelagian heresy. NAB would claim to depend on Greek *thelein* for *desire*. In 5th century B. C. Attic it did have only that sense. But in 1st century A.D. koine it has also often the sense of *will*. If it meant only desire here, we would have Pelagianism.

[7]St. Augustine, Epistle 194. 5. 19. PL 33. 880. *Cf.* words of St. John Vianney, the Curé of Ars when someone asked how he could stay humble with all the applause. He replied: "I once asked for it [full knowledge of his own wretchedness] and obtained it. If God had not upheld me, I would have fallen instantly into despair." He told Frère Athanase that God left him enough in-

We can begin to see now how, on the fundamental level *i.e.*, considering what good I myself originate and do not receive from God, the Saints could find no good in themselves. In fact, we could speak in an even worse way. Suppose we think of a ledger, with a page for credits, and a page for debits, for me, all on this fundamental level. On the credit side, what can I write in to my credit? Not a thing: For there is utterly no good—not the good that I am, not a good thought, not a good decision of will, not the carrying out of a good decision—that is mine in this basic sense. Hence I write in zero. Now: What measure of self-esteem matches this zero? Obviously, zero self-esteem.

But then I must fill in the debit page. There I enter a number to indicate what evil I have done, my sins. We each have different numbers, but we all have them: we are all sinners. And now comes the frightening thought: If the credit page took me down to zero self-esteem, the debit page, with my sins, takes me below zero! I am, strictly, literally, worse than nothing. I not only have produced no good in the basic sense: I have done much evil. No wonder the Saints could say dreadful things about themselves, and say them in all truth. If the mentally sane person is the one who sees things as they are, instead of thinking he is Napoleon, or imagining people are after him, then the sanest of men are the Saints, for they have seen the shattering truth about themselves on this basic level.

But it is psychologically important for us not to have too bad an image of ourselves. Some react more strongly to such images than others. We think of the old saying: "Give a bad dog a good name and he will live up to it." The reverse is true: A bad self-image can lead a person to act badly. So therefore we must look on the secondary level. There we find a totally different picture. We need only recall it now, for we saw it fully chapter 2, on Sons of God. For that is what we are by His grace. We are not only adopted by Him—adoption in human affairs is a thing that is kind, but still only a legal fiction—but we are given a share in the divine nature itself by grace!

Suppose a delegation from Podunk came to the White House, and gave the President a scroll saying: "The good people of Podunk have made you Honorary Dogcatcher of Podunk." Being a good politician, the President would smile, and hand the document to his secretary. But when those people had left, he would say: "What do they think? I am the President—and they make me Honorary Dogcatcher!" Clearly, his new title would not go to the President's head. But to be

---

sight into his nothingness to make him understand that he was capable of nothing. He was only a tool in God's hands. Cited from: Margaret Trouncer, *Saint Jean-Marie Vianney*, Sheed-Ward , NY, 1958, p. 249.

made President or King after already being made partly divine involves an even more gaping distance. No human dignity can compare to ours; and no earthly honor ought to distract us from our true worth.

So we are creatures of incredible contrasts! On the primary level, we are nothing, really, worse than nothing because of sin. No matter how much good we may do later, God still "loses money on us". For our good works cannot make up for our sins, or rebalance the scales (which we saw in chapter 4). Yet, on the secondary level, we are wondrous, with a dignity that far eclipses all human honors. St. Augustine says well of human honor that it is "smoke without substance."[8]

But we have not yet finished. We would still like to know precisely how to reconcile what we saw from St. Paul with the fact that we are free. Namely, on the one hand, St. Paul insists we cannot even get a good thought, or make a good decision of ourselves. Yet, on the other hand, we know we have free will. This is clear all over Scripture, and St. Paul himself wrote (2 Cor 6:1): "We urge you not to receive the grace of God in vain." So, in some way I must be able to control whether or not it comes in vain. Similarly, all Scripture urges us to repent, to turn to God. . . .

Just how can we fit these two facts together, our freedom, and our total dependence on God? Neither Scripture nor the Church has told us. So we must fall back on our own speculations.

Some theologians[9] have simply said this: When a grace comes to me, it at once gives me the previously missing power to make a good decision. This may be possible, but there seems to be a better way, one that fits more closely with the words of St. Paul.

This other view begins by considering at first only two possibilities for me when a grace comes to lead and empower me to do a certain good thing right now. The two are these: to decide to accept that grace, or to reject it.[10]

But: to decide to accept is a good act of will, and the words of St. Paul in Phil 2:13 tell me I do not have such a power: "It is God who works in you both the will and the doing."

Of course, I can reject grace. But if I had only that one power, I would not be free. There is no freedom with only one option.

So there must be another possibility, one within my power. That, clearly could only be this: to *non-reject*. Someone will say: "Does not that amount to the same as deciding to accept?" We answer: It has the

---

[8]St. Augustine, *City of God* 5. 17. PL41. 161.

[9]This is the view of the Molinists. On it *cf.* Most, *New Answers to Old Questions* ## 9 and 328-29.

[10]Most, *ibid.* ## 336-84.

same effect, but uses a different process to get it.

We notice further that this process of non-rejection must not include an act of will or decision. If it did, Phil 2:13 would stop us.

So that non-rejection must consist merely in this: When grace has come and given me the good idea, and a favorable attitude (not a decision)—suppose that at the very point at which I could reject—I simply do nothing, no decision. To do nothing is of course in my power. But yet, that doing nothing, at the very point where I could reject can serve as a condition. When that condition is present, God causes His grace to move ahead, so as to "work both the will and the doing." The idea is really very simple: At the precise point where I could reject, I merely make no decision against grace. Then it works both the will and the doing.[11]

Does this seem to make me totally passive? Not really, for two reasons: first, I omit rejection at the very point where I could have rejected; second, we notice something additional about the second stage (that is, the stage after I have nonrejected). At that point, I am both being moved by grace, and moving myself by power currently coming from grace. It is obvious that our proposed theory fits neatly with every statement of St. Paul.[12]

A further consideration on non-rejection is still needed. The very framework of that nonrejection—a situation in which I have felt the attraction, given by grace, of the good, is a precondition for that non-rejection. For grace at the start produced in me a favorable attitude—not yet a decision—to the good thing it proposed. This favorable attitude as it were supports the very possibility of non-rejection of the grace. Further, my previous spiritual condition which leaves me open to this non-rejection is, in turn, owed to many instances of graces, with the process we have just described. Our indebtness reaches back endlessly, infinitely!

The early Fathers of the Church often made use of a philosophy to deepen their understanding of divine revelation. They used Plato, with much profit. But St. Thomas Aquinas began to use Aristotle in the

---

[11]Even our non-resistance or non-rejection is made possible by grace. For we have the inclination to evil or sin from original sin, and that inclination increases with personal sins. Grace, by showing God's will as good to our mind, compensates for these inclinations, and so makes non-resistance possible. Yet there is freedom, because this work of grace does not determine whether or when the will will non-resiSt. *Cf.* also St. Thomas *Summa* I-II. 111. 2 ad 3.

[12]It fits easily with 2 Cor 3:5—since God causes the good thought; with Phil 2:13—since God moves the will; with 1 Cor 4:7—since all the good we are and have and do is His gift. *Cf.* DS 1554.

same way, with even better results. We are going to sketch some ideas of Aristotle to help us to penetrate more deeply into what we have just seen from St. Paul.

Aristotle noticed that if I am at one place on the earth, and wish to travel to another, before going, there must be the capacity to go. If the trip is made, that capacity will be filled or fulfilled. Aristotle liked to name these two things *potency* and *act* or *actualization*. We would not have to use his words, but they are convenient.

But next we notice that this same matter of capacity and fulfillment (potency and act) also appears any time there is any change made. Before the change, there is the potency, then if it goes through, that potency will be actualized.

We need to note this too: at the top of the rise from potency to act, there is more or higher being on hand. For before the change, there was an empty capacity, which would like to be filled. Therefore we ask: Where did this extra, added being come from? No one can lift himself from the floor by pulling his shoelaces; or, no one gives himself what he does not have. So where, again, does the extra come from?

Perhaps some other part of me (if I am the one causing the change) has the needed extra. But even so, where did that other part of me get it? It had to move up from potency to actualization too. So I must look outside myself for a source for the added being—in some other cause. But where did that cause get it? It too had to arise from potency to act.

We could put as long a chain of causes in place as we might wish—but we have not solved our problem at all, of where, finally, the extra being comes from, until we see that there has to be a Being that does not have to go from potency to actuality—a Being that simply *is* actuality. Aristotle called that the First Cause—sometimes he even used the word *God*, which is obviously right.

Now we are in a position to make a tremendous discovery: even when I get a good thought, that involves progressing from potency to act, and I need the First Cause to bring that about. Even more surprisingly: even when I make a free decision of my will, that too involves going from potency to act—which means I need the First Cause, God, for that. But this is precisley what St. Paul said: "It is God who works in you both the will and the doing . . . we are not sufficient to think anything of ourselves as from ourselves: our sufficiency is from God."

When the First Cause (God) has caused me to see a thing as good and to be favorably disposed, if at that point I simply non-reject (*i.e.*, make no decision), His movement goes ahead, as we said above, and actualizes the potency of my will to make a good decision.

Just ahead of the words we quoted from Phil 2:13, St. Paul said: "Work out your salvation with fear and trembling, because it is God who works in you both the will and the doing." This does not mean servile fear and trembling; rather the phrase had come to mean "with reverence." So I must act with reverence. Why? Because when I do anything good, it is His power that is at work in me. But—even more strikingly and fearfully—when I do evil it is also His power that is at work in me . Not that He causes the evil orientation—no, I do that,[13] but the power of added being still comes from Him, without whom I can do nothing (*cf.* Jn. 15:5). It is indeed a fearful thought that I really handle the power of God, using it as I please—for good, or even for sin! No wonder St. Paul calls for reverence!

We notice too that our ability to do good comes to us from God in two phases as it were. A comparison will help here. Imagine I am standing in a TV store, admiring a set, priced at $500. The storekeeper comes to me: "I see you like that set. Why not buy it?" I tell him: "Yes, but it is $500, and I don't have any money." He replies: "Here, I give you $300." But I still do not buy—I am short $200. A day later I am there again, looking at the same TV, and the owner comes again: "I see you like that set, why not buy it?" I reply: "I have only $300, and it costs $500." "Do not worry," he says," Here is another $200." So now I put together the $300 and the $200, and pay him. I can really claim it is mine, since I have paid for it. But yet, I have paid him with his own money.

Somewhat similarly God gives us at the start of our existence our body, soul, faculties, our permanent equipment as it were. But that is not enough—new or higher being appears at the time of acting, as we said. So He must supply more at the time of acting. He does it. Every bit of good I am and have and do is His gift, as we said before (*cf.* 1 Cor 4:7). I pay Him with His own money. Yet I do pay Him, and so, in a secondary sense I have paid, and the act is mine. My faculties, as it were, do churn it out. So there is strong temptation, which I need to fight against constantly, to think the good is mine. It is mine only in the

---

[13]There is a philosophical problem with rejection, since it involves a decision, a passage from potency to act. We solve it thus: At the start, God actualizes the potency of my mind to see a thing as good and partly actualizes the potency of my will—not as far as a decision, but as far as a favorable attitude. Suppose then, when these things are in place, the picture does not please me. Then the favorable attitude of will drops back from actuality to potency—we do not need God to drop. That serves as the condition. When it appears, He actualizes the potency of my will to reject. He supplies only the power in the order of being; the rejecter supplies the evil orientation, by the drop described.

secondary sense, not in the basic sense. We recall what we said above about how we are in the basic sense: we produce no good, only evil. Yet in the secondary sense, we pay Him with His own gifts. So St. Augustine is right, terribly right, when he says: "When God crowns your merits, He crowns nothing other than His own gifts."

This does not, of course, mean that I am a mere robot: my own faculties, which God gave me long ago, really do produce good, even though they can do it only under the divine motion. We recall too, that in the second stage of the process (described above) we are both being moved by grace, and moving ourselves by power being received at that very moment from grace.

To pursue the TV store comparison again: why do I not, on receiving the final installment of the money, go and do something else with it, instead of what the storekeeper had in mind? As we said above, it is the attraction of grace that makes possible our very non-rejection—plus our more general spiritual condition, which in turn, is the effect of many encounters with grace on the pattern we decribed above.

When, however, I acquire and even accumulate merits through good works, this fact is a great ground of hope for me—not because I have produced any good by myself. No, the hope rests on the fact that His giving me these claims or tickets, as it were, proves His love for me.[14]

We begin to see now why Jesus could not stand pride: pride implicitly claims to be God. For if I really could produce, could originate any good, I would have to have infinite power, for this reason: If I produced some good, that good before I acted did not exist. Yet it came into existence. What power is required to start with nothing and bring good into existence? The rise from nothing to some good is an infinite rise—it is, literally, making something out of nothing—it is *creation*. So, if I could really originate any good by my own power, that same power—being infinite—would also enable me to create a universe. Perhaps, then, when I am tempted to be proud, I should ask myself: How many universes have I created lately?

It is tremendously helpful spiritually not to merely know these things, but to meditate on them constantly. For as we said, since our faculties do turn out good things at times, we get the impression that the good comes from ourselves. We can see from St. Paul, and from

[14]*Cf.* St. Thomas, *Summa* I. 19. 5. c, which says that God "vult hoc esse propter hoc, sed non propter hoc vult hoc." That is: God wants one thing to be there to serve as a title for another thing, even though the title does not move Him. The titles He gives me serve His love of objective order, and His love of me. His promise, "Ask and you shall receive" serves both purposes similarly.

Aristotle, that the good does not really come from us—only the evil orientation comes from us.

Should we say, on seeing another sinning greatly: "There but for the grace of God go I!" There is danger here. It is true that every bit of good we are or have or do is simply His gift to us. But it is also true, as we saw, that in some way (which we tried to explain) we do control whether or not a grace comes to us in vain (*cf.* 2 Cor 6:1). In depreciating ourselves, we must not also depreciate God: If it were true that grace was the sole reason why we are not as sinful as someone else we may see, then we would be blaming God.

It is important in trying for humility to watch out for a sort of "chesty feeling" when we do something good.[15] That sort of feeling can serve as the somatic resonance (*cf.* chapter 16) to pride, the deadliest of all vices. Again, pride logically implies a claim to be God. Only He can produce the "higher being" in good actions in the basic sense. Yet the sinner feels and thinks he produces it.

We should watch out too for something like the submarine motives we mentioned in chapter 15. The Saints knew they were doing great good—yet realized it all came from God. But the Pharisee in the Temple (Lk 18:11) prayed: "O God, I give you thanks that I am not like the rest of men. . . ." And he enumerated his good deeds. His lips said he gave the credit to God. But, at least subconsciously, he was grabbing credit for himself, as if he produced the good in the basic sense. Hence Our Lord said the Pharisee went home unjustified.

Jesus also said (Mt 6:3): "In giving alms, let not your left hand know what your right hand is doing." Of course, our hands have no knowledge. But Jesus seems to mean: Beware. Do not think much on the fact of doing good—to avoid the subconscious grabbing of credit we saw in the Pharisee.

There is a special way in which we may be tempted to think ourselves better. A young child sometimes, on seeing his brothers or sisters misbehaving, takes pleasure in the thought: "Now Mother will think more of me." No. Each must stand on his/her own deserts, and not want to grow by others' losses. This is a lack of both love and humility.

So, we need to pray much for humility, to meditate much on what we saw in this chapter. And we need to act on our own knowledge of our powerlessness in good, but our ability to do evil. Action tends

---

[15]We distinguish a feeling of "chestiness," which can be resonance for pride, from a mental satisfaction at doing some good, which is not such a resonance. Even so, we need to be careful pride does not creep into the legitimate satisfaction.

greatly to strengthen our interior beliefs,[16] and God is ever ready to put both the will and the action into us.

Jesus said (Mt 18: 3): "Unless you become like little children, you will not enter the kingdom of heaven." Children know they do not earn their place in their Father's house—they get it not because they are good, but because He is good. It is humility that teaches us to live in this awareness.[17]

---

[16]The experience of being rejected of course helps humility, and increases our likeness to Jesus, if we accept it as such: even though I may not deserve this particular slight, yet my sins deserve more than the equivalent.

Persons in positions of great power—such that others fear to tell them anything unfavorable—gradually lose their bearings, like the men who were put into experimental space capsules at the beginning of US space program. They lacked light and sound, and had only bland temperature inside. So they all got hallucinations. People with great power, since they do not have the correcting input normal people have (criticism from friends and enemies) grow able to accept even outrageous flattery.

[17]In the basic sense, God needs no creature—He did not need to create any at all. But in a different sense, He can need us. For though He could do anything directly, by omnipotence, yet that would often involve use of extraordinary or miraculous power. He should not make the extraordinary ordinary (else someone could ask why He made laws He intended to violate regularly). Hence He uses us to do in the ordinary way things He could do only in the extraordinary mode. Angels serve a parallel purpose. They can do things for us without a miracle that God would need a miracle to do, since their nature has great powers, greater than ours.

Chapter 19:
Why the Cross?

Jesus insisted (Mt 18:38): "Whoever does not take up his cross and follow me, is not worthy of me." St. Paul expressed the same idea with his well known *syn Christo* framework, which, as we saw before, could be summarized: A person is saved and made holy, if and to the extent that he is a member of Christ, and is like Him. Now in the life of Jesus there are two stages: first, a hard life, suffering, and death; second, eternal glory. Of course we are still in stage one. So the more we are like Him in His suffering now, the more will we be like Him in glory in the next world. Hence St. Paul also said, as we saw earlier (2 Cor 4:17; Rom 8:18): "That which is light and momentary in our tribulations, is working for us an eternal weight of glory. . . . I judge that the sufferings of the present time are not worthy to be compared to the glory that is to be revealed to us."

We can, then, take comfort in this, and even, with St. Paul, rejoice in our tribulations. But yet, also with St. Paul, we should be pleased to be more conformed to Jesus. To see this, we need to realize deeply who He is. If He just seems to be some man of centuries ago who had a horrid death, which we say redeemed us from sin, this may not impress us much at all, for our age has certainly lost the sense of sin.[1] So, if we do not *deeply* realize who He is, we will not likely feel an attraction to imitate Him. St. Paul, and the first generations with him, could grasp this more easily. They had seen the cross in its horror, whereas so often our crucifixes depict Him as quite comfortable! But they, even pagans, felt the immense shock that God should deal with man at all. As we saw

[1]Pius XII, Radio Message to National Catechetical Congress of U.S., Oct 26, 1946. *Cf.* John Paul II, *Encyclical on Holy Spirit*, May 18, 1986, #47.

earlier, the great Plato wrote: "No god associates with men."[2] The still greater Aristotle said that friendship of a god with a man is impossible, since the distance between them is too great.[3]

They had in mind poor things, hardly deserving the name of a god. What would they think if the omnipotent, infinite God became man—still more, if He allowed Himself to suffer so terrible and shameful a death! This is why St. Paul wrote (1 Cor 1:23): "We preach Christ crucified—a scandal to the Jews, and nonsense to the gentiles." Our problem is that we have grown up with these doctrines, and they have lost their edge for us—really, we never did even in earlier life feel that edge. We need to work to try to recover it. Then, if we know and realize who He is, what He did for us, we will readily want to be like Him even in His suffering—by way of mortification.

We have to try to realize deeply too that it is our sins that caused His suffering and death. Since each of us can say with St. Paul (Gal 2:20): "He loved me and gave Himself for me," we must also say: He died because of me, because of my sins.

There are other reasons for mortification. One very important one is the need of developing our spiritual eyesight. Imagine two men going to the Louvre in Paris, one of the world's greatest art galleries. It could easily be that one is thrilled by the art; the other is bored, and hopes his friend will not stay long. He just wants to see the Follies. The reason would be that one was conditioned to appreciate the beauty of that art; the other was not.

Similarly, we need to be conditioned to appreciate the divine truths. Several things contribute to that conditioning. We just saw one of them, humility. Now we try to see the facts about mortification.

We can approach it this way: Adam and Eve had more than the essentials of humanity (a body and soul, having mind and free will); they had a coordinating gift. Without it, we now need mortification. For there are many drives in both body and soul. These are legitimate in themselves. God made them good. But they each seek their own satisfaction, working blindly, without respect to the whole person. (As noted earlier, we can see the effect of the loss of this coordinating gift, this *integrity*, in the fact that Adam hid himself after the fall, because he was naked. Before the fall he also was naked, but the sex drive was not erupting spontaneously; it obeyed his reason.)

We think of a piece of springy metal. It is not enough to just push it straight once—it takes long repeated effort to finally get it into place. Similarly, long repeated efforts are required to push our disorderly

---

[2]Plato, *Symposium* 203.

[3]Aristotle, *Nichomachean Ethics* 8.7.

drives into the right positions. For they keep on rebelling. Bending them back beyond the middle by depriving them of some things they otherwise could have reasonably had is the way to finally tame them, so far as can be done in this life.

Jesus once said (Mt 6:21): "Where your treasure is, there is your heart also." In the narrow sense this would mean a box of coins a man might hide under the floor of his house. If he had such a stash, he would of course enjoy thinking of it. It would be like a magnet, pulling his thoughts and heart to itself.

But we can put our treasure not only in a box of coins; wc can put it in anything: in huge meals, in gourmet meals, in sex, in travel, in power, even in studying theology. All these things are lower than God, some farther down than others. But even more importantly, a person may be attached, or addicted to them, in various degrees. Some are pulled by these things only to the extent of imperfection; others to the point of occasional venial sin, or habitual venial sin, or occasional mortal sin, or habitual mortal sin. The farther below God a thing is, and the more we let it grip us, the more difficult it is for thoughts and heart to rise to the divine level, to the thought and love of God.

A modern comparison makes a good supplement: we think of a galvanometer, which is just a magnetic needle on its pivot, so it can swing freely, like a compass. There is a coil of wire around it. If we pass a current through the coil, the needle will swing in the right direction and the right amount. It measures the current.

My mind is like such a meter. When God sends an actual grace to me (recall chapter 18 and the words on Phil 2:13) to lead and enable me to do a certain good thing here and now, the first thing grace needs to do is to put into my head the good idea of what God wishes me to do. Grace stands for the current in the coil, which is gentle in that it respects my freedom. But the outside pulls of creatures, even legitimate use of creatures, can also exert a pull, in the proportions we indicated. Whereas grace respects my freedom, these pulls may not do so, if I let myself become heavily addicted to them, on the scale we just drew.

By now it is obvious: if we want to be fully responsive to the movements of divine grace, we will need to cut down, so far as is possible, the pulls of creatures on us, so that grace can register on us.[4] It is

[4]This detachment from pulls does not rule out affection for parents, etc. Jesus at the tomb of Lazarus, only a good friend, allowed Himself to weep. So St. Augustine was wrong in thinking himself probably sinning in weeping over his Mother's death (*scor*

Confessions 9.12-13). We distinguish love in the will, from feelings of love. Love in the will, if in the right direction (directed to the right persons), is

mortification that reduces those pulls. The Saints tried to keep as free as possible of those pulls: hence some even moved out into the desert. They wanted not only to avoid the pulls that would lead to small sins: they wanted to avoid even imperfections. Here is where we can see the value of celibacy/virginity. Sex is a most powerful pull. In marriage it is not only legitimate, but, given the right conditions (not too hard to provide), it can even be meritorious. But even when legitimate, it does provide a pull, making it so much less easy for the thoughts and heart to rise to the level of God. Hence St. Paul in 1 Cor. 7:5 suggests to married people to abstain from sex at times, by mutual consent, "So you may be free for prayer." This does not mean St. Paul looks down on marriage. No, he calls it a grace (1 Cor 7:7) and says the union of spouses is an image of the union of Christ with His Church (Eph. 5:32). But there can be two aspects to a thing; *e.g.*, in the parable of the sower (Lk 8:14) some seed falls on ground on which thorns are growing. They choke off the growth. The Gospel explains that the thorns are riches and pleasures of this life. Now earthly goods are not evil; they are good in themselves, and can be used well. Yet they have another aspect: they are thorns. So they make it less easy for thoughts to rise to the divine level. Hence surely one must not let his heart be set on them, but rather, to some extent at least, he should give up some of them, to be the more free of pulls.

We can see then the spiritual value of virginity/celibacy, and of poverty at least in spirit. They help the soul to be the more free to rise to the thought of God, and to respond to the least breeze of His inspirations. Obedience, similarly, helps to control our self-will. These three—poverty, chastity, obedience—are called the evangelical counsels. This means that Jesus Himself recommended them. Hence Vatican II wrote that they "contribute not a little to purification of heart and spiritual freedom, they constantly stir up the fervor of love and can make the Christian more in harmony with the virginal and poor life that

---

positively good, unless of course it becomes excessive, so as to lead a soul into violating God's law or wishes. If this love were not good, then our supernatural love for these persons would not perfect, but destroy nature. But, grace does perfect nature. Love of feeling can more easily interfere with adherence to God's will. This is because of our weakness in the present life, but in the future life, there will be no such conflict. Here we recall that St. Paul (1 Cor 7:5) suggests that married partners at times refrain from the lawful use of marriage "so you may be free for prayer," as we explain in the body of this chapter.

Jesus Himself, as Pius XII explains in *Haurietis aquas*, has even a love of feeling for all of us (not based on sensory attraction, but resonance to His love in His will for us).

Christ the Lord, and His Virgin Mother, embraced."[5]

The Eastern Fathers of the Church note specially at this point that it is not enough for one to separate self from the pulls of even legitimate sex; one needs to try to be free from every kind of pull from creatures. So someonoe who gives up marriage needs to take care that in giving up one thing he/she does not think it is enough. Complete detachment is needed for full likeness to Jesus and His Mother, and for 20/20 spiritual eyesight.

We should even add this: Marriage, as we explained in chapter 16, contains powerful providential means to get a person out of the shell of self and deeply interested in another for the other's sake. Those who abstain from marriage do not have this help. So they will need to take definite care to supply for it in other ways. This does not of course deny what St. Paul insists on so clearly and strongly in chapter 7 of First Corinthians: abstention from marriage provides a spiritual aid that is not found within marriage, even though marriage is good, and has the advantages we just spoke of.

Over a period of time, our somatic resonance—we recall it from chapter 16—will become gradually adjusted so as to find it easier to resist the pulls of creatures, and to register the divine invitation that grace offers us. This is the same as saying that when things become habitual, they become easier to do.

Some today are saying: let us just be positive, be loving to people, and since love is greater, we do not need all those negatives of giving things up. But this does not really work out. For just as we need many different food elements for bodily health, even though some are worth less than others, so too we need negative mortification too, for it affects the bodily side, and hence does more to adjust our somatic resonance. Further, the harder mortificaton is on our bodily side, the more somatic resonance can be adjusted, and so the more are we capable of even large growth when advancing from one plateau to a higher one. When we say the harder the better, we presuppose prudence, great prudence. In practice most people will go to extremes in this matter of negative mortification—either they do nothing, or they do too much. It is obvious, then, that the help of a good spiritual director is priceless, needed more for this matter than for many other things. It is hard to be objective in one's own case.

There is still another reason for mortification: the rebalancing of the objective order, of which we spoke in chapter 4. The Holiness of our Father wills it. So if we love Him, we will want to do what we can towards rebalancing the weight of sin. We recall in this connection that

[5]Vatican II, *On the Church* #46.

love of God in practice is the same as doing His will. This is a very important part of His will, so dear to Him that it is one of the reasons why He sent His Son to so dreadful a death. (The other is His love of us.)

A desire for likeness to His Son also moves us to want mortification for rebalance. He was willing even to die for that. Love of Him should make us want to be like Him in this work most dear to His Heart. Again, St. Paul tells us we are saved and made holy if and to the extent that we are not only His members, but are like Him in all things—including this essential part of His work.

And something like personal feeling should also impel us in this direction, namely, the desire to make up to Him for what He suffered for us. St. Margaret Mary tells us that in one of the great revelations of the Sacred Heart to her He complained of people's ingratitude, and said: "I feel this more than all that I suffered during My Passion. If only they would make Me some return for My love, I should think but little of all I have done for them, and would wish, were it possible, to suffer still more."[6]

At this point we should try to understand something beyond our power to visualize, namely, that in view of the fact that His human mind was necessarily joined to the divinity from the first instant of its human existence, that mind saw, in the vision of the divinity, all sins of all centuries—but also saw all reparation that would be offered to Him in later times. It is evident that this would give Him some consolation. Hence Pope Pius XI in his Encyclical, *Miserentissimus Redemptor*, tells us: "Now if the soul of Christ [in Gethsemani] was made sorrowful even to death on account of our sins, which were yet to come, but which were foreseen, there is no doubt that He received some consolaition from our reparation."[7] As we said, we cannot stricly visualize this, yet our theological deduction, confirmed by the Pope, shows us inescapably that it is true. By acting *today*, we can console Him *then*. Love and gratitude should impel us to do that, most abundantly.

This also follows: since He most earnstly desires the salvation of all men—so much so that St. Paul could write in Galatians 2:20 that He "loved me and gave Himself for me," that is, for each individual soul—then if we love Him, we will want to work to save souls for Him. For that, the Holiness of the Father calls for reparation, *i.e.*, for rebalancing, in union with His Son.

Words of our Blessed Mother at Fatima underscore this. In the vision of August 13, 1917, she told the three children: "Pray, pray much, and make sacrifices for sinners for many go to hell because they have

[6]St. Margaret Mary, *Autobiography* #55, p.70.

[7]Pius XI, *Miserentissimus Redemptor*, May 8, 1928, AAS 20.174.

no one to sacrifice and intercede for them."[8]

How can it be that this soul is lost because someone else does not pray and sacrifice for it? It is because some souls make themselves blind; they so give themselves to the pulls of creatures that the gentle impulse of grace cannot register at all.[9] Then, clearly, grace cannot even begin to move them, if it cannot do the first necessary thing, to put the good thought into their mind. Of course, no one can be saved without grace, so if a soul makes itself impervious to grace, it is surely lost. Yet the Blessed Mother holds out a possibility: sacrifice and much prayer. Her words imply that even blinded and hardened souls can be rescued from going to hell if they receive an extraordinary grace, one that is comparable to a miracle in the natural order.

Under what conditions is such an extraordinary or miraculous grace given? The Holiness of Our Father considers the balance in the objective order. If someone else puts an extraordinary weight, as it were, into the scales, it will call for and make suitable the grant of even a miraculous grace, to rescue hardened sinners. Love of our Father, and of souls, urges use to do what we can to rescue even hardened sinners from hell. The three Fatima children went to heroic lengths spurred by this motive.

In chapter 17 we saw that souls who are very faithful to our Father receive a lasting peace, that nothing can take away, on what is often called the "fine point of the soul." There may be storms and blackness on the lower levels of our being, but this peak is ever in the brightness of the sun. The factor that chiefly contributes to getting this condition is simply generosity in mortification. Faith tells us that the things of this world are not worth much at all compared to the goods to come. St. Paul even boldly says that for the sake of Christ, he has taken the loss of all things, and considers them as "dung" (Phil 3:8) to gain Christ. As we know, St. Paul knew that God's creatures are good—he did not deny that. But he wanted to say that on a relative scale, comparing this world with the next, things here are worse than worthless, since they can distract us from our true goal. The book of Wisdom said it well (4:12):

---

[8]Cited from Lucy's *Memoirs*, in *Documentos de Fatima*, ed. A.M. Martins, Porto, 1976, p.345, reporting on apparition of August 13, 1917.

[9]Hardness develops specially rapidly from presumption, *i.e.*, if a person says, in effect, I will commit this mortal sin now, and continue to commit them, but before I die, I will go to Confession. There is not likely to be a real change of heart, when the pattern is planned in advance. This is the kind of case we see when people live in a hopelessly invalid marriage, and plan to go to confession at the end. We do not suggest despair, for grace can do wonders, and the fear of death can bring some sense. But the risk is immense.

"The witching spell of things that are little, makes it hard to see the good things." If we put this into the framework of the pulls on our mental meter that we saw earlier in this chapter, it obviously makes sense.[10]

To act on such faith is, of course, the way to strengthen it, to attain to the lasting contentment and peace on the fine point of the soul. So we should understand the eight Beatitudes given us by Jesus (Mt 5:3-10) to refer not only to eternal happiness, but even to happiness in this world. Those who follow His program—which involves much detachment and mortification—will find themselves well-off and happy even here.

In contrast, a person who always pursues fleeting happiness, will find it runs away from him. We used to hear of the bored, sated rich, who had used up every pleasure they could imagine, and found only boredom at the end of the search. Literally, they had nothing to look forward too—they had given themselves everything and found what St. Augustine proclaimed: "You have made us for yourself, O Lord, and restless are our hearts until they rest in you."[11] Those who deny themselves have much, even in the worldy sense, much to look forward to even in this world. It is so true that as the popular saying tells us: "Anticipation is greater than realization."

Really, everything created can lose its edge. Suppose, for example, someone buys for himself a new tape or recording. It is a great pleasure the first few times it is played, but after many plays, it becomes boring. The person does not care to hear it even if someone else plays it on the air. Many today who try for constant pleasure find instead not only not much pleasure, but even nervous strain, a fatigue from asking the senses to respond so strongly and so constantly.

Even sex can lose much of its edge—hence manuals for the "Joy of Sex", and some even turn to perversions, in a vain attempt to recover a lost thrill. But those who practise a certain abstinence in Natural Family Planning, find that sex keeps much of its pleasure, and marriages are strengthened.

The pagan philosopher Epicurus, who said that pleasure was the goal of life, seems to have understood this at least to some extent. For it is certain that he lived very sparingly. The Roman philosopher Seneca reports that Epicurus said that "at times he would withdraw from pleasure," and "that he boasted that he could eat for less than a penny,"[12]

---

[10]Suffering can help bring wisdom. *Cf.* the great Greek tragedian Aeschylus, *Agamemnon* 177: "By suffering comes learning." *Cf.* also Herodotus, *Histories* 1.207

[11]St. Augustine, *Confessions* 1.1. PL 32.661.

[12]Seneca, *On Leisure* 1.7; Epistle 18.9.

while Diogenes Laertius, in his life of Epicurus, quotes a letter of Epicurus saying, "Send me a little pot of cheese, so when I wish, I can have a feast." Hardly Epicurean, we would say today![13] It was his later followers who gave the bad name to Epicureanism.

Our Father is infinite Generosity. If we give up things for Him here, He gives us, even in this life the hundredfold that His Son promised (Mk 10:30; Lk 18:30).[14]

[13]Cited in Diogenes Laertius, *Life of Epicurus* 10.11. *Cf.* also chapter 16, references in note 15.

[14]*Cf.* Cicero *Tusculan Disputations* 1.31.75: "For what else do we do when we recall the soul from pleasure, that is, from the body . . . except we call the soul to itself. . . . This, while we are on earth, will be like that heavenly life." *Cf.* also A. Solzhenitsyn, in *Time* Feb. 18, 1980, p.48: "There are two reasons for this string of capitulations [of the West to Russia]. First is the spiritual impotence that comes from living a life of ease; people are unwilling to risk their comforts."

Chapter 20: How to Follow the Cross

The material of the last chapter, if we meditate deeply on it, will lead us to want to take up our cross and follow Him, and to join in the sufferings of Our Lady too. But the next question is: How does one carry this out.

First we need to notice that there are two great categories of mortification: self-imposed, and providential.

Providential mortification is that which God sends or permits to come to us; clearly, we should make best use of it, joining in His will for us. Self-imposed mortification is that which we voluntarily and freely take upon ourselves.

At once the proponents of an unfortunate new tendency in spirituality will object that while providential mortification is good, since sent by God, self-imposed mortification is not good. In fact, some forms of giving up things are even harmful, and obedience prevents our making the decisions needed for spiritual maturing.[1] (This movement does not often get a name, though it is all around us. We will follow the current penchant for alphabetic names, and invent the name: Give-up-nothing spirituality, abbreviated GUN.)

They reach this conclusion by noticing—a thing confirmed by Vatican II, in section 7 of its Decree on the Lay Apostolate—that all creatures of God are good for three reasons: (1) God made them good, and after creating each thing said: It is good; (2) Creatures are all destined for the use of humans: we are the peak of visibile creation; (3)

[1]The problem of obedience *vs.* decision making comes only at one age, about the teen age period. Even then, there are so many decisions to make that one can cultivate both values, since obedience will not take in everything.

Christ in the Incarnation took on a created nature, and used created things—hence a tremendous added dignity for creatures.

Now it is true that all creatures have this threefold dignity or goodness.[2] It is true that Vatican II affirmed this. But we need to notice a large leap made by the GUN Spirituality advocates. They say, in effect: Since all creatures are so good, therefore there is no value in giving up any of them. Instead, they lead us to God, showing us His perfections.

It is, as we said, a very large leap to go from the goodness of creatures to saying there is no value in giving up anything voluntarily. Vatican II did not make that leap. Instead, as we saw in chapter 19, it said that the three evangelical counsels, poverty, chastity and obedience, "contribute not a little to purification of heart and spiritual freedom, they constantly stir up the fervor of love."[3] These things, poverty, chastity and obedience, are of course, three great ways of giving up creatures. Hence the GUN Spirituality is sadly in error. Further, it does not seem to understand what we saw in chapter 19 about the effects of the pulls of creatures. Even if they are good, even if they can, if carefully used, lead us to God, yet they can be like the thorns in the parable of the sower (they stood for the riches and pleasures of this life, so there were two aspects, one good, one harmful).

In passing, we notice that to practice the GUN Spirituality can be devastating in two respects. First, it can readily lead to marriage failures, or even invalid marriages. Marriage is not just a grand round of sexual indulgence: it requires much give and take (recall what we said in chapter 16). A person who has lived all his/her life up to the day of marriage without giving up anything, is in no condition for such give and take. Really, since marriage by nature must be a permanent commitment, and since a self-indulgent person is not really capable of something permanent that requires self-sacrifice, there may be no marriage at all; in extreme cases, it might simply be invalid from the start. In any case, clearly, it will not have much chance of success.

The same damage appears in vocations. Imagine a young person considering any form of priesthood or religious life. If properly lived, these involve much giving up of things. But then the same person comes to believe, with the GUN Spirituality: It does me no good to give up

---

[2]Vatican II speaks on the absolute scale of creatures in themselves; one can also speak, as St. Paul does in Phil 3:8 on the relative scale, comparing creatures now with the things of eternity.

[3]Vatican II, *On the Church* #46. *Cf.* also *On Missions* #40, where the Council praises the institutes of contemplative life which go so far in giving up so many things.

anything. Who would be such a fool as pursue such a vocation? And if when already in a convent, for example, a nun comes to believe this error, she will, logically, either leave, as thousands have done in recent years, or will try to revamp her institute to match the GUN Spirituality—no inexpensive habit (poverty is useless), no obedience (so have only a president, not a superior), and so on.

In addition, one who practices the GUN Spirituality cannot be very happy. For only the really mature can be happy. But one who lives on the principle of self-indulgence, never giving up anything, does not mature. As we saw in chapter 16, even the pagan Socrates knew this: Over and over again he said that one who wishes to find truth should have as little as possible to do with the things of the body. And, as I have already observed elsewhere, pagan Romans as a whole, up to about 265 B.C. held to and really lived out an ideal of *frugalitas*, sparingness, in their mode of life. They thought—rightly—that they were happier that way.[4] We think again of the wise words of St. Augustine: "Every disordered soul is its own penalty."[5]

Clearly self-imposed mortification is strictly essential, nor can it be made up for by just being "nice" to people, on the grounds that charity is the greatest of all virtues. As we saw in chapter 19, just as we cannot eat only one food element and omit the rest, so neither can we omit negative mortification, self-imposed.

St. Paul understood this well. Even though he had a great abundance of providential hardships in his work, yet he added fasting, as we learn from his recital in 2 Cor 11:27.

There are in general two types of self-imposed mortification, which we might call the great way and the little way. In the great way, one takes on physically very difficult things, even the use of a discipline. These things, used with prudence (in practice the help of a sound director is indispensable for this), can be very good. Even Pope John XXIII, who is often thought of as cutting out restraints, and opening windows, and is considered a pleasant companion with whom to drink beer of an evening, yet wrote some strenuous words in his Encyclical on the Curé of Ars. St. John Vianney had heard a fellow priest complain of the slight effectiveness of his ministry. The Curé, as quoted by the Pope, replied: "You have prayed, you have wept, you have groaned, you have sighed. But have you fasted, have you stayed awake, have you slept on the hard floor, have you given yourself the discipline? So long as you have not reached that point there, do not think you have done everything." The Pope commented:

[4]*Cf.* also note 17 on chapter 16, and notes 12, 13, 14 on chapter 19.
[5]St. Augustine, *Confessions* 1.12. PL32.670.

> We turn to all priests who have charge of souls and we beg them to hear these strong words. May everyone, according to the supernatural prudence that must always guide our actions, appreciate his proper conduct with regard to the people entrusted to his pastoral solicitude.[6]

The little way has its chief exponent in St. Thérèse of Lisieux—her autobiography lets us see into her way of life almost as if she were living in a goldfish bowl. She preferred little things, *e.g.*, if a letter came from home in the morning, she would not open it until evening. If she liked a certain kind of food, she might at times eat something else instead. When well-meaning Sisters served her dishes they thought she would enjoy, but which she actually disliked, she would not let them know the truth about her tastes.[7] And we must not forget that St. Thérèse had as a base to which she added all these little things the hard life of a Discalced Carmelite. These things, provided one uses prudence so as not to generate too much stress by the very accumulation, can be of wonderful spiritual value.

Here again, the help of a good spiritual director is priceless. On the other hand, we could notice that some are excessively concerned about effects on health. St. Teresa of Avila makes the sage observation: "This body of ours has one fault: the more you indulge it, the more ailments and needs it discovers." And with delightful humor she also says: "We begin to imagine that our head aches when we should go to choir—which would not kill us—[we skip] one day because it does ache, and another because it has ached and three more so it won't ache."[8]

Routine life offers us many an occasion for accepting mortifications that come our way without being sought: discomforts that we meet from crowded trains or busses, or late planes, or having to submit humbly to an irritable boss. Doctors or nurses may have to put up with unpleasant or even repulsive patients. Clerks in stores must deal with customers who at times can be unreasonable—yet it is an axiom for successful business people to act as though the customer is always right.

---

[6]John XXIII, *Sacerdotii nostri primordia*, August 1, 1959. AAS 51.569.

[7]*Cf. St. Thérèse, By Those Who Knew Her* (testimonies at process of beatification) ed. C. O'Mahony, Our Sunday Visitor, Huntington, 1975, esp. pp. 64, 67, 31, 33, 37, 38, 49, 51.

[8]St. Teresa of Avila, *Way of Perfection* 11.2 & 10.6, BAC edition pp.110, 108. When we judge how much we are giving up, it is useful to compare our living to that of even ancient kings and emperors, whose material comforts were much less than even people considered rather poor in the U.S. today have: no cars, no electric fans, no air conditioning, no TV, no radio, no screens on windows, no central heating, etc.

Students may have to put up with boring teachers; professors put up with so many students who pay no attention at all in class. Assembly-line workers have to endure a monotony more suited to machines than to humans. Marriage partners may suffer much from the normal differences of male and female psychology, or from positively unreasonable wishes of the spouse—not to mention the troubles with children of various ages. Or, suppose a friend drops in in the middle of our favorite TV program. Will we perform a mortification worthy of the Fathers of the desert, or tell him to watch along with us, when he has not seen the needed earlier parts of the program? And the list could go on almost without end.

We might note that some seem to find it easier or more agreeable to take large difficulties than to take small hardships. There is a subtle danger here. One might find himself feeling heroic from doing large things. Without such an appeal to vanity, he might not be much inclined to accept the small things.

One can, for certain, take without risk a one-a-day spiritual vitamin. That is, we can all do one or two of these little things per day. This should harm no normal person. But to go very far calls for the advice of a prudent spiritual director.

Even the followers of the GUN spirituality often agree that we should accept, even gladly, from the hand of God, whatever hardships and sufferings He either sends or permits to come to us. Since they are as it were handpicked by Him, they are good in general, and good for us in particular.

We thought earlier about conformity of our will with the will of God, and noticed that since the only thing free in me is my will, if I could make that totally aligned with the will of God, that would be all that is possible. We noted too that we cannot achieve this perfect conformity by just one prayer of resignation to His will, however sincere we might try to be. No, we cannot foresee all He may ask of us in the rest of our lives; and there is need for gradual development of somatic resonance, which we explained in chapter 16.

Providential mortification is really the chief concrete application of this conformity of will, in which we accept His will even when it is hard to do so, and are prepared in advance to accept whatever He may send or permit to come to us.

There are different levels of acceptance. First, one would merely refrain from complaining against the things God sends. But the fullest acceptance means positively being glad to have the suffering, as it were, embracing it. In passing, let us notice that to embrace the hardship is the opposite of the attempt to fly away from reality—a thing not only spiritually bad, but psychologically unsound as well. So this acceptance is, as we would expect, beneficial to us psychologically, and makes for happiness, for that deep peace on the "point of the soul" of which we spoke in chapter 17. In fact, St. John of the Cross says one cannot really enjoy even creatures unless he is detached from them: "One will find greater joy and refreshment from creatures in being detached from them."[9]

In what sense can we positively embrace suffering? We do not think suffering is good in itself, but we like its effects: it makes us more like our Savior; it pleases our Father because it makes us more open to His gifts, which His Generosity loves to give; it makes reparation for our sins and the sins of others, so that they and we may also in this way be more open to receive what He loves to give.

The noted scholar J. Bonsirven reports a remarkable instance of this attitude among ancient Jews: "If a righteous person is afflicted, sufferings are called 'corrections of love,' and they are gladly accepted. Some men are even sad if such sufferings are absent for a prolonged time."[10]

There are two areas in acceptance or aligment of will: first, in the things where His will is already clear; second in the area in which His will is still at least partly not known to us.

Where His will is clearly known, of course we should not be just passive, but should actively embrace what He sends, in union with His Divine Son. It is, of course, clearly known when a suffering or difficulty is already at hand. Then there can be no doubt that He has either sent or permitted it. This does not mean we may not or should not take ordinary remedies against illness or other things. We should use at least ordinary means. but when we have used these, and some hardship or suffering is left, then we do know it is the will of the Father for us, at least for a time. (Note that this does not rule out the possibility of, for example, a miraculous healing at some point, for God may also wish to use an infirmity or other difficulty to show forth His glory—which is also for our benefit.)

A special comment is needed on anxiety, so common today. Deep trust in the Father can do much to alleviate it, yet it cannot do everything. (The basis of much of it is biochemical as we saw in chapter 16.)

---

[9]St. John of the Cross, *Ascent of Mt. Carmel* 3.20.2. BAC ed. p. 758.

[10]J. Bonsirven, *Palestinian Judaism in the Time of Christ*, tr. W. Wolf, McGraw-Hill, NY, 1964, p. 115. Bonsirven refers to Mekilta on Exodus 20:23, which he says is "reporting a generally accepted doctrine." *Cf.* Genesis Rabbah 32 (on 7:1) cited in J. Neusner, *Midrash in Context*, Fortress, Philadelphia, 1983, p. 155.

Should we think it is just a loss? Not at all. We need to remember, as we saw in chapter 8, that Jesus Himself suffered from anxiety, looking forward all His life to the terrible ordeal He would have to undergo. So we should accept even anxiety, and offer the suffering to our Father.

But His will in many things is not yet clear, or not entirely clear. What then? We cannot actively will what we do not yet know; rather, our attitude is one of plasticity, being ready to accept whatever He may send, as soon as, and to the extent that, it becomes clear.

Suppose, for example, someone were given an assignment by lawful authority to take up a collection for some great charity. If it is commanded by authority, it is clear that our Father wills him/her to start out and work diligently. But will such a labor always bear maximum fruit? Not at all. So even though we know in general that a good work is His will, yet we may not know just what degree of success He wills us to have, at what time, by what means. In all these aspects, we remain pliable, waiting for His will to appear.

How acquire such plasticity? By cutting down the strength of the outside pulls of which we spoke earlier. They prevent us from registering the most delicate impulses sent by the Holy Spirit. This is done, of course, especially by self-imposed mortification, by giving up some things we might otherwise have lawfully had.

Especially we need at this point mortification of our desires. St. John of the Cross considers this more important than even great penitential practices:

> We must greatly deplore the ignorance of some who burden themselves with extraordinary penances and other voluntary practices and think that this or that will be enough to bring them to union with Divine Wisdom. That will not happen, if they do not take great care to mortify their desires. If they spent half the effort on it [mortification of desires] they would make more progress in one month than by all the other exercises in many years.[11]

St. John does not mean that we should not desire the glory of God and our salvation and that of neighbor. Of course we should. But as we said above, by what means and at what time, and to what extent these things are to bear fruit—on these matters we need the plasticity we spoke of, or lack of specific desire. St. Francis de Sales compares souls that are full of desires to a hunting dog in the spring. There are so many scents that the dog can hardly find the game: "Those souls that always are full of desires, designs, and projects never desire holy heavenly love

---

[11]St. John of the Cross, *Ascent* 1.8.4. BAC ed. p. 582.

as they should, and they fail to pick up the delightful strain and scent of the Divine Beloved."[12]

So one reason why it is so important to mortify desires is obvious: ideally, we should actively want things only to the extent that the will of our Father is clearly willing them. Beyond that, we may be in discord with His will.

But furthermore, desires cause us to stretch ahead, and thereby to leave aside the goodness of things present. Creatures, well used, can be a means to spiritual growth. We already mentioned that St. Francis of Assisi found occasion to praise our Father for His delicate kindness in giving us such lovely creatures as birds. Similarly, we should thank our Father for the favor of His inspiration to great composers or other artists, for the beauty they put before us, which is simply too lofty for mere unaided human ability to generate.[13]

However, in using creatures to help us praise God, we need to watch out that they do not hold us onto themselves so strongly as to cause any hindrance to the ascent of our minds and hearts to God. There are two classic, and obvious, principles about music at Mass that show this point well: (1) The music should lift us above the everyday level(so, music designed to appeal precisely at this level lacks the needed value. It can be tolerated temporarily, while we try to raise people's spiritual level); (2) It should not hold us so strongly as to impede the rise of our minds and hearts to God. It is only a stepping stone, not a stopping place.[14]

However, when the good things are not yet present, they do not give the same opportunity. Then we leave aside what good is at hand, and emptily push to a future that is not yet to be had. This straining ahead is especially harmful when it leads us to hurry Mass or prayers, as we have seen.

Should we positively ask God to send us sufferings, as a means of likeness to Jesus and His Blessed Mother? He Himself on entering into this world said (Heb. 10:7): "Behold, I come to do your will O God." He did not positively ask for such great suffering; but He accepted it. Similarly in Gethsemani He prayed (Lk 22: 42): "Father, if you are willing, take this chalice away from me; however, let not my will but yours be done." In the same way, His mother, when the angel asked her to be the Mother of the Redeemer, simply said: "Be it done to me ac-

---

[12]St. Francis de Sales, *Traitté de l'Amour de Dieu* 12.3. *Oeuvres*, Nierat, Annecy 1894. Let us note that it is specially good to aim mortifications at those particular desires to which we seem specially attached.

[13]*Cf.* comments on natural inspiration at the end of chapter 23.

[14]*Cf.* Pius XII, *Encyclical on Music*, in *The Pope Speaks* 3, 1956, p.13.

cording to your word." She knew, as we explained earlier, much of what that would entail. She did not ask for that suffering, but she accepted. St. Thérèse of Lisieux is reported to have said on August 11, 1897: "I would never ask God for greater sufferings for then they would be my own sufferings, and I should have to bear them all alone."[15] (She said this less than three weeks before her death, which came on Sept. 30, 1897.)

What do we gather from this? First, it is one thing to desire suffering; another thing to rejoice in it when God has actually sent it, as a means of greater likeness to His Divine Son, and union with His Blessed Mother. What of asking for suffering? We may do so in a general way, with, of course the provision: If it pleases our Father. But we should not be specific, asking for a particular suffering at a particular time. For we do not know if that would please Him.

Yet there is something we can do to come more close to actively willing what He wills on this point. Our Blessed Mother knows—even though we do not know—what it might please Him to have us offer at a given time. So we could if we wished give her, as it were, a power of attorney, saying in effect: "I do not know what specific offering it might please Him that I should make at this moment. But you know. Therefore, I appoint you to speak in my name. Please speak for me." If we once make this offering, give her this authority, we should never retract it. Rather, it is good to renew it, particularly at times when things are difficult: "Mother, please speak for me."[16]

Certainly if we want our mortifications to have value and to be profitable, we should join them with the sufferings of Jesus and His Mother. Alone we are nothing. but if we ask her to come and add her dispositions to ours, and join all to those of her Divine Son, then what we do is supremely worthwhile.

---

[15]*Novissima Verba. The Last Conversations and Confidences of Saint Thérèse of the Child Jesus*, tr. Carmelite Nuns of New York, Kenedy, N.Y., 1951. p. 96.

[16]For a somewhat similar attitude, cf. *St. Thérèse of Lisieux, Her Last Conversations*, tr. J. Clarke, ICS Publications, Washington. Cited from *Our Lady's Digest*, Sept-Oct. 1978. p.40; "Asking the Blessed Virgin for something is not the same thing as asking God. She really knows what is to be done about my little desires, whether or not she must speak about them to God. So it's up to her to see that God is not forced to answer me, to allow Him to do everything He pleases."

Chapter 21: Mental Prayer

Prayer in general seeks direct contact or union with God in mind and will. We have already considered liturgical prayer, in chapter 11, and have stressed the essential part of it, the interior participation, while also saying that exterior participation is objectively very good, even though without the interior it is worthless. The importance and value of liturgical prayer comes from the fact that it is the prayer of Christ, or, the whole Christ, Head and members.[1]

But we must not think that since liturgical prayer has this excellence, we could neglect other prayer, especially mental prayer. As we pointed out in other connections, if someone would eat only the one food element that is the best, he would incur deficiency diseases. So too, to limit oneself to liturgical prayer would result in a great loss.

Further, any kind of prayer without the support of mortification and humility would be almost if not entirely devoid of value. St. Jane de Chantal points out that there is even danger of delusion: "A person to whom God gives [special or high] graces at prayer, should give good heed to accompany them with true mortification and humility . . .: if they do not, the graces will not last, or are nothing but illusions."[2] This sound advice is especially needed today, when some are trying to reach advanced stages of prayer almost solely by means of special techniques, without the needed accompanying spiritual development—often because they follow that false spirituality, already discussed, which denies any value in self-imposed mortification; or else they are taken in by the

---

[1]Vatican II, *On the Liturgy* #7.

[2]St. Jane Frances Fremyot de Chantal, *Exhortations, Conferences, and Instructions*, Newman, Westminster, 1947, p. 261.

false "angel of light" (*cf.* 2 Cor 11:14) who deludes them with a false concept of love of neighbor.

So we intend in this chapter to first review the chief time-tested means of mental prayer, and then to consider also some more recent proposals.

To set the stage for any mental prayer, it is highly desirable to first try to recall the fact that we are, even though we are not always aware of it, in the presence of God our Father. If we could live in the constant realization of that presence, what a difference it would make in our lives! This leads logically to the thought of who we are and who He is—let us recall our earlier considerations on His Infinite Majesty. The great St. Teresa of Avila, even after receiving so many extraordinary favors, still liked to refer to Him as "His Majesty". This attitude is really adoration, and is most basic. If we find our thoughts and hearts occupied well with this adoration, there is really no need to move on to any further stages of mental prayer—for this is in itself enormously valuable spiritually and pleasing to our Father. This same thought naturally leads us to pray for light and help to pray well (if we do not mind using that word "help", which, as we saw in chapter 18, is really too weak an expression: it tends to imply we are the chief doers, with God only as a sort of side-line assistant! This is the opposite of the real situation).

Then, realizing our own weakness and insufficiency, we also ask for the help of our Blessed Mother. We ask her to come with her perfect adoration, to supplement our deficient dispositions.

There are many ways to go forward after this point—for there are great individual differences in our response to grace.

Formal method is a rather new thing in the history of the Church. This does not mean there was no meditation in earlier times. There definitely was, but it was not so formal, and often would come in connection with thoughtful reading of the Scriptures privately.

Some will be attracted to very methodical procedure; others will not. The important thing is to try for union of our minds (including imagination) and wills (including even feelings, with the qualifications we saw in chapter 17) with God. Whatever method helps a given person at given time will be good for that person.

One way is what is called discursive meditation. Most people will find a good spiritual book almost necessary at this point. They will read until they find some thought that impresses them. Then they pause either to soak it in, as it were, or to develop it, almost as if they are reasoning with themselves, somewhat as one might do in giving a sermon to another. Further, it is very good to intersperse—or put at the end of the period—attempts at free conversational prayer with our Father, with Jesus, or with Mary, or even with other Saints. This conversation may be purely mental, or even vocalized. In general, people at an early stage find this less easy than the mental part of the prayer. but there are great individual differences here, as elsewhere. Some too like to compare themselves with an ideal they have seen in their reading, in a sort of self-examination—which readily leads into a prayer of regret for not doing too well, and a petition for help to do better in the future.

When one spot in the reading has been exhausted, some will reread it, and try to use it all over again. Others will go on to find another passage that helps them, and so on, for the full period they have chosen for meditation. At each such point, of course, the various supplementary things we have mentioned above will still apply.

As their book, some will use Holy Scripture, especially the Gospels. Those who have a stronger imagination might like to pass the entire scene through their minds. Some can even picture themselves taking part in the episode, even making remarks to the principal actors in it. It is good too to simply gaze at Our Lord in the scene we have pictured to ourselves—watching out that this gaze does not degenerate into mere vagueness or blankness.

Still others may prefer to use some vocal prayer, especially the Our Father, and to go through it a bit at a time, dwelling on one phrase or line after another. This too is a good method, suitable even for more advanced stages of meditation.

Some find it helpful to have pen and paper at hand. They may first write out some opening line, without much idea of what to write next. For some psychological reason this will often, in some people, lead on to a good development of an idea, in a process which is basically meditative.

At the end of the meditation, it is very desirable to add a prayer for help to do better on the matters we have just considered, and even to form a rather specific resolution to improve in the matters we have considered.

In this first type of meditation, with which most persons will begin their experience of meditation, the work of the mind or imagination takes up most of the time and effort; the use of the will and feelings in collloquy, free conversational prayer, is apt to be much less. But there may come—again, souls are different—a period in which these proportions shift, so that now free conversation takes up much or most of the meditation period. This is often called affective meditation.

After these first two stages, discursive and affective, there may come what is sometimes called the prayer of simplicity (unfortunately not all authors use this term in the same way, so care is needed in reading to see what the author has in mind). It comes only in perspns who are working generously toward making progess in the love of God, especially by detachment, mortification, humility. With these must go much habitual recollection, that is, frequent awareness of the presence of God. The person too should be working for purity of motive—*cf.* our remarks on submarine motives—in all actions. Of course, we do not mean a person must be perfect, but it does mean solid sustained effort at spiritual growth. If these preconditions are not present, what might appear to be the prayer of simplicity is more likely to be an illusion—we think again of the prudent remark of St. Jane de Chantal which we saw earlier in this chapter.

The term prayer of simplicity is a very good description. In affective prayer, the work of the mind and/or imagination is simplified, *i.e.*, just one thought may serve as a basis for the whole meditation period. But now in the prayer of simplicity, the work of the will and feelings and conversational prayer is also simplified. We mean that a person may take just one suitable thought, along with a matching attitude of heart, and use it repeatedly over the entire period, renewing it each time it sinks down into mere vagueness or reverie, which it does naturally.

For example, one might picture Jesus sitting crowned with thorns, with spittle on His face, being mocked by the soldiers. The attitude of heart is simply expressed: It is because of me—it is for me—I am sorry—any one of these serves. Or again, one might think of the words of Psalm 8: "O Lord, our Lord, how marvelous is your name in the whole earth!" Along with this goes an attitude of adoration, or admiration.

As we said, this prayer begins when the person takes up one such thought, with mataching attitude of heart or will. How long will this be sustained? Only a rather short time, perhaps even two minutes. Then it begins to dissolve into vagueness. As soon as the person notices this fact, he deliberately recalls the opening thought and attitude, and can then re-use it for another stretch, until that too begins to dissolve. So there is a sort of wave pattern, up and down, for the whole period of meditation. Yet that one thought and one response serves over and over for the entire period.[3]

When the prayer of simplicity first appears, the thought used may be anything at all in the sphere of religious things. But as time goes on, there will be a tendency—if the person continues to grow spiritually in general—to move towards an almost abstract and general thought of the Divinity. We do not mean that one wants to leave aside the Sacred Humanity of Jesus. Not at all, but the soul is still in the process of de-

---

[3]*Cf.* Poulain, *op.cit.* pp. 8-51.

velopment. A stage comes when the thought of that Humanity cannot be handled simultaneously with the next emerging stage. Later it will return, most fruitfully. We will see more of this in the next chapter.

During this phase bits of infused light are apt to appear—on which we will say more later. Such light may strike abruptly at any time, even outside the time of formal prayer. It often consists in a deep realization—not just a feeling—of the nothingness of creatures as compared to the things of eternity. In this light St. Paul told the Philippians (3:8) that compared to Christ, everything in this world seemed like so much "dung." St. Teresa of Avila said things of this life seem like mere toys.[4]

It is obvious that good spiritual reading outside the time of meditation provides nourishment for meditation.

The importance of meditation is very great. In fact, Pope Pius XI wrote: "We must say without reservation that no other means has the unique efficacy of meditation and that, as a result, nothing can substitute for it."[5]

Is meditation only for religous and priests? Not at all. As Pius XI said, nothing else can replace it. No one who wishes to grow spiritually can afford to neglect it.

What if one does not have time for it? Long periods are good, but not essential. If only one could take time out for even five minutes per day, there would be much fruit. Many people who are busy find that just a slight nap, only enough to just drift off briefly, refreshes them greatly to go ahead with their work. Similarly, even a short meditation can work wonders.

Today there are many proposals of techniques that are unfamiliar to most people, and are at least in that sense new. Some of these claim to be revivals of ancient traditions; others are more clearly new. What are we to think of them? First, it is good, as usual, to make distinctions.

Especially well known is Transcendental Meditation. But it is neither transcendental, nor meditation. Some practitioners attach many Hindu trappings to it, giving each person a *mantra*, which is supposed to be secret, designed for just that person. It is often a Hindu word. But this seems to be just mystification. Dr. Herbert Benson, of Harvard University Medical School, found a group of teachers of TM who were anxious to cooperate. He checked them carefully, and reported first of all, that if one leaves off the Hindu trimmings, it is a purely natural process, which he described, in his book, called *The Relaxation Response*.[6]

---

[4]St. Teresa of Avila, *Life*, 28.

[5]Pius XI, *Menti nostrae*, Sept 23, 1950. #47, NCCW Edition.

[6]Herbert Benson, M.D., *The Relaxation Response*, Avon, 1976

Dr. Benson says it is very valuable for relaxation, producing measurable effects on mental and even, indirectly, physical health.

The method, as he describes it, is very simple. One should sit in a comfortable chair, but not slouching. If need be, one might relax or let go the tension in one limb after another. But that is only preliminary. One begins the "meditation" itself by closing the eyes. Then the meditator begins to say interiorly, without vocalizing, the word *one*. (Dr. Benson picked this word merely to show that no mystic mantra is needed.) It is best to say this word with each exhalation of the breath. All attention is focused on that one word. If distractions come, as of course they do, they are brushed aside gently. It often takes about 10 minutes to get into the state, and it is recommended to stay in it for another 10 minutes. Best effects come with two such periods per day. (One may look at a clock just a few times to check on how long the period is running.)

It is obvious that this is not prayer, but a natural relaxation technique. Can it be of any use for prayer? Perhaps it might help develop concentration as a preliminary to meditation, not as meditation itself, for it essentially focuses just on an empty word.

At this point we naturally think of what is called Centering Prayer, especially as promoted by Basil Pennington.[7] It too calls for two 20 minute periods per day. It opens with taking a minute or two to quiet down—for this, the practice of TM could be useful. Then the person thinks of God dwelling in his depths, using just a single simple word, perhaps the word Jesus. This word is repeated, or refocused as needed. If distraction come, one brushes them gently aside—as in TM—and then returns to the single word. At the end one should come out of the relaxed state, by mentally praying the Our Father or some other prayer.

What should we think of this? Two chief comments are in order. First, if one really does focus on the thought of God dwelling within the soul, there is a spiritual content—unlike TM. But one needs to watch out for mere vagueness, almost blankness, which could come in place of the thought of God, especially since the repetition of one word can tend to have a mild hypnotic effect. Secondly, if all these things are done well, we would have something similar to the Prayer of Simplicity which we just described above. But: the repetitions in this proposed prayer are much closer together than those in the true Prayer of Simplicity, and further, that Prayer of Simplicity is not something that just any per-

---

[7]M. Basil Pennington, *Centering Prayer*, Doubleday, N.Y., 1980, p. 45. H. Benson has also suggested in his newer, *Beyond the Relaxation Response* (esp. pp. 103-11) that one can add "the faith factor" to his previous proposals, by using a religious word or line, such as the Jesus prayer. *Cf.* comments above on the ideas of Pennington.

son can take to at once. No, there is need of a spiritual deepening, by much mortification, humility, some degree of habitual recollection and other things. St. Jane de Chantal's comment which we quoted at the start of this chapter applies well here.

In other words, one cannot use mere technique[8] to substitute for spiritual growth, and get "instant contemplation," as it were. It is apt to be just an illusion—even though the one who practices it may praise it and say it brings deep peace. A feeling of calm, yes, but it is apt to be the calm of a blankness that approaches that of TM. As such it can bring no spiritual growth.

A step farther than what we have just described is proposed by A. De Mello, in his book *Sadhana*.[9] He asserts:

> Many mystics tell us that, in addition to the mind and heart . . . we are, all of us, endowed with a mystical mind and mystical heart, a faculty which makes it possible for us to know God directly and intuit him in his very being, though in a dark manner, apart from all thoughts and concepts and images. . . . What do I gaze into when I gaze silently at God? . . . a blank.

Is there such a faculty? Definitely not—though there is, as we shall see in chapter 22, a lack of image in infused contemplation that has some small resemblance. But there is no blankness in infused contemplation, and it is not something we induce in ourselves, but is given by God when and as He wills. It lasts normally but a few minutes. For certain, it is not the act of a third power of the soul, which can be brought on at will.

Pope John Paul II spoke against such proposals of blankness, in a homily given at Avila, for the Fourth Centenary of the death of the great mystic St. Teresa of Avila. He said that St. Teresa opposed books of her day which presented contemplation as a vague assimilation into divinity or thinking about nothing. The Pope added that her reaction ". . . applies also in our days against some methods of prayer which . . . practically tend to prescind from Christ in favor of an empty mental state." He said that the contemplation taught and lived by St. Teresa was not "a search for subjective and hidden possibilities through technical methods which are without interior purification."[10] This, of course, is

---

[8]*Cf.* Benedict J. Groeschel, *Spiritual Passages*, Crossroad, N.Y. 1983, p. 104, speaks of "the current vogue to learn methods of meditation aimed at producing religious experience apart from the imperatives of moral conversion."

[9]A. DeMello, *Sadhana*, Institute of Jesuit Sources, 1978, pp. 25-29.

[10]Pope John Paul II, Homily at Avila, Nov. 1, 1982, in *The Pope Speaks*

precisely what St. Jane de Chantal observed.

St. Teresa herself comments on proposals to suspend the intellect in prayer:

> In the mystical theology which I began to describe, the understanding ceases working because God suspends it.... [if we] presume not to think and to suspend it ourselves ... we remain boobs and arid, and attain neither the one nor the other.[11]

That is, we neither advance towards the state in which God Himself will suspend the working of the mind in infused contemplation, nor do we have the fruit of basic meditation.

Finally, we include here a word on the Rosary. We need not give any proof of the importance of the Rosary—so many Popes so many times have strongly recommended it. Vatican II did so implicitly when it wrote:

> This most Holy Synod admonishes all the sons of the Church that the cult, especially the liturgical cult, of the Blessed Virgin be generously fostered, and that the practices and exercises of piety, recommended by the Magisterium of the Church toward her in the course of centuries, be considered of great importance.[12]

Pope Paul VI, in *Christi Matri Rosarii*, pointed out specifically that this general recomendation of Vatican II included the Rosary.[13]

Our special reason for speaking of the Rosary here is the fact that it should include meditation on each of the 15 mysteries.

First, we must notice that we are not asked to be fully attentive to the meaning of each word of the 50 Hail Mary's and the 5 Our Father's in the Rosary. No, that would be beyond human ability, even with the help of usual actual graces. Rather, the vocal prayers form a sort of background. Along with those vocal prayers, we are to meditate on the various mysteries.

This is, of course, difficult, as even some of the Saints have admitted. Yet it can be done. There are two chief methods of trying to do it.

---

28 (1983) pp. 114-15.

[11]St. Teresa of Avila, *Life* 12.5. BAC edition I. p. 660.

[12]Vatican II, *On the Church* #67.

[13]Paul VI, *Christi Matri Rosarii*, Sept 15,1966. AAS 58.748.

Pope John XXIII in his autobiography, *Journal of A Soul*, tr. D. White, Mc Graw-Hill, N.Y. 1964, 1965, p. 315, says that since 1953 he increased his Rosary to 15 decades daily, and that he continued that even in the busy work of the Papacy.

One way is to use a set of inserted phrases or lines between the Hail Mary's, so that the narrative of the mystery advances a step with each one. Some can do this on their own; others will find useful one of the several books designed for this purpose.

Others can make a sort of discursive meditation simultaneously with the vocal prayers. This, as we said, is not easy. Yet it is so valuable spiritually that we cannot omit at least trying to do it. As a means of working into this, it is good to take a few moments before each of the decades, to get the meditation started. For some, this will be in one of the forms of discursive meditation described earlier in this chapter. Many will moving from one thought to another, or picture the episode unfolding. Others will find it easier and better to absorb the main thought of each mystery.

For example, in the first joyful mystery, one can dwell on the marvel that God saw fit to take on our nature; in the second, that He was willing to dwell in the womb of Mary for nine months—with awareness too, for even though His physical brain was not yet entirely formed at the early stages, yet His human soul had a spiritual intellect which was joined directly to the vision of God, through which all knowledge was available to Him (as we saw in chapter 8). In the third mystery we try to realize He was willing even to be a helpless baby; in the fourth, we think of His offering Himself to the cross in the presentation in the Temple, and His Mother's joining her *fiat* to His, continuing the acceptance she had made at the annunciation. In the fifth, we admire His restraint in not overwhelming the Doctors in the Temple, and His mysterious way of furthering the spiritual advance of His parents by His puzzling reply when they found Him there. With this kind of start, one can more readily continue during the decade.

Of course, the meditation can develop, as one advances, into the affective form, or that of the prayer of simplicity.

Some[14] have even suggested that the recitation of the Rosary may cease altogether. We distinguish: (1) If infused contemplation comes during the saying of the Rosary, then the Rosary is put aside for that time; all vocal prayer needs to be dropped because of what is called *ligature*, which we will discuss in the next chapter; but, (2) even if such contemplation does come, the Rosary can and should be continued outside the brief periods of infused contemplation.

One's whole spiritual life can be transformed if this meditation in

---

[14]*Cf.* A. B. Calkins, "A Point of Arrival, The Rosary as Contemplative Prayer" in *Civitas Immaculatae*, April, 1987, special edition, p. 11. Unfortunately, some of the ideas of Sadhana, cited in note 9 above, seem to appear in part in this article.

the Rosary is made habitually and well. The Rosary or other meditative prayer is essential for growing union with God.

Chapter 22: Mystical Rose

Beyond the realm of the meditations we have described lies a much longer stretch of spiritual growth, leading even to infused contemplation.

At this point we must admit that there is a large difference in the pictures given by reputable theologians. All agree that there are three stages or ways in the spiritual life: the purgative way, the illuminative way, the unitive way. All would agree that the forms of meditation we have just described belong within the first, the purgative way. But after that, disagreement begins.

The key question is this: is infused contemplation[1] a normal part of spiritual growth, such that if a person advances very far, he must inevitably meet with it? We find some theologians saying it is a necessary part of growth;[2] others deny this, and say that contemplation is something extraordinary,[3] not necessarily part of normal development. Both sides try to claim the support of St. John of the Cross and St. Teresa of

---

[1]Some speak also of acquired contemplation. Unfortunately, not all use terms the same way. Some use it to mean the prayer of simplicity (we favor this way, if the term is used at all). Others use it even for the initial infused contemplation of the first night, which we will describe in this chapter.

[2]*E.g.*, R. Garrigou-Lagrange, in *Christian Perfection and Contemplation*, tr. T. Doyle, Herder, St. Louis, 1946 and in *The Three Ages of the Interior Life*, tr. T. Doyle, Herder, St. Louis, 1949, and Gabriel of St. Mary Magdalen, *St. John of the Cross*, tr. A Benedictine of Stanbrook Abbey, Newman, Westminster, 1951.

[3]*E.g.*, Poulain, *op. cit.* and A. Tanquerey, *The Spiritual Life*. B. Groeschel, *Spiritual Passages* at least seems to hold a position similar to this. He has many helpful things from the standpoint of experimental psychology.

Avila, who are clearly the greatest mystical theologians the Church has produced.

Those who say infused contemplation is a necessary stage say it first appears at the transition from the purgative way into the illuminative way; this first passage they name the dark night of the Senses. Still higher forms of contemplation are found in the illuminative way. But at the end of that way, as a transition again, there is found the dark night of the Spirit, leading into the highest forms of contemplation to be found in this life.

The other school tend to say that the purgative way is the period in which we, and God's grace, are working to cleanse ourselves of our faults; the illuminative way is the period of receiving graces of light; the unitive way is one of rather constant union with God in this life. If infused contemplation appears at all, they say, it is extraordinary, and would be found in the unitive way. These theologians sometimes do speak of the two nights, but they understand them in a much reduced way.

In this chapter we will follow those who hold that infused contemplation is a necessary step in spiritual growth. The reasons for this view will become clearer throughout the chapter.

To make the connection to chapter 21, we recall that at the end of it we saw the prayer of simplicity. We noted too that that prayer tends to develop in such a way that the topic used tends more and more to be restricted to the divinity in an almost abstract way—whereas in the early phases of the prayer of simplicity, almost any religious subject could serve for meditation. We noted too that, temporarily, the soul will find itself unable to meditate much if at all on the Sacred Humanity of Jesus. This is because the soul at that stage is too weak to do that and at the same time advance another step. Later, devotion to His Humanity returns, with great spiritual profit.

Simultaneous with this development in prayer must go growth in humility and mortification. If these do not accompany the development of prayer, that growth in prayer will be mere illusion—we recall again the helpful words of St. Jane de Chantal quoted in chapter 21.

Besides these things there will appear—at quite unpredictable times, even when one is at work—bits of the infused light of the Holy Spirit, sent through the Gifts (we will speak more of these Gifts in chapter 23). One very frequent effect of this light is to give the soul a deep realization, not attainable by usual meditation, of the awful nothingness of all things, even ourselves, compared to God. When such bits of light come, the soul needs to know that if at all possible, it should drop other things, and simply pay attention to and receive the full effects of the light. Other prayer, especially vocal prayer, might disturb this special favor. How long will it last? Only a couple of minutes, ordinarily, although there often are trail-off effects for a still longer time.

Next, if the soul advances further, three signs should appear of approaching infused contemplation.

The first sign is a great aridity, such that the soul finds no pleasure in either the things of this world, or even in spiritual things.[4] This can be very wearisome to the soul, and can leave it open to temptations. It can suffer from relatively slight causes. It is important to distinguish this aridity from the aridity that comes from spiritual sluggishness in general. The difference is that one who is spiritually slothful or very sinful does still find pleasure in things of sense, but not in the things of God.

The second sign is the fact that the soul has an awareness of God that returns persistently in spite of distractions.[5] No one can have a constant awareness of Him in this life—apart from very special graces—but yet in this second sign, the thought of God returns as it were spontaneously as soon as one is free from necessary occupations that demand one's full attention. This consciousness of God is indistinct and obscure, but yet very real. It leads the soul to want closer union with God. The soul may be inclined too to think it is not serving Him well enough—which will be very true, for the soul even at this point is still only in the purgative way, and has a long road to travel before reaching the peak of spiritual devepment possible in this life.

Again, we can see the difference between this condition and the ordinary aridity coming from laxity or sin. The ordinary aridity does not lead to the increased desire to serve God, or to the persistent return of the thought of Him.

Finally the third sign is inability to carry out the older form of discursive meditation, in which the mind or imagination moved from one point to another.[6] In strongly developed cases, it will seem as though the mind and imagination will not move. A person might even be unable to comprehend a book. Yet, outside of prayer, one can carry on

---

[4]The aridity and other features are more intense in some souls than in others. In general, the higher God wills to lead a soul, the greater the trial.

[5]In *Ascent* 2, 13 St. John of the Cross gives the three signs in a different form from that which we are following (we follow his *Dark Night* 1.9-10). The chief difference is on the second sign, which in the *Ascent* is replaced by the fact that the soul takes pleasure in being alone and waiting on God without any specific meditation. Probably both versions are for the same thing: the picture given in *Night* is still inchoate, in *Ascent* it is fully formed.

[6]As we see from St. John of Cross, *Ascent* 2.15, the soul is still able to return at times to discursive meditation when there is no active special influence of the Gifts of the Holy Spirit at the moment.

ordinary duties well enough.[7] However, in many cases, especially less well developed cases, the soul will find it possible at times—still within the area of the three signs—to return to the older forms of discursive meditation.[8]

This great aridity betrays the fact that God Himself is at work in the soul. Humans by their own efforts, aided by the usual actual graces, can go only so far in the work of purification of the soul. Then, for further development, God must take over, in such a way that the soul is more passive. (We will see more of this activity/passivity question in chapter 23.)

When the stage is thus set by the three signs, infused contemplation itself may appear. It can come about in either of two patterns. In one pattern, the prayer of simplicity may as it were melt into infused contemplation, blending with it. For the prayer of simplicity, in its more developed forms, involves a loving gaze at God. However, that gaze in the prayer of simplicity is produced actively by the soul, with the aid of ordinary actual graces; the gaze of infused contemplation is passive, produced by the operation of the Gifts of the Holy Spirit.

In the other pattern, there is a more sharply defined pattern of the onset of infused contemplation. The soul suddenly finds welling up in it from the depths of the spirit a perception of contact with God which is much different from the consolations we saw in chapter 17, which are basically from the sensory realm. There is no image of Him, nor is there any sound from Him. It is all obscure, and in the darkness of faith, yet it comes in such a way that we could almost say the soul feels the presence of God. We hesitate to use the word feels, for this is not at all in the region of sense, though there may be an overflow into the sensory area, if the contemplation comes in what is called a sweet, as contrasted with an arid, form.[9]

This experience can come during a time of prayer; it can equally well appear during other times, even when the person is somewhat busy—though not totally absorbed—with routine things. We note here that the tendency for the thought of God to recur persistently sets the stage for this happening.

When it does come, the person, even without instruction, will seem to know almost instinctively that it is important to drop all else and simply pay attention. Even vocal prayer, even interiorly worded

---

[7]G. Belorgey, *The Practice of Mental Prayer*, tr. E. Boylan, Newman, Westminster, 1952 gives a helpful description on pp. 110-11.

[8]All three signs should be present at once before the director can be confident a soul is in the transition to the illuminative way.

[9]*Cf.* St. John of the Cross, *Ascent* 2.13.7 and *Dark Night* 1.9.6.

prayer, would be an obstacle. This phenomenon is called *ligature*, meaning a sort of binding.[10]

We said the soul should hold itself attentive, for it is quite possible for it to interrupt the contemplation by doing other things, or even by distractions, which are possible even at this point.[11] (Even though the soul may enjoy the contemplation, especialy if it is in sweet form, yet the body may find no comfort in it unless there is a strong overflow, as it were, into the sensory region.)

How long does this contemplation last? A rather short time ordinarily, much like the case of the bits of infused light we spoke of earlier. When will it return again? It will come when God wills—for we can do nothing to bring it on. In fact, we should not even attempt to do so—out of fear of illusion, or going counter to the will of God. For while we should desire to grow ever more in pleasing Him, we should not desire a particular means at a particular time—as we saw in chapter 20. That we must leave up to Him.

St. John of the Cross, in a context in which he speaks of infused contemplation, even says:

> When the soul empties itself of all things in this way and comes to be empty and detached from things—which is, as we said, that which the soul can do [actively], it is impossible . . . that God would fail to do His part, communicating Himself to the soul at least in secret and in silence. . . . Just as the sun gets up early to enter your house if you open the window, so God . . . will enter into the soul that is emptied and fill it with divine goods.[12]

These words imply of course, that infused contemplation is a normal part of spiritual growth, for if the soul does its part, God will not fail to grant it.

Do only those in monasteries or convents experience this contemplation? Not at all. Some persons in the world meet with it, those who are devoted to God and who use, so far as is compatible with their state in life, the means we have been explaining. Obviously, there will be differences in the form these things take between souls in contemplative houses, and those engaged in the world.[13]

After this passage is completed in the way in which God wills, the soul enters into the illuminative way, in which a higher form of contem-

---

[10]On ligature see Poulain pp. 178-99 and Belorgey pp. 125-26.

[11]*Cf.* St. John of the Cross, *Ascent* 2.13.3.

[12]St. John of the Cross, *Living Flame* 3.46. BAC ed. p.1239.

[13]There are cases of persons engaged in busy active life who have had some experiences of infused contemplation.

plation appears, which is called the prayer of quiet, in which the perception of contact with God is comparable to that of a hand placed on a table.

At first this kind of prayer appears only occasionaly, and for a few moments at a time, perhaps for the time needed to say one Hail Mary. In some persons this grace comes abruptly, when not expected. They are suddenly seized with an unusual recollection, so that the divine seems to penetrate them. Then suddenly it vanishes. The intensity of this prayer also varies from time to time.

After the first appearances of this grace it may not be had again for a long time, even for some years. The interruption may come from lack of fidelity in the soul, or simply because God so wills. In others there are not these interruptions.

Even when this stage is reached, the soul is still far from the peak of growth that is possible in this world. Hence a further, more terrible purification, largely passive, is needed, which is called the dark night of the Spirit. In it commonly great trials and temptations come—against any virtue, even faith or hope or purity. Not a few comentators think temptation against purity was the "thorn of the flesh" of which St. Paul speaks in 2 Cor 12:7.

This night may run for years. It is needed because the first night, that of the senses, worked chiefly on the faults that are rooted in the sensory area, still leaving in place many faults whose roots lie deep in the spirit. The object is to bring the soul to such a point that it can be moved only by the Holy Spirit, though the Gifts (more on this in chapter 23).[14]

When the soul finally emerges from this severe night, it moves on into the highest forms of contemplation possible in this world, leading to the transforming union, in which not only the will, but all faculties of the soul are in effect taken over by the divine action.

As we indicated in passing, there are some souls in which the contemplation comes in an enjoyable or sweet form; in others, it is arid, that is, lacking in pleasure, though this does not exclude a sort of satisfaction at least on the fine point of the soul (*cf.* chapter 17 on this latter). St. Thérèse of Lisieux sems to have been that type of soul, and she liked to think the Blessed Virgin was such also.

Another kind of contemplation is often referred to as "Marian contemplation." We can use the term either to mean that which the Mother of God had, or the contemplation in which other souls may perceive her.

St. Luke tells us more than once that Mary pondered these things

---

[14]*Cf.* St. John of the Cross, *Ascent* 3.2.10.

in her heart. *Ineffabilis Deus*, in which Pope Pius IX, defined the Immaculate Conception makes the matter clearer. Speaking of her holiness at the very beginning, at the moment of her conception, the Pope tells us that the Father

> attended her with such great love, more than for all other creatures, that in her alone He took singular pleasure. Therefore He so wonderfully filled her, more than all angelic spirits and all the Saints, with an abundance of all heavenly gifts taken from the treasury of the divinity, that she, always free from absolutely every stain of sin, and completely beautiful and perfect, presented such a fulness of innocence and holiness that none greater under God can be thought of, and no one, except God, can comprehend it.

That is: Even if we say that God could make a creature capable of understanding her holiness, yet, as a matter of fact, He has not done that. Not even the highest of the archangels or the seraphim can comprehend it—only He Himself can. It is evident then, that she began where other souls leave off at the end of a life of surpassing virtue. What her contemplation must have been is, then, beyond our ability to grasp. And yet this did not keep her from doing her duties in the home at Nazareth in such a way that those who saw her would not suspect, even though she was clearly a specially good person.

There is also a contemplation, reported by a few souls, in which the Blessed Mother seems to be part of the object of infused contemplation. Theologically, this is clearly quite possible. If a soul in infused contemplation is given as it were direct contact[15] with God, then, since Mary is more closely united with Him than any other being, more closely than the highest angels and the Seraphim, it follows that if God so wills, the soul could be given a perception of her along with that of God. This clearly happened in the case of Venerable Marie of St. Thérèse, a 17th century mystic in the Netherlands. She writes that she was given "a contemplation, an enjoyment of Mary inasmuch as she is one with God and united to Him. In tasting God, I taste also Mary, as if she were but one with God."[16] Father Emil Neubert, in his outstanding work, *Life of Union with Mary*, says that since the definition of the Im-

---

[15]*Cf.* W. Most, "Maria Conservabat Omnia Verba Haec" in *Miles Immaculatae* 21, 1985, p.164.

[16]Marie de Sainte-Thérèse, "L'Union Mystique à Marie," *Cahiers de la Vierge* 15, Cerf, Juvisy, 1936, p. 50, translated as: "Union with Our Lady," *Marian Writings of Ven. Marie Petyt*, tr. T. McGinnis, Scapular Press, NY, 1954, p. 33. *Cf.* Also Michael A. S. Augustino, *Introductio ad Vitam Internam*, Collegio S. Alberti, Rome, 1926.

maculate Conception, there have been more souls than before favored with special union with Mary.[17] His book is a splendid guide for those who wish to develop, on any level, a Marian spirituality.

Venerable Marie even says she at times experienced a contact with St. Joseph in a similar way.[18] This is clearly theologically possible, since now in the glory of Heaven, St. Joseph is most closely united with God. In fact, there is no reason why God could not, when and if He so willed, grant a contact with even lesser souls that have reached the divine vision.

When and whether a soul attains this special favor of Marian contemplation, is, of course, entirely the decision of our Father. It is obviously not a necessary part of the spiritual ascent the way basic infused contemplation is. In regard to Marian contemplation, as in all things, we should be entirely pliable and conformed to His will.

---

[17]Emil Neubert, *Life of Union With Mary*, tr. S. Juergens, Bruce, Milwaukee, 1959, pp. 243-46.

[18]*Cf.* Marie de Sainte-Therese, *op. cit.* in note 16 above, p. 78, or McGinnis translation, p. 50.

Chapter 23: Spouse of the Holy Spirit

Infused contemplation, of which we spoke in chapter 22, comes through the Gifts of the Holy Spirit, chiefly wisdom and understanding. But there are other functions of these Gifts, especially in letting us be guided by the the Holy Spirit Himself.

To make the matter clear, we notice that there are three guides, or levels of guides, that we may follow in making our decisions.

The first and lowest level is that in which the soul is led by the whim of the moment, by that which gives pleasure. The great pagan philosopher Aristotle said that to make pleasure our guide is to have a life "fit for cattle."[1] A dog's life is a helpful comparison. Dogs are completely predictable. If a dog has something to eat, and happens to feel like eating, he will surely eat. If a dog has a chance to sleep, and happens to feel like sleeping, he will surely sleep. And so on for sex, and everything else. A dog always does whatever he happens to feel like at the moment; he follows the whim of the moment, in pursuit of pleasure.

Not a few humans have greatly misunderstood this: they have thought that to do what they want, when they want, as they want it, is the glorious "freedom of the sons of God" of which St. Paul speaks. Far from the truth!. They are living, literally, a dog's life, or a life fit for cattle.

Clearly, we ought to go higher than a dog's life. On the second level the guide a person follows is reason. This is a life more fit for humans. Of course, thanks to the goodness and generosity of our Father, when a person tries to follow reason sincerely, he or she will in practice also have the help of actual graces, the kind of which we spoke in ex-

[1] Aristotle, *Nicomachean Ethics* 1.5.

plaining St. Paul's words in Philippians 2:13 (chapter 18).

But there is a much higher level: that of the Gifts of the Holy Spirit.[2] On this level, one has the higest kind of guide. Let us compare the second and third levels, to make the difference clear. On the second level, one follows reason, with, as we said, the help of actual graces. On this level one commonly has to think things out step by step. For example, suppose I come to see that since I have sinned, I ought to do penance, in reparation for the pain I have caused our Lord, and to help rebalance the damage my sins have done to the objective order, which the Holiness of our Father loves, and to help correct the pulls of creatures (*cf.* chapter 19) which make it less easy for my thoughts and heart to rise above creatures to the level of our Father Himself. After coming to realize that I need mortification or penance, I would next ask myself: How much do I need, considering my sins? What sort of mortification is prudent considering my whole life situation? I would go through several steps to finally reach the conclusion of what I should do. As we said, this is a process carried on basically by human reason, with the help of actual graces, which the generosity of our Father always offers, which we actually have if we do not reject them. After I have reached my conclusion, if someone should ask me: Why did you decide on this? I could give a rational explanation, precisely since I arrived at the conclusion by a step-by-step process of reasoning.

But when guidance comes to us through the gifts, there is no such step by step process. Rather, the answer is, as it were, dropped ready-made into the hopper of our brain. It is the Holy Spirit Himself who provides it. He does this, we might say, on the special wavelength of His gifts. They make it possible for me to receive such guidance. As a result, if someone should ask me why I propose to do what I have come to see in this way, I would probably reply: "I don't know how to explain. I just know it is good." This happens since I did not reach the conclusion by a step-by-step process.

Clearly, we can see both a great advantage and a danger here. The danger is that a person might just deceive himself, and mistake feelings for the guidance of the Holy Spirit. (Some writings on this subject speak of instincts or impulses from the Holy Spirit. There is a sense in which this is true, but we must not take it to mean one waits for a feeling to jab him, and then decides it is the Holy Spirit.)

How avoid the danger? Experience shows that when guidance comes through the gifts, it sometimes gives an interior certitude, sometimes does not. Usually it does not give a certitude, but leaves some

---

[2]We might compare the Gifts to receptors, fitted on top of the infused virtues, making them receptive to the special wavelength of the Holy Spirit.

doubt. This is because the Holy Spirit wants us to ask the advice of a superior or prudent spiritual director. St. Teresa of Avila received a commission from the Holy Spirit—by way of a special revelaton—to found a stricter branch of the Carmelites. Yet she did not dare to begin without consulting more than one spiritual director.[3] In general, the more important or far-reaching the proposal that one seems to receive is, the more need of consultation. Further, one should not readily suppose he or she has received such an inspiration unless he or she is already far advanced in the spiritual life. These gifts do not make their influence felt much, if at all, in the earlier stages, though there may be a latent effect, as we will explain shortly.

It is only when something must be decided, and yet there is no chance to check with a superior or director, that the Holy Spirit gives real certitude. Even when He seems to do so, we must be careful, for the seeming certitude could come from self-deception. If one is humble, cultivates mortification and meditation, and asks the help of our Blessed Mother, there is great protection against such deception.

We mentioned that there is a latent operation of the gifts at times. In the full instances of the operation of the gifts, the soul is largely passive—its faculties do little more than assent to be moved by the Holy Spirit. In contrast, under ordinary actual graces, of which we spoke in chapter 18, the soul is more active: the movement of grace causes the person's faculties to turn out the results actively. In the latent mode there is an intermediate picture, more passive, yet not as fully passive as when the gifts work in the fullest way. For example, a soul that is in the gradual transition from the prayer of simplicity to the first experience of infused contemptation may have the light from the gifts intermingling with human activity aided by actual graces. The contribution of the gifts will probably not be noticed, at least not clearly. Or suppose one is deliberating using the infused virtue of prudence. An inspiration from the gifts might add a sudden light, or might put before him a thought from the Gospels. This sort of aid could blend in so well with the work of deliberation by reason as to pass unnoticed.

In any case, we said there is a great advantage in having this highest kind of guidance, since it comes from the Holy Spirit Himself. St. Thomas Aquinas holds that the help of the gifts is indispensable for eternal salvation, since the goal of salvation is the direct vision of

---

[3]*Cf.* St. Teresa of Avila, *Cuentas de Conciencia* (Spiritual Relations) 4.10: "She never acted on what she has learned through prayer; if her confesssors said the contrary, she always then acted [on what they said] and told them everything." She had a healthy fear of self-deception and deception by the evil one. *Ibid.* 4.6. BAC edition II, pp. 520 and 518.

God—a thing entirely beyond the natural capabilities of any conceivable creature. Hence the need of a "superhuman" mode of acting, provided by the gifts.[4] The Holy Spirit will lead a soul to decide on things that are not contrary to reason, but are higher than the point to which reason would reach. Jesus Himself, even though divine, even though His human soul had the direct vision of God, yet was habitually led by the Holy Spirit, as we find many times in the Gospels, e.g., the Spirit led Him into the desert for His 40 day fast before he began His public mission: Lk 4:1. Again, on another occasion, Lk 10:21 tells us that He "rejoiced in the Holy Spirit."

Since our Father loves to observe good order in all things, He willed that the human faculties of Jesus be guided and moved through these Gifts, even though His divinity could have done all directly.

A specially clear instance of the fact that this guidance of the Holy Spirit can lead one not to points contrary to reason, but to things above reason, is to be seen in the conduct of our Blessed Mother right after the Archangel had asked and obtained her consent, her *fiat*, to be the Mother of the Redeemer. If she were acting in a merely natural way, following just reason—which St. Paul would call the mode of the "natural man" in contrast to the "spiritual man" (1 Cor 2:14-15)—she probably would have thought the following way: "My people have been waiting for centuries for this day; they have desired the coming of the Messiah. Now I know from the words of the Angel that He is already conceived within me.[5] I should not just keep this joy to myself; I should tell our people; especially I ought to tell the authorities in Jerusalem. And what of Joseph my husband—it is only a question of time until he will have to see that I am with child. What would he suspect! I really ought to tell him right away."

But yet we know from the Scriptures what she really did: none of these things at all. The Holy Spirit led her higher, on the lofty path of humility. She told no one, not even Joseph who, quite reasonably, was worried. God had to send an angel to Joseph to keep him from divorcing her quietly.

St. John of the Cross speaks eloquently on her fidelity to the Holy Spirit:

> God alone moves the powers of these souls . . . to those deeds which are suitable, according to the will and ordinance of God, and they cannot be moved to others. . . . Such were the actions of the most glorious Virgin, our Lady, who, being elevated from the beginning [of her life] to this

[4]St. Thomas Aquinas, *Summa* I-II 68.1.

[5]On her knowledge, *cf.* W. Most, *art. cit.* on chapter 22, note 15.

lofty state, never had the form of any creature impressed on her, nor was moved by such, but was always moved by the Holy Spirit.[6]

Creatures do make their imprint on ordinary souls, and the attractions of creatures often lure them to act on the level of animals, or at least to fall short of the highest level. But as for our Blessed Mother, we recall the words of Pope Pius IX in his document defining the Immaculate Conception, in which he taught:

He [our Father] attended her with such great love, more than all other creatures, that in her alone He took singular pleasure. Wherefore He so wonderfully filled her, more than all angelic spirits and all the Saints, with an abundance of all heavenly gifts taken from the treasury of the divinity, that she, always free from absolutely every stain of sin and completely beautiful and perfect, presented such a fulness of innocence and holiness that none greater under God can be thought of, and no one, except God, can comprehend it.[7]

If such was her holiness even at the start, what must it have been after a long, most difficult life of absolute fidelity to the Holy Spirit![8] So it is quite fitting that many theologians today speak of her as the Spouse of the Holy Spirit. St. Maximilian Kolbe, a few hours before his final arrest on February 17, 1941, leading to his martyrdom, wrote down on paper these theologically splendid and beautiful comments:

Who is the Holy Spirit? The flowering of the love of the Father and the Son. If the fruit of created love is a created conception, then the fruit of divine Love . . . is necessarily a divine "conception."[9] The Holy Spirit is, therefore, the "uncreated eternal conception" . . . this thrice holy "conception", this infinitely holy Immaculate Conception. This eternal "Immaculate Conception" (which is the Holy Spirit) produces in an immaculate manner divine life itself in the womb (or depths) of Mary's soul, making her the Immaculate Conception [for thus she named herself at Lourdes], the human Immacaculate Conception. If among human beings the wife takes the name of her husband because she belongs to him, is one with him . . . and is, with him, the source of new life, with how much greater reason should the name of the Holy Spirit, who is the divine Immaculate Conception, be used as the name of her in whom He lives as uncreated Love, the principle of life in the whole supernatural

[6]St. John of the Cross, *Ascent* 3.2.10; *cf. Living Flame* 1.4; 1.9 and 2.34

[7]Pius IX, *Ineffabilis Deus*.

[8]Even though she was full of grace at the start, yet her capacity could grow.

[9]The Holy Spirit is the love of the Father and of the Son for each other.

order of grace?[10]

No wonder then that Pope Pius XII could write of her in the cenacle before the first Pentecost: "She it was who, by her most mighty prayers, obtained that the Spirit of the Divine Redeemer, already given on the Cross, should be bestowed on the newborn Church on the day of Pentecost, in the company of miraculous gifts."[11]

It is obvious too how her prayers can gain the riches of the workings of these same gifts for those devoted to her. As St. Louis de Montfort said: "When the Holy Spirit, her Spouse, has found Mary in a soul, He flies there, He enters there in His fulness, He communicates Himself to that soul abundantly, and to the full extent to which it makes room for His Spouse."[12]

We all receive these gifts at baptism, or even earlier; if baptized in adult life, we receive when we first gain the state of grace. Why then, we must ask, is there not more effect from them in our lives? It is basically a lack of receptivity, of needed dispositons. Only when a soul is rather advanced will the effects of the gifts show clearly (as contrasted with the latent action described above). It follows that whatever promotes spiritual development favors also the activity of the gifts. The chief things of course are humility, mortification, meditation—all of which make room for love. To these we add deep devotion to the Mother of God.

A particularly important obstacle is what is sometimes called affection to venial sin, which we spoke of in chapter 15. As we have seen, this is a kind of gap in the person's resolve to please God, the attitude that given a certain degree of difficulty, one fully intends to offend Him by venial sin. Of course, little or no progress can be made in this context. Lesser but similar is the obstacle from attachments to any creatures. We recall the dramatic comparison given by St. John of the Cross of the bird on a string[13] and our comparison of the mental meter (chapter 19).

St. Thérèse of Lisieux made it a practice to obey any Sister in the convent, even those without authority. The reason seems to have been mortification, and this was also a means to avoid acting on the low, first level which we spoke of earlier in this chapter, the level on which one

[10]Cited from H. M. Manteau-Bonamy, *Immaculate Conception and the Holy Spirit*, Prow Books, Libertyville, 1977, pp. 3-5.

[11]Pius XII, *Mystici Corporis*, June 29, 1914 3. AAS 35.248. We note again the Father's love of objective order: Mary's prayers provided a special added title for the sending of the Holy Spirit.

[12]St. Louis de Montfort, *True Devotion* # 36.

[13]St. John of the Cross, *Ascent* 1.11.4. (cited in chapter 15 at note 8).

follows the whim of the moment. In obeying another she would at least stay clear of that low way of deciding. Those who do not live in circumstances like hers cannot of course use such a means. But one can follow the spirit of the Beatitudes and related ideals presented in Matthew 5, which urge us not to press our own will.

Further, it is a great help to have what we might call a set of private policies (it used to be called a private rule). For this one works out, with the help of a good spiritual adviser, a set of policies: what devotions, specifically, one will follow each day, and perhaps even the times for each, so far as the life situation of each one permits; it will also include definite general principles on what kind of mortification and how much a person will cultivate. Such a policy on mortification is much needed, precisely because it is especially hard to be objective about mortification; people tend to do nothing, or to do too much. Obviously, the advice of a good director is priceless here. Once such a set of policies has been prudently determined, it should be held to without wavering until the time comes when it seems a general change is in order—again, to be worked out with a good director. What of exceptions to such policies? Of course, exceptions are possible, but if we recall the astute comment made by St. Teresa of Avila[14] that our body tends to find it needs more and more, we will be inclined to be very tight, to reject reasons for exceptions unless they are very strong and very clear. Otherwise, the exception tends to become the rule.

One final note, on a phenomenon called *natural inspiration*, is in order. The very first thing the action of the gifts does is to cause the soul to see something as good which mere reason would not be likely to show. Then, as needed, the gifts provide the strength to carry out this good—which is most conspicuous in the case of martyrs, who hold up with cheer, even seeming joy, under the most atrocious physical tortures.

As we said, the gifts can lead one to strictly superhuman heights. Now in natural matters there is also a kind of action of God, not through these gifts, but in the natural order, which can and does lead some to see things in a superhuman way. This is what we mean: His action can cause a musician to see a vision of musical beauty, and to write it down for performance by an orchestra, or a single artist, or a group. It is in this way that great masterpieces seem to be created. Let us take an example. Suppose we would take a young child and give that child the maximum possible musical training from the earliest years on up. Could we in that way produce another Beethoven, or Mozart or other great composer? Hardly. Yes, there is work involved, often hard work, on the

[14]Cited in chapter 20 at note 8.

part of great composers. Yet the vision of beauty they see and capture for us is at least at times above and beyond what ordinary human powers could reach—it is, strictly, superhuman.[15] Really, it is a touching act of special goodness on the part of our Father to provide such inspirations, to give us an elevated perception beyond ordinary human reach.[16] We ought to thank Him when we hear great music—or see other great art forms.

There can be parallel superhuman virtue in the natural order shown also in courage, as Aristotle points out:

> As the opposite of beastlike behavior, it is very suitable to speak of virtue that is above us [above ordinary humans], just as Homer repesents Priam saying of Hector that he seems to be exceedingly brave, "He did not seem to be the son of a human, but of a god."[17]

---

[15]*Cf.* St. Thomas, *Summa* I-II 68.1.c.

[16]*Cf.* Pius XII, Encyclical on Music. In *The Pope Speaks* 3. 1956, esp. p. 13.

[17]Aristotle, *Nicomachean Ethics* 7.1.1, citing Homer, *Iliad* 24.258-59.

Chapter 24: Consecration to Jesus and Mary

All practices of spiritual growth can be summed up and brought to perfection in the living of a complete consecration to the Hearts of Jesus and Mary.

Pope Leo XIII in 1899 consecrated the world to the Sacred Heart of Jesus. He explained the basis for that consecration:

> For we, in dedicating ourselves, not only recognize and accept His rule explicitly and freely, but we actually testify that if that which we give were ours, we would most willingly give it; and we ask Him to graciously accept from us that very thing, even though it is already His.[1]

We can see at once that this is a consecration in the full sense of the word—for often, not illegitimately, the word consecration means merely "entrusting." The Pope said, in effect, that we already owe most complete service to the Heart of Jesus. We owe that on two grounds: He, as God, has made us out of nothing, has created us; and, as Redeemer He has bought us back from the captivity of the evil one, by paying the price of redemption (*cf.* chapter 9). Hence Leo XIII said that what we give is not really ours to give, for we already owe it to Him. Yet we can and do ask Him to graciously accept it all on a new title, that of love, as if we were to say: "We already owe you everything; but

[1]Leo XIII, *Annum sacrum*, May 25, 1899, ASS 31.649. The beginnings of consecration appear in the Old Covenant, which made the people *qadosh*, set aside for God. However, it brought out only the negative side explicitly: avoiding sin. It did not explicitly demand positive fulfillment of everything in His will. Baptism tended to imply more. *Cf.* the remarks on Baptism at the end of this chapter.

even if we did not, we would want, out of love, to give you our full service anyway." Inasmuch as His claims on us are total, we can see how it is true to say that consecration sums up everything.

In speaking of "service" however, we need to keep constantly in mind that, as we said in chapter 1, our "service" does Him no good. It is mere kindness on His part—for our service makes us open to receive what He so generously wishes to give—and love of objective goodness, that leads Him to want and value it.

Some may wonder why we specified that this devotion is to the Heart of Jesus. Pius XII, in his great Encyclical *Haurietis aquas* told us that devotion to the Sacred Heart of Jesus is not just an optional matter, like devotion to St. Anthony and other favorite Saints.[2] This is quite obvious, for devotion to the Sacred Heart is really devotion to the love of God for us, without which we would not exist at all, without which we could not reach eternal happiness. There is nothing more central than this. Of course, certain external features often found in that devotion need not be considered as essential, such as the Nine First Fridays, even though the Church highly commends them. It is the honor to the love of God expressed in and found in the Heart of His Son that is indispensable.

There is a parallel consecration to the Immaculate Heart of Mary, for she too, in union with Him, has a parallel claim to our service. She is not the Creator, but she is the Mother of God who created us; she is not by herself the Redeemer, but she shared most intimately with Him in redeeming us, as we saw in chapter 10.

Pope Pius XII brought this fact out beautifully in a broadcast over the Vatican Radio to pilgrims assembled at Fatima on May 13, 1946: "He, the Son of God, reflects on His heavenly Mother the glory, the majesty and the dominion of His kingship"—which sums up His claims to our service.

> For, having been associated with the King of Martyrs in the unspeakable work of human redemption as Mother and cooperatrix, she remains forever associated to Him with a practically unlimited power, in the distribution of the graces which flow from the redemption. Jesus is King throughout all eternity by nature and by right of conquest; through Him, with Him, and subordinate to Him Mary is Queen by grace, by Divine Relationship, by right of conquest, and by singular choice; and her kingdom is as vast as that of her Son and God, since nothing is excluded fom her dominion.[3]

---

[2]Pius XII, *Haurietis aquas*. AAS 48.337.

[3]Pius XII, *Bendito seia*, May 13, 1946. AAS 38.266.

We notice the Pope said that her kingdom is just as vast as that of her Son. We should not think of two powers, one infinite, the other subordinate. Rather, she and Her Divine Son form a sort of unit, with one power, for her will is always most perfectly in union with His. Hence in *Haurietis aquas* the Pope added: "So that more abundant benefits may flow upon the Christian family, and in fact, on the whole human race, from this worship of the most Sacred Heart of Jeus, let the faithful take care that devotion to the Immaculate Heart of the Mother of God also be closely joined to it."[4] God has joined her to His Divine Son at every point in the mysteries of His life and death; what God has joined, let no one put asunder.

Vatican II in its long Marian Chapter (VIII) of the Constitution on the Church, highlighted this fact wonderfully, as we can see from the following synthesis of texts from that chapter. (All words in quotes are from the Council. We have added explanatory comments at suitable points.) "The Blessed Virgin, planned for from eternity as the Mother of God along with the incarnation of the divine Word, was the loving Mother of the Redeemer on this earth, His generous associate, more than others, and the humble servant of the Lord." That is, her union with Him was from all eternity: since the Father always planned for the incarnation of His Son, necessarily He also planned for the Mother through whom it could take place.

"She is already prophetically foreshadowed in the promise given our first parents of a victory over the serpent." The Council refers to the prophecy of the Protogospel, Genesis 3:15.[5] We see that the Father not only planned for her from eternity, but began to speak of her at once after the fall of our first parents. "Similarly, she is the Virgin who is to conceive and bear a Son...." This is of course, the prophecy of Isaiah 7:14.[6]

"The Father of Mercies willed that the acceptance of the planned-for Mother should precede the Incarnation." This is the same thought as that of Pope Leo XIII, who said she was asked to consent "In the name of the whole human race'."[7] "... in this way, just as a woman contributed to death, so also a woman should contribute to life." Here the Council builds on the New Eve theme, found in practically every major Father of the Church, according to which just as the first Eve shared in involving our race in the ruin of original sin, so

[4]Pius XII, *Haurietis aquas* AAS 48.352.

[5]*Cf.* John Paul II, *Redemptoris Mater*, March 25, 1987, #24.

[6]*Cf.* W. Most, *art. cit.*, "Maria Conservabat..." pp. 143-46.

[7]Leo XIII, *Fidentem piumque*, Sept 20, 1896, ASS 29, 206. Citing St. Thomas, *Summa* III.30.1.

Mary, the New Eve, shared in reversing that damage. . . ."[8] "This union of the Mother with the Son in the work of salvation is evident from the time of the virginal conception of Christ even to His death." The Council, we notice, says her union with Him became "evident" at the annunciation. Before that it was not evident, though it was there eternally, as the Council itself had taught.

"In the first place, it is evident when Mary, arising in haste to visit Elizabeth, is greeted by her as blessed because of her faith . . . [and] when the Mother of God joyfully showed her firstborn, who did not lessen but consecrated her virginal integrity, to the shepherds and the Magi." In passing, we notice the Council speaks in a matter of fact way about the shepherds and the Magi. And her virginity is not merely a spiritual symbol, but is physical, for the Council speaks of her "integrity" which can refer only to physical condition.[9] "[It is evident also] when she presented Him to the Lord in the temple." There He, for His human mind had the vision of divinity and so was fully aware, made the offertory of the Mass of the Cenacle and Calvary, as we saw in chapter 8. She for her part continued and repeated her fiat of the day of the annunciation. "And [that union was evident] when she heard Simeon foretelling that her Son would be a sign of contradiction, and that the sword would pierce her Mother's heart, so that the thoughts of many hearts would be revealed." She, of course, had known, painfully known, long before this. The words of Simeon would increase the pain of the ever-present wound.[10]

"In the public life of Jesus, His Mother appears remarkably . . . at the very beginning when, at the wedding in Cana . . . moved by pity, she obtained by her intercession the beginning of the miracles of Jesus. . . . During the course of His preaching, she received His words in which He, her Son, praising the kingdom more than ties of flesh and blood, proclaimed blessed those who heard the Word of God and kept it, as she herself was faithfully doing." Her Son dramatically explained that of two forms of greatness—being the bodily Mother of God, and hearing

---

[8]The New Eve theme is found in chiefly the following Fathers of the Church: St. Justin Martyr, St. Irenaeus, Tertullian, St. Cyril of Jerusalem, St. Jerome, St. Ambrose, St. Augustine, St. Theophilus of Antioch, Origen, St. Gregory Thaumaturgus, St. Gregory of Nyssa, St. Amphilocus, St. Ephrem, St. Epiphanius, St. Maximus, St. John Chrysostom, St. Peter Chrysologus, St. Proclus, St. Eleutherius Tornacensis, Epistle to Diognetus. *Cf.* T. Livius, *The Blesssed Virgin in the Fathers of the First Six Centuries*, London, 1893, pp. 47-59 and. G.M. Roschini, *Mariologia*, 2d ed. Rome, 1947, II.300-01, 304-09.

[9]*Cf.* G. Owens, "Our Lady's Virginity in the Birth of Jesus," in *Marian Studies* 7, 1956, pp. 43-68.

[10]*Cf.* W. Most, *art. cit.* "Maria Conservabat . . ."

and keeping His word—the second was the greater. Yet, as the Council said, she was greatest in both categories.

"In faith she bore with her union with[11] her Son even to the Cross." Yes, her union, the continuation of her fiat was difficult, so it is right to say she endured or bore with it. "There she stood in accord with the divine plan." She was not just an ordinary person, like St. John. She was there really officially, appointed to cooperate in the redemption as the New Eve. "She joined herself to His sacrifice with a Motherly heart, consenting to the immolation of the Victim that had been born of her." It was the will of the Father that He die, die in such a way; it was the will of her Son also. So she had to positively and actively join in that will, willing His death! This was to save us and for the rectification of the objective order. "In suffering with her Son as He died on the Cross, she cooperated in the work of the Savior, in an altogether singular way, by obedience, faith, hope and burning love, to restore supernatural life to souls." We recall all the rich content that we saw on this cooperation of hers in chapter 10. "As a result, she is our Mother in the order of grace." An ordinary Mother must share in bringing a new life, and then take care of the new life. She shared by her participation in the Great Sacrifice itself. Now today she continues to take care of the brothers of her Son, for even in heaven "she has not put aside this saving function, but continues by her manifold intercession to win the gifts of eternal salvation for us ... the brothers of her Son, still in pilgrimage, and involved in dangers and difficulties, until they are led to the happy fatherland." Therefore rightly she is "invoked in the Church under the titles of Advocate, Auxiliatrix, Helper and Mediatrix."

Further:

> Before the day of Pentecost, we see the Apostles persevering with one heart in prayer with the women and with Mary the Mother of Jesus and His brothers, and Mary too with her prayers imploring the gift of the Spirit, who already at the annunciation had overshadowed her. Finally, the Immaculate Virgin ... having finished the course of her earthly life, was taken up, body and soul, to heavenly glory, and was exalted as Queen of the universe by the Lord, so that she might be more fully conformed to her Son, the Lord of Lords, and Victor over sin and death.

Fittingly we add the words of Pius XII here, on the extra joy every blessed soul will have from seeing her too in heaven:

> Surely, in the face of His own Mother, God has gathered together all the splendors of His divine artistry.... You know, beloved sons and daughters, how easily human beauty enraptures and exalts a kind heart.

[11]The Latin here is *sustinuit*.

> What would it ever do before the beauty of Mary... ! That is why Dante saw in Paradise, in the midst of 'more than a million rejoicing Angels ... a beauty smiling—what joy! It was in the eyes of all the other saints.'—Mary![12]

What a magnificent perspective has the Council put before our eyes. Literally, from eternity to eternity—that is, from eternity before time began, in which she was joined to her Son in the eternal decree of the Incarnation, to eternity when time shall be no more, when she will be forever Queen of Heaven, and a marvelous added joy to all angels and saints—and at every point in between, in every one of the mysteries of His life and death and resurrection, we find her, "always sharing His lot"[13] as Pius XII summed it up. In the approach of our Father to us, she is everywhere, her role is all-pervading.

Now obviously, since we cannot do anything better than to imitate the ways of our Father Himself, the ideal would be for every one of us to give her, in our own spiritual lives, a place corresponding to the place our Father has given her—an all-pervading place. To do that would be to live out most fully a consecration to her Immaculate Heart, in union with the Heart of her Son. Vatican II really did recommend such a life of consecration for it also wrote:

> This most holy Synod deliberately teaches this Catholic doctrine [the previous parts of Chapter 8 which we have seen] and it admonishes all the sons of the Church that they should generously cultivate devotion, especially liturgical devotion, towards the Blessed Virgin, and that they should consider of great importance the practices and exercises of piety toward her that were recommended by the Teaching Authority of the Church over the course of centuries.[14]

Included among those recommendations of course is consecration. In fact, Pope Paul VI on the floor of the Council itself, at the close of the third session, renewed publicly the consecration of the Church and the world to her Immaculate Heart. He said that his thoughts turned to the whole world "which our venerated predecessor Pius XII ... not without inspiration from on high, solemnly consecrated to the Immaculate Heart of Mary.... O Virgin Mary, Mother of the Council, to you we recommend the entire Church."[15] When he visited Fatima on May 13,

---

[12]Pius XII, To Italian Catholic Action Youth, Dec. 8, 1953. From *The Pope Speaks*, 1954. 1. p. 38. Citing Dante, *Paradiso* 31.130-35.

[13]Pius XII, *Munificentissimus Deus*. 42.768.

[14]Vatican II, *On the Church* #67.

[15]Paul VI, Speech closing third session of Vatican II, Nov. 21. 1965. AAS 56.1017.

1967, the same Pope recalled this

> consecration which we ourselves have renewed on November 21, 1964—we exhort all the sons of the Church to renew personally their consecration to the Immaculate Heart of the Mother of the Church and to bring alive this most noble act of veneration through a life ever more in accord with the divine will and in a spirit of filial service and of devout imitation of their heavenly Queen.[16]

At this point we must inject a special comment. The force of the logic we have just seen, namely, that since our Father has put her in an all-pervading role in His approach to us, therefore it would be ideal for us to give her the same place in our spiritual lives—this impresses many souls as a command, as something mandatory. But we must be honest and make a distinction. Devotion to the Sacred Heart of her Son—with the qualifications expressed above—really is mandatory, for that is at the very center of our faith: He is, after all, God. To have at least some devotion to her is also clearly required; we could not, after seeing the place our Father has given her, say in effect: But I do not care to bother with her at all. That would be gravely wrong.[17] But to go all the way, to live a life such as we have indicated—and in the way we are about to unfold further—this is not required of all. It falls under the principle of diversity of spiritual graces, which we spoke of in chapter 17. So each one, according to the varied dispositions and graces of that soul, will go into this, some farther than others.

Before making a consecration, it is most desirable to make a careful preparation, extending over some period of time. One good way to make that is described in the last part of St. Louis de Montfort's *True Devotion* book.

The most essential thing is not making an act of consecration, with or without some solemnity, though that is important. The essential thing is to live that consecration.

There are several ways of describing how to live a consecration. Major work on both theory and practice has been done by Father Chaminade,[18] St. Louis de Montfort, and St. Maximilian Kolbe.

All are excellent, all have strong similarities and much in com-

---

[16]Paul VI, *Signum magnum*, May 13, 1967. AAS 59.475.

[17]Leo XIII. ASS 30.133: "Such is the greatness of Mary, such her power with God, that he who when needing help would not turn to her would want to fly without wings." Pius XII, AAS 39.628: "Devotion to the Mother of God is . . . a fundamental element of Christian life."

[18]*Cf.* E. Neubert, *Life of Union With Mary*, tr. S. Juergens, Bruce, Milwaukee, 1959.

mon, in spite of certain variations. But let us sketch a generic way, as it were, of carrying out a consecration. We will speak most directly of the Marian phase of consecration, understanding that she is to lead us to the Heart of her Son, which she will surely do. However, in view of the diversity of spiritual attractions, of which we have already spoken, some souls will begin with living a Sacred Heart consecration, and move from that to the Marian phase.

Living a consecration could be described as following three attitudes or spirits: union, dependence, and obedience.

Union with Mary and with the Heart of her Son calls for chiefly two things: imitation of Him and her, so as to become like them, and trying to develop as constant as possible a realization of His and her presence.

Somewhat in the way in which St. Paul could say (Gal 2:20): "I no longer live, but Christ lives in me," St.Maximilian Kolbe spoke in a lyrical or poetic way of "becoming her or being in her" so that we "forget ourselves" and are "annihilated in her."[19] This is done by imitating Jesus and Mary, and also through, in the higher reaches, being so fully taken over by the action of the same Spirit who led Jesus, the Spirit whose spouse she is, that what St. John of the Cross said becomes true: "God alone moves the powers of these souls . . . to those deeds which are suitable . . . and they cannot be moved to others."[20]

He, inasmuch as He is God, is of course present everywhere, most especially in the Holy Eucharist. One who really lives a consecrated life cannot fail to develop a deep attachment to that Eucharistic Presence.

In what sense would we say that Mary is present to us? She is not a mere spirit, yet, in view of her assumption, her glorified body functions according to the principles of spirits. We, with our untransformed bodies, are present somewhere by physically taking up space. But a spirit does not take up, does not even need space—we think of the glorified body of Jesus after the resurrection coming through closed doors of the upper room. We say a spirit is present wherever that spirit is producing an effect.[21] So she is present wherever she is causing an effect. What effect? All graces come through her.[22] And we need these

---

[19]*Cf. Gli Scritti di Massimiliano Kolbe* Florence, Citta di Vita, 1975-78, #'s 579, 432, 508.

[20]St. John of the Cross, *Ascent* 3, 2, 10.

[21]Thus we can speak of God or the Holy Spirit as "coming" several times—in Baptism, in Confirmation, in Holy Orders, etc.—since each time He begins to produce added effects.

[22]St. Thomas thinks the sacraments are physical instruments of the transmission of grace: *Summa* III. 62.4. Some papal texts seem to indicate

graces constantly as long as we are in this world, So in that very real sense, she is always present to those devoted to her. There is also a sort of affective presence, almost a presence via feeling; when two people have strong mutual love, that love can create a sort of presence even at a distance.

No one without a most extraordinary grace can have a strictly constant, uninterrupted awareness of the presence of God, of Jesus, or of Mary. But we can cultivate a frequent awareness, one that returns almost spontaneously after interruptions forced by attention to our duties. One way is to make use of conditioned reflexes. If we repeatedly tie together two things, a reflex connection is built up. For example, if one lives in a place where he must climb or descend stairs often, it is possible to get in the habit of beginning to say some aspirational prayer, formal or informal, as soon as we feel our feet on the steps. Or one can tie it to entering or leaving any room, or to many other things. Some too will like a method we might call the small-talk way. If two persons are together in a room, and yet are somewhat occupied with some task that does not demand all their attention, they may exchange comments at intervals: how a thing is going, what one hopes for, what is not turning out well—a host of trivia, really. Now we can use this format to speak to Jesus or His Blessed Mother. This of course is not the highest form of prayer, but it is a prayer, a means of contact, and can serve as a start to better prayer.

There is, secondly, a spirit of dependence. On Jesus, inasmuch as He is God, we have the most absolute dependence; let us recall what we saw about Philippians 2:13 in chapter 18. But if we want to make our consecration as full as possible, we will have given to Jesus and Mary the right to dispose of everything we have, temporal and spiritual. We cannot of course, put their names on our bank account. But we can develop the attitude of taking seriously the fact that we should not, within a total consecration, use any of our money in a way that would not please them. This of course needs adjustment to various states in life; a priest can and should go much farther than a father of a family, who by no means should impose an almost monastic spirit of detachment on his wife and children.

We give too, in a complete consecration, the right to dispose of what spiritual goods we have. Our spiritual goods include condign and congruous merit—the former, condign merit, is so personal that we cannot alienate it at all. But the latter means a claim we can acquire—in a secondary sense, given God's promise (we recall chapter

---

Mary is also a physical instrument: Leo XIII, Sept 8, 1894. ASS 27.179; St. Pius X, Feb. 2, 1904. ASS 36.454.

5)—to good things from Him; we have also the satisfactory power of good acts (rebalancing the scales of the objective order for ourselves and others, as noted in chapter 4, and the power of prayer to obtain favors especially in view of the promise of Our Lord, "Ask and you shall receive."[23] In a total consecration we do not stop asking for specific favors especially for particular persons towards whom we have obligations. No. Jesus and Mary respect these obligations. It is from Him as God that we have, for example, the command: "Honor your Father and Mother" which includes not only obedience, in proper limits, but also psychological and perhaps if needed financial support in old age.[24] Really, Jesus and Mary love our parents, and others to whom we are indebted, even more than we do, and surely want us to satisfy our obligations to them. In fact, in a total consecration we enter in to a sort of pooling arrangement: we put our poor goods into a pool with those of Jesus and Mary. But in this, we give the last word, the final determination into their hands. So when I pray, I may and at times should ask for particular things for specific persons, but I always have the condition at least understood, sometimes expressed: "If this pleases you. You may use it in other ways if you wish."[25]

In prayer, we are free to speak directly to Our Father, for He Himself loves us. Yet even when we do that, we should be aware of our dependence on Jesus and Mary, on what they have acquired for us by the Great Sacrifice. To speak of prayer through Mary, there are two ways. In one, I address my words directly to her, asking her to speak for me. In the other, I may speak directly to the Father, or to His Son, trying to realize that even in this I depend on her sufferings and labors. It

---

[23]St. Teresa of Avila urges her Sisters not to waste time praying for minor things when there are so many great intentions, when the heretics would raze the Church: *Way of Perfection* 1.5. Really, the promise of Christ does not cover such things as victory in sports events; it basically refers to salvation and things needed for it. Yet we may pray for the lesser things, but without such an assurance.

[24]We might speak of this commandment as the divine social security system. When we are young, parents take care of us; when they are old and failing, it is our turn.

[25]It is good at times to have a Mass offered for the intentions of our Blessed Mother. Here there is a theological point: the priest himself must determine what the Mass is being offered for. But he can apply it "for the intentions of the giver." So we can give an offering marked "for the intentions of the giver, and then form our own intention that we want it to be for the intentions for which Mary wishes it offered. A priest who accepts a stipend, however, even with this consecration, must simply apply the Mass directly for the intentions the giver asks for, without putting it through the hands of the Blessed Mother.

is good to pray sometimes directly, sometimes indirectly, as the Holy Spirit leads us.

It is obvious that we still may, and in general should, pray to individual favorite Saints, again, with the qualifications we have just expressed.

Recall too that in chapter 22 we pointed out that we can give to her a sort of power of attorney. We do not directly ask for specific trials or sufferings, even though these are a special means of likeness to Him and to her. But since we do not know in a specific time and case what would please our Father to have us offer, we say to Her: "Mother, please speak for me. I have ratified in advance any offer you make in my name."

Lastly, there is a spirit of obedience to our heavenly King and Queen. they have, as we said, the right to ask us to do anything at all, even without reward—though they are most generous in giving to us. In consecration, we recognize that right, and give it on a basis of love, and plan to carry it out with fullest generosity.

When we speak of obeying, what do they want us to do? Some things are clear, others less so. Surely, they want us to obey all legitimate comands from lawful authorities. They want us also to be wholehearted in fulfilling the duties of our various states in life, whatever they may be.[26] Clearly too they want us to try to actively align our wills with the will of the Father insofar as that is clear at a given time; insofar as it is not yet clear, we are to take, as we explained in chapter 20, an attitude of a sort of plasticity, waiting and ready to carry out His will as soon as it appears.

However there are other things not covered by these comments. We often have to make decisions on what would please Jesus and Mary at a particular juncture. What do we do then? We do pray first, of course, but then we do not wait for a feeling and take that as an inspiration. That would be folly; it would leave us open to autosuggestion, and to the deceits of the evil one. Rather, after praying, we try to reason out what Jesus and Mary would do if placed in our particular circumstances—which may be quite different from those of first century Palestine. We try to imitate their virtues, their way of doing things.

In important decisions, or decisions that are to cover many smaller things, we should take more care than on little things. We ask: Is this proposal in harmony with our state in life? If a light seems to come in prayer we ask: Is it conducive, at least in the long run, to peace and gentleness of heart? Here the rules of what is called discernment of

---

[26] *Cf.* the wise counsels of St. Francis de Sales on the various states, in his *Introduction to a Devout Life* 1.3.

spirits, provided by such writers as St. Francis de Sales and St. Ignatius Loyola, are priceless.[27] Still further, especially on important things, we ought to consult with a good spiritual guide, when we have the opportunity. Our Father loves obedience: His Son saved the world by His obedience. Within it, we are safe; outside of it, there is danger.

St. Maximilian Kolbe liked to speak of the relation of consecration to our baptismal promises, in which we promised to renounce satan and all his works, and to follow Jesus, by whom we are "sealed"[28] in baptism as His property. Consecration is the fullest kind of response to and carrying out of these promises. Mary, in view of her Immaculate Conception, was most fitted to respond most fully, and that she did, with a fullness and perfection beyond our ability to visualize—for we recall that Pius IX told us that even at the start of her existence, her holiness was so great that "none greater under God can be thought of, and no one but God can comprehend it."

Living such a consecration most fully will not dispense us from trials or make life easy. Rather, the added likeness to Jesus and Mary may involve more trials. But it will make this life much happier, by giving us on the point of the soul (*cf.* chapter 17) that peace which no man can take from us, and which will lead to a consummation beyond anything we can imagine—where eye has not seen nor has ear heard, nor has it entered into the heart of man what things God has prepared for those who love Him.[29]

---

[27]*Cf.* St. Francis de Sales, *Treatise on the Love of God* 8.10-14; St. Ignatius Loyola, "Rules for the Discernment of Spirits" in his *Spiritual Exercises*; Garrigou-Lagrange, *The Three Ages of the Interior Life* II. pp. 241-48.

[28]The Fathers of the Church often spoke of Baptism as a seal marking us as God's property. After Baptism, we should never sin again, *cf. e.g.*, *Shepherd of Hermas*, Mandate 4.3.1-6.

[29]The Brown Scapular is an excellent external sign of Marian consecration. *Cf.* the letter of Pius XII to Major Superiors of Carmelites for the 700th anniversary of the apparition to St. Simon Stock.

Chapter 25: End Without End

Our first parents, at the start of our race, wanted to be like gods, but in their folly threw away the participation in divinity they already had, thinking thereby they would get what they cast away. But our Father, who, as the old Portuguese proverb says, can write straight with crooked lines, at once set in motion His plans so that we might indeed finally become partly divine by sharing in His own nature, and have it more abundantly, for the redemption was to be greater than the fall (Rom 5:15-19) since He would send His Son so we might have life and have it more abundantly (Jn 10:10). He announced, mysteriously but truly,[1] that He would "put enmity between you [the serpent] and the woman." Her offspring would crush the head of the serpent and open up to our race a greater sharing in divinity through fullest participation in His covenant.

The Father, the One who is "best known by unknowing," who "should not even be called inexpressible, since when we say that word we say something" (*cf.* Introduction)—He, the incomprehensible, willed to be comprehended[2] through His only Son, who would be "our peace" (Eph. 2:14). During the long ages of waiting until He should appear, people still were to become His members, members of His Church, by anticipation,[3] by faith in Him who was to come. For faith is a

---

[1]Vatican II, *On the Church* #55 (cited in chapter 6) says that Gen 3:15, in the light of later revelation, gradually brings into view the Mother of the Redeemer and her son.

[2]*Cf.* Leo the Great, DS 294.

[3]Somewhat similarly, Mary was preserved Immaculate by anticipation of the merits of her Son.

total adherence of the person to God, in mind and will.[4] Even though so many had never heard word of Him, yet it was His Spirit who "wrote the law on their hearts" (Rom 2:15; Jer 31:33) so that in accepting that word, they would be joined in will to the Divine Word—accepting His word written in their hearts, without clearly understanding that they were doing so.[5]

But at last came the fulness of time, planned for by the Father, who "in manifold and varied ways spoke of old to our fathers, in the last days spoke to us through His Son, whom He apppointed heir of all things" (Heb. 1:1). At last, when the Holy Virgin spoke her fiat to the Father's messenger, "the Word was made flesh, and dwelt among us." Then "although He was in the form of God, He did not consider equality with God something to be clung to, but He emptied Himself, taking on the form of a slave, being made in the likeness of men, and in appearance was found as a man" (Phil 2:6-8), so that He might even—a folly to the Greeks, a scandal to the Jews (1 Cor 1:22)—become "obedient even to death, death on the cross."

By this very birth He gave us the beginning of brotherhood with Him, for "to those who received Him, He gave power to become sons of God" (Jn 1:12)[6] as His brothers, since we were to have one and the same Mother with Him. As Pius XII put it, it was necessarily true that "the Mother of the Head would be the Mother of the members,"[7] of those who by participation in His covenant become His brothers, members of His body, which is the Church.

He told us, "I am the way, the truth and the life" (Jn 14:6).

He is the way to the Father—for He also said, "I and the Father are one" (Jn 10:30), so that he who sees Him, sees the Father (Jn 14:9). We enter the way by becoming His members, whether fully and consciously, or by only "an unknowing will"[8] by which those who follow the law written on hearts (Rom 2:15, *cf.* Jer 31:33) adhere to Him substantially, even if unknowingly. For it is only inasmuch as we are His members, and like Him—thus we could sum up the Christian regime as St. Paul presents it—that we are saved and made holy. Hence the true teaching: No salvation outside the Church,[9] that is, without being at least in this basic way His members.

He is the Truth. In English we speak of things as being "true to

---

[4]On the full Pauline sense of the word faith, see chapters 14 & 15.

[5]The appendix will develop this point fully.

[6]*Cf.* the Patristic concept of physical-mystical solidarity, in chapter 7.

[7]Pius XII, to Marian Congress of Ottawa, 1947. AAS 39. 271.

[8]*Cf.* chapter 12 and the appendix.

[9]*Cf.* the appendix.

form". In saying this we do not refer to speech that matches our minds—no, we mean that a thing matches the pattern to which it should conform. But He is the Truth, since He Himself is the pattern, the model to which every human being should conform, so as to be true to form. Hence St. Augustine said that it is not enough for us to "live according to man,"[10] that is, just in conformity to a purely human pattern; no, we should live according to God, copying in varied ways, in varied degrees, the pattern of the incomprehensible Father Himself, of whom His Son is the Word, the "Image of the invisible God" (Col 1:15). This, in sum, means imitating Him, "having that attitude in us which was also in Christ Jesus" (cf. Phil 2:5), the attitude of doing the will of the Father, just as His Son came down from Him not to do His own will, but the will of Him who sent Him (Jn 6:38), so that He could even say: "My food is to do the will of Him who sent me" (Jn 4:34). It is precisely when we join Him in the renewal of the New Covenant,[11] which is the Mass, that we are to join our conformity to the will of the Father with His obedience even to death.

He is the Truth too in that He teaches us divine truth, and has sent us His Holy Spirit, who leads the Church into all truth (Jn 14:26) and will teach it all things, so that the Church can with divine authority fulfill the words of the Divine Master (Lk 10:16): "He who hears you, hears me."

He is the Life. It is only by Him that anyone can be spiritually alive—even those who, in this world in the ages before His coming, adhered to Him unknowingly, by carrying out the law written on their hearts. For He is the vine, we are the branches (Jn 15:5). If we are not engrafted into Him (*cf.* Rom 11:19) we are dead branches, for we then would not be joined to the Head "from whom the whole body [his Church] nourished and knit together through its joints and ligaments, grows with a divine growth" (Col. 2:19).

We who have the blessing of full membership in His Body, the Church, enter through the gate of Baptism, which, as the Fathers of the Church so often said, echoing St. Paul (2 Cor 1:22), seals us with the imprint of the Spirit of His Son. At the suitable point, we are strengthened by a further coming of His Spirit in Confirmation, to give the resources needed for strength since "our wrestling is not against flesh and blood, but against the principalities, against the powers, against the world-rulers of this darkness, against the spirits of evil in heavenly places" (Eph 6:12). Should we at times, in human weakness, slip or fall,

---

[10]St. Augustine, *City of God*, 14. 4.

[11]Vatican II, *On Liturgy* #10 speaks of the Mass as the renewal of the new covenant. See also chapter 11.

He gave to His Apostles such power that "whose sins you shall forgive, they are forgiven them" (Jn 20:23). We can have not only the lesser security of merely interior forgiveness, but the declaration with power that our sins are forgiven us.

But the peak of the fulfillment of His words "I have come that they may have life, and have it more abundantly" (Jn 10:10), the center of our participation in Him, comes in the Mass, the renewal of the New Covenant, in which we are asked to join our obedience to the Father with His obedience even to death, "so that in one and the same offering of the Victim . . . they may be presented to God the Father"[12] in the offering of twofold obedience, of Head and members, melting into one, and united with the cooperation of the Mother of Jesus, who, since she shared intimately in the making of the New Covenant on Calvary, continues to share with the Divine Victim in each Mass (*cf.* chapter 11). So that our offering in the Mass may not be just empty words, as if saying "Lord Lord, we offer thee," we remember His words that "not everyone who says to me, Lord Lord, shall enter the kingdom of Heaven, but he who does the will of my Father" (Mt 7:21). To be open to and capable of that obedience/love (*cf.* chapters 14 & 15) we need the recollection of which chapter 21 spoke; we need the preparation and emptying of self for obedience that is achieved by following after His Cross through mortification (chapters 19 & 20), and by a humility (chapter 18) that recognizes with His Mother that every bit of good we are and have and do is the gift of the Father (*cf.* 1 Cor 4:7). We are greatly helped in all these things by the total dedication of a life of consecration to the Hearts of Jesus and Mary (chapter 24).

St. Augustine said well of the Mass that in it the Church, "since it is the body of this Head, learns through Him to offer herself."[13]

Varied are the walks in life that the Father may will for each one. If it is marriage, which is, as Paul VI told us, "a long path to sanctification"[14] if used as our Father planned, there is the Sacrament He blessed at Cana to give present helps, and asssurance of future helps as needed (sacramental graces) to fulfill the role the Father has assigned to spouses.

If our lot is the ordained priesthood, the Sacrament of Holy Orders gives an imprint of the Spirit for indelible conformity to Christ precisely as Priest, for the benefit of His members, and for the human priest himself.

Finally, He who is our Life has prepared for us the sacred oil of

---

[12]Pius XII, *Mediator Dei*, cited and explained in chapter 11.

[13]St. Augustine, *City of God*, 10. 20.

[14]Paul VI, cited and explained in chapter 16.

anointing, to strengthen us for our crossing over to the Father, to even forgive sins if that be needed, provided that our dispositions are just sufficient. That crossing is indeed momentous, for the state in which we are at the moment of passage sets our pattern forever.

With the help of Holy Scripture, and the addition of principles of the great minds to whom the Father has willed to give special lights for our sake (*cf.* chapter 23), we can to some extent get some notion of what that crossing is like.

Aristotle, that pagan philosopher to whom the Father gave the greatest insights, tells us that "time is a measure of change on a scale of before and after."[15] In this life, we are immersed in change, and so we are in time. Within our bodies, every cell is constantly being torn down and rebuilt, so that we are literally full of change. We are on a planet that revolves on its axis once every 24 hours, and in addition travels around our sun once each year—while the sun and all its planets, part of the Milky Way galaxy, are rushing through space at a tremendous rate, to what destination we know not.

We are, then, full of change interiorly and surrounded by change outside us. But the point of contact with all that change is the body. When we are freed form the body, we lose contact with all that change. Then we are no longer in time, which is the measure of that change. Popular speech speaks of the departed as in eternity. In the strict sense of the word, eternity applies only to God Himself, "with whom there is no shadow of change" (Jas 1:17). So for Him, there is no past, no future—He simply *is*. We, after our crossing, still have had a past, and to some extent face some changes in what lies ahead, but not the unceasing motion that puts before us constantly a moment we call future, which quickly changes into present, then into past; no, then we can know only some relatively shallow changes, and those not constantly, but at some hard-to-define intervals. There will be no substantial, that is, deep change, and so no possibility that our basic stance toward the will of the Father—for or against it—can ever change.

Some imagine death as if it were a turning off of the lights. Rather, it is a turning on of the light into a brilliance we have never yet known. Hence the same Aristotle wrote that only then—when separated from the body—is the mind fully itself.[16] For in this life, our intelligence has two components: the physical brain, a marvelous instrument, which the best scientists understand only imperfectly; plus the spirit intellect that is natural to our soul. Such a spirit intellect is, obvi-

[15]Aristotle, *Physics* 4. 11. On a sort of natural inspiration given special persons, *cf.* the last part of chapter 23.

[16]Aristotle, *Psychology* 3. 5.

ously, far more powerful than the physical intrument in our heads, for spirit is immeasurably above matter. Yet in the present life, those two components are inescapably tied together, so that if there be severe damage to our physical brain, we may lack all consciousness. Hence the power of our spiritual intellect is restrained, greatly hampered in this life.[17]

But when we have crossed over, when we have shaken off this mortal coil, then the natural power of the spiritual intellect asserts itself. Then we shall know—even if we do not at once reach the direct vision of God—what God is like, in a way we never knew in this world. For our spiritual memory retains data, once very poorly grasped, but then illumined by the brilliant light of the spirit. Further, in this life we find it so easy to do without the thought of God. The reason is that our senses are constantly bringing into us input, reports saying that the physical world is the thing that counts, the only fully real thing.[18] But then, lacking the body, we will lack those senses, and so will lack that distraction. The glaring light of the spirit intellect will know what He is like. Therefore it will most intensely want Him with a desire we cannot really feel in this life, even though the greatest Saints have approached that point. The soul makes its own the words of Psalm 42: "As the hart pants after the flowing water, so my souls longs for you, O God... When shall I come and behold the face of God?"

Even those who are eternally lost will feel this longing—except in them it is never to be satisfied. Rather, they both long for Him, and hate Him, for they have left this world with their wills opposed to His will—a condition that never will be, never can be corrected. In that lies the worst pain of hell. We might speculate that it would be like a sick, twisted state, both wanting and hating, like the state of a person who tries to awake in the middle of the night, yet, from sickness, is not able to reach fully the level of consciousness, and so is in anguish in a horror state between sleep and waking.

At the resurrection, there will also be what the Church speaks of as a "repercussion on the whole being of the sinner,"[19] that is, the body

[17]There is an advantage for us, in that since we do not at the time of acting see everything with the maximum possible clarity, there is always room for us later to reconsider and say: I now see I should not have done that; I wish I had not done it; I do not want to do it again. In an angel the absolute clarity of intellect means there never was a chance to repent. *Cf.* St. Thomas, *Summa*, I. 64. 2.

[18]This makes clear again the need of mortification. *Cf.* chapter 19. The pagan Socrates also understood this: *cf.* note 17 on chapter 16.

[19]S. Congregation for the Doctrine of the Faith, May 17, 1979. AAS 71. 941-42.

will suffer in some mysterious way, which it deserves since it has shared in sin, even incited the soul to sin. This "repercussion" must be dreadful, for Christ Himself described it as "fire."

But those whose will is basically in accord with the will of the Father, know, thanks to the judgment already given them by Christ, that at least eventually they will reach that vision, they will behold the face of God. But they may lack the needed preparation. They may not have fully done their part to rebalance the objective order (*cf.* chapters 4 & 19) damaged by their personal sins; their soul may not have achieved that high degree of purity and elevation needed to be able to see the face of God. Ideally, they should have reached that perfection in this life. If they did not, thanks to the mercy of the Father, there is purgatory, which can remedy both deficiencies. Were there no purgatory, they could never come before the face of God.

There is no time in purgatory, yet there surely are some mysterious stages in the purification. One can, as it were, drop a line from the curve on the graph representing the duration (not time) of purgatory to the curve below representing time on earth. A corresponding point can be found. If we can believe some of the private revelations to some of the Saints, such as St. Catherine of Genoa, for small faults there may be need of a purification that is very long, comparable to many years on earth.

Souls in that state are really incomplete persons, for a human person consists of both body and soul. They lack body until the resurrection. Those in hell have to wait but one instant for the resurrection day with its increased pains forever, for there is no change in hell. Those who at once reach the vision of God in heaven also wait but one instant. But in pugatory, there is prolonged waiting.

When finally the soul is purified, refined enough to be able to stand the vision of God, then what is it like? As we saw in chapter 2, it is participating in infinite streams of knowledge and of love, a thing possible for no conceivable creature, only for one made partly divine by grace, which then turns into the light of glory. Then God joins Himself directly to the created intellect, with no image in between, for no image could show Him as He is (*cf.* chapter 2).

That vision is infinite—the soul there is a finite receptacle, trying to take in the infinite, comparable to the butterfly image used by Arendzen which we saw in chapter 2. Will it become dull as endless ages pass? No, because the vision is infinite, and we are finite, incapable of taking in all. But also, because as St. Augustine says, we shall be partakers of His eternity,[20] in which there is no sucession of future-

[20]St. Augustine, *City of God* 10. 7.

present-past. We, by participation in Him, will simply *be*, will be blessed, unimaginably happy, satisfied.

Here too shows the mercy of our Father. Yes, hell is endless, but we should not picture it as an old popular image did—a bird comes once every ten thousand years, takes one peck at a granite mountain: when it has the mountain gone, eternity is only beginning. No, even the souls in hell will simply be, be *miserable*. There is no dragging out endlessly, as it were. This does not make it less than terrible. We cannot visualize it, even for the bodiless soul, still less when that misery causes a repercussion on the whole being of the sinner that is comparable to fire.

For those in the vision of God, there will be a secondary, but wondrous joy from being able to go anywhere in the universe to see the marvels of our Father, by merely willing it, without the restrictions of the speed of light, which seems to be the speed-limit of the universe now. There will be the joy of being with all our dear ones, and all other marvelous souls of Saints. And greatest in this category will be the sight of Mary, which, as we saw in chapter 24, Pius XII pictures splendidly:

> Surely, in the face of His own Mother, God has gathered together all the splendors of His divine artistry.... You know, beloved sons and daughters, how easily human beauty enraptures and exalts a kind heart. What would it ever do before the beauty of Mary! That is why Dante saw in Paradise, in the midst of 'more than a million rejoicing Angels, a beauty smiling—what joy! It was in the eyes of all the other Saints': Mary!

As Vatican II tells us, "The Church will attain her full perfection only in the glory of heaven."[21] Then the promise of the covenant will be most completely fulfilled, the promise of which the Father spoke already at Sinai (Ex 19:5): "If you really obey my voice and keep my covenant, you shall be my special possession, more than all people," the People of God of whom our Father said through Jeremiah (31:33): "I will be their God and they will be my people." For we shall be forever members joined to our Head, through whom we are eternally blessed.

It is highly suitable to borrow the words with which St. Augustine closed his *City of God*:

> Then, being at rest, we will see that He is God[22]—that which we wanted to be ourselves, when we fell from Him in listening to the seducer, 'You shall be like gods' and going away from the true God, by whose action we would be gods by participation, not by desertion.... Being remade

[21] Vatican II, *On the Church* #48.

[22] Ps. 46:10 as Augustine read it said: "Be at rest and see that I am God."

> by Him . . . we will be at rest forever, seeing that He is God, by whom we will be filled, when He will be all in all. . . . There we shall be at rest and we shall see; we shall see and we shall love; we shall love and we shall praise. Behold what will be at the end without end![23]

And I add with St. Augustine: "I seem to myself, with the help[24] of the Lord, to have paid the debt of this large work. Let those for whom it is too little or too much forgive me. Let those for whom it is right, give thanks not to me, but to God. Amen. Amen."[25]

---

[23]St. Augustine, *City of God* 22. 30.

[24]The word *help* is much too weak, as chapter 18 explains. *Cf.* also chapter 23 on the special modes in which God may move some persons, such as St. Augustine. He does this chiefly for the benefit of others. Why God picks a particular person does not depend on the person's merits. Rather, He seems to follow at least largely the principle taught by St. Paul in 1 Cor 1:27-29.

[25]St. Augustine, *City of God* 22. 30.

Appendix: Is There Salvation Outside the Church?

A recent study by Gustave Thils, *Pour une théologie de structure planétaire*, has pointed out some new possibilities for the solution of the vexing and long-standing problem, the salvation of those who are or seem to be outside the Church.[1]

The question is difficult, because salvation requires not only a su-

---

[1]Gustave Thils, *Pour une Théologie de Structure Planétaire*, in *Cahiers De la Revue Théologique de Louvain*, 6, 1983. The literature on the general problem of the salvation of pagans is immense. Especially significant also are: P. Damboriena, *La Salvacion en la Religiones No Cristianas*, Biblioteca de Autores Cristianos, Madrid (hereinafter BAC), 1973, esp. pp. 19-54; Paul Hacker, "The Religions of the Gentiles as viewed by the Fathers of the Church" in *Zeitschrift für Missionswissenschaft und Religionswissenschaft* 54 (1970) pp. 253-78; *idem*, "The Religions of the Nations in the Light of Holy Scripture," *ibid.* 54 (1970) pp. 161-85; A. Luneau, "Les Pères et les Religions non-chrétiennes," in *Nouvelle Revue Theologique* 89 (1967) pp.821-41; 914-39; J. N. D. Kelly, *Early Christian Doctrines*, Adam & Charles Black, London, 1968; L. Caperan, *Le probleme du salut des infidèles*, 2d ed. 2 vols, Paris, 1934; R. Lombardi, *The Salvation of the Unbeliever*, tr. D. M. White, Newman, Westminster, 1956; K. Rahner, "Christianity and the Non-Christian Religions," in *Theological Investigations* 5, pp. 115-34, Helicon, Baltimore, 1966; J. Patout Burns, "The Economy of Salvation: Two Patristic Traditions," in *Theological Studies* 37 (1976) pp. 598-619. On Patristic exegesis of Romans 2:14-16, especially important are: Max Lachmann, *Vom Geheimnis der Schöpfung*, Evangelisches Verlagswerk GMBH, Stuttgart, 1952, esp. pp. 95-135; 285-305; Karl Hermann Schelkle, *Paulus, Lehrer der Väter*, Die altkirchliche Auslegung von Römer 1-11 2d ed. 1959, Patmos-Verlag, Düsseldorf.

pernatural faith in God who requites justly, and adherence to the moral code, so far as the person knows it, but even membership in the Church. Not a few Fathers of the Church,and even Popes and Councils, have insisted on this requirement of membership.

From merely popular level mission magazines to more scholarly works, one so often finds mere despair about this requirement of membership. For example, a seminar on Christology at the 1984 convention of the Catholic Theological Society of America shows not a few participants not only thought the Church could be dispensed with, but even Christ Himself. Doubt was even raised over the "non-contradictory notion of truth" with a tendency to think that "truth is always perspectival."[2]

At the other end of the spectrum, one finds the pessimistic notion of St. Augustine that most persons are lost without really a chance and—though Augustine did not seem to share this second facet—the fundamentalistic understanding of the membership requirement, leading to heroic missionary zeal on the part of not a few Saints, anxious to rescue pagans from otherwise certain eternal ruin.

Yet, the Fathers of the first centuries, on closer study, reveal the start of a way out of this impasse. They did not, it seems, reach the complete solution, but they pointed in the right direction.

To understand their thought we need to notice that so many of them were remarkably faithful to an essential facet of theological method. They knew that in divine revelation it is not strange if one meets two conclusions which, even on rechecking, turn out to be both true, so that we must hold on in the dark, as it were, until somehow the day may dawn that will show the way to reconciliation. A striking example of this appears in the way the Fathers wrestled with two most dificult Scriptural texts:[3] Lk 2:52, which asserts that Jesus grew even in wisdom as well as in age, and Mk 13:32, in which Jesus Himself is quoted as saying He did not know the day of the end.

The result was that in a very large number of major Fathers, we find two groups of statements on the question of the human knowledge of Jesus. One group seems to admit ignorance in Him, so He could literally grow in wisdom, and have a lack of knowledge of the day of the end. The other group of texts firmly asserts there was no ignorance in

---

[2]*Cf.* E. A. Johnson, "Seminar on Christology" in *Proceedings of the Catholic Theological Society of America*, 39 (1984) pp. 153-55. *Cf.* also J. Peter Schneller, in a review of J. P. Theisen, "The Ultimate Church and the Promise of Salvation" in *Theological Studies* 38 (1977) p. 777.

[3]*Cf.* W. G. Most, *The Consciousness of Christ*, Christendom College Press, Front Royal, 1980, pp. 93-133.

Him on either of these points.

With remarkable fidelity, the Fathers went on for a long time in making both kinds of assertions. On the one hand, they did not wish to flatly contradict what Scripture seemed to say; on the other hand, they knew that there could not be ignorance in His human intellect. This situation went on until finally a way was found to reconcile the seeming contradiction. St. Athanasius first discovered that we could distinguish between actual growth in knowledge, and growth in the manifestation of what was always there—showing it "before God and men." Much more time had to pass before Eulogius and St. Gregory the Great found the solution to the knowledge of the last day, in saying that He knew it *in* His humanity but not *from* His humanity.

A diligent search in the Fathers shows a similar situation in regard to "no salvation outside the Church." We find again two sets of assertions, very often by the same writers. One group of statements speaks very strongly, and almost stringently, about the need of membership; the other group softens this position by taking a remarkably broad view of what membership consists in.

As we said, in the problems of the human knowledge of Jesus, the Fathers eventually did find out how to reconcile the two kinds of assertions. On our present question of membership in the Church, they seem to have found only part of the answer. But, with their help, we will, at the end of this appendix, propose a new Scripturally-based solution.

Before going ahead we need to notice one more principle of interpretation. It is this: the only things guaranteed in statements of the Magisterium, and protected in lesser ways in the works of the Fathers, are the things explicitly set down on paper. We may indeed know historically that certain thoughts, more extensive, were in the minds of the writers. Yet Divine Providence has committed itself to protect only the explicitly written texts, not what is merely in the mind and unexpressed.

We might say that God practices a sort of brinkmanship. He has made two commitments that go in opposite directions. First, He has made humans free; second, He has guaranteed this protection of teaching. Therefore He often, as it were, draws a very tight line, protecting only what is explicit on paper, not what is implicit, or only in the minds of the writers. For example, some statements made near the time of St. Augustine and even later were written by those who may have believed at least part of his *massa damnata* theory. The fact that we know they had these things in mind does not commit the Church to that theory. Again, the writers of some teachings on the Eucharist had in mind an Aristotelian framework of substance and accident. But these words can be understood in a non-technical, everyday sense. So the

Church did not guarantee Aristotelianism. Further, Pius IX and Gregory XVI (and perhaps Leo XIII also) may well have had more extensive ideas in mind on religious liberty/indifferentism than what they set down in writing. But the Church is committed only to what they actually wrote.

We need to keep this principle firmly in mind in reading conciliar statements on our question.

For the sake of clarity, we will go through each of the two sets of statements separately, beginning with the seemingly rigid texts.

Restrictive Texts of the Fathers

Perhaps the earliest of these comes from the *Shepherd* of Hermas:

> These apostles and the teachers who preached the name of the Son of God, when they fell asleep in the power and faith of the Son of God, preached also to those who had fallen asleep earlier, and they gave them the seal of the preaching. They therefore went down into the water with them, and came up again.[4]

Hermas clearly takes the requirement of physical Baptism so rigidly that it had to be given even after death, or there could be no salvation. Yet, we shall meet Hermas again in our second series, with a very broad text.

About the same time as Hermas, we meet a statement from St. Justin the Martyr, from the middle of the second century, "Then they [converts] are led by us where there is water, and are regenerated.... For Christ said: Unless you are born again, you will not enter into the kingdom of heaven."[5] In context, of course, Justin is speaking of converts. Yet the insistence on Baptism is strong. On the other hand, as we shall see, Justin has some of the most important texts of a broader type.

St. Irenaeus who also has many broad passages, has one which might be considered restrictive: "God places in the Church apostles, prophets, doctors ... those who are not partakers of these, who do not run to the Church, deprive themselves of life through evil opinions and wicked working."[6] Yet he seems to have in mind those who culpably

---

[4]Hermas, *Shepherd, Similitudes* 9.16. From Greek text in D. Ruiz Bueno, *Padres Apostolicos*, BAC, 2d ed. 1967. pp. 1071-72.

[5]Justin, *First Apology* 46. From Greek text in D. Ruiz Bueno, *Padres Apologistas Griegos* BAC, 1964. pp. 250.

[6]Irenaeus, *Against Heresies* 3.24.1. SC 1952 ed. (no number given) p.400. *Cf.* also *ibid.* 3.19.1.

reject the Church.

Clement of Alexandria, who has many texts in our second series, quotes verbatim the text we saw from Hermas,[7] and seems to agree, in *Stromata* 2. 9. Clement also wrote: "He who does not enter through the door ... is a thief and a robber. Therefore it is necessary for them to learn the truth through Christ and to be saved, even if they happen on philosophy."[8] Here however, we might wonder if Clement means that only those are lost who by their own fault reject the faith.

Clement's great pupil, Origen, also gives us both kinds of statements. Strongest is that from his Homily on Jesu Nave:

> If anyone of that people wishes to be saved, let him come to this house, so that he can attain salvation, to this house in which the blood of Christ is a sign of redemption.... Therefore let no one persuade himself, let no one deceive himself: outside this house, that is, outside the Church, no one is saved: for if anyone goes outside, he becomes guilty of his own death.[9]

Origen is allegorizing the house of Rahab in Jericho. But it seems that those who went outside did so by their own fault.

Most stringent of all is St. Cyprian: "Whoever separates himself from the Church ... is separated from the promises of the Church.... He cannot have God as his Father who does not have the Church as his mother. If anyone was able to escape outside the ark of Noah, he too who is outside the Church escapes."‡ Even more sternly:

> The power of baptism cannot be greater or more powerful, can it, than confession, than suffering, such that someone who confesses Christ before men, is baptized with his own blood. And yet, neither does this baptism profit a heretic, even though after confessing Christ, he is killed outside the Church.[11]

However, the testimony of St. Cyprian is quite marred because he

---

[7]*cf.* note 4 above.

[8]Clement of Alexandria, *Stromata* 5. 12. PG 9. 128.

[9]Origen, Homily on Jesu Nave 3. 5. PG 12. 841. *Cf.* also *idem* in Rom 2. 9-10.

[10]Cyprian, *De Catholicae Ecclesiae Unitate* 6. PL 4. 502. *Cf.* Pierre-Thomas Camelot, *Die Lehre von der Kirche, Väterzeit bis ausschliesslich Augustinus* in *Handbuch der Dogmengeschichte* (ed. M. Schmaus, A. Grillmeier, L Scheffczyk) Herder, Freiburg, 1970, III. 3b. pp. 18-27; and A. D'Alès, *La Théologie de Saint Cyprien*, Beauchesne, Paris, 1922, esp. pp. 91-242.

[11]Cyprian, Epist. to Iubianus (#73) 21, in J. Campos, *Obras de San Cipriano*, BAC, 1964, pp. 688-89.

himself broke with the unity of the Church in contradicting Pope St. Stephen on the validity of baptism given by heretics, the very point underlying these statements. Really, if God had taken Cyprian at his word, Cyprian should have been lost, even though a martyr.

Lactantius has a similar, though less sweeping text: "Whoever does not enter there [the Church], or whoever goes out from there, is foreign to the hope of life and salvation."[12] It is just possible that this could be taken to refer to those who are culpably outside.

In view of his pessimistic belief in his *massa damnata* theory, we might expect St. Augustine to give us many stringent statements. Actually, he does the opposite, as we shall see presently. His restrictive texts are fewer and less clear. In *De natura et gratia* he wrote: "If Christ did not die for no purpose, therefore all human nature can in no way be justified and redeemed from the most just anger of God . . . except by faith and the sacrament of the blood of ChriSt. "[13] Yet even this statement is softened by his words a few lines earlier: "God is not unjust, so as to deprive the just of the reward of justice, if the sacrament of the divinity and humanity of Christ was not announced to them."[14] He thought only a few places by his day had not heard the preaching—not dreaming of a whole added hemisphere, and of so many other places in his own hemisphere.

Again, in his *Contra Julianum*, Augustine comments on Romans 2:14-16, which seems to speak of the salvation of pagans without the law. He takes the gentiles mentioned to be converted gentiles, and adds: "Nor can you prove by them that which you want, that even infidels can have true virtues."[15] Similarly, in commenting in Epistle 164. 4. 10 on the mysterious words of 1 Peter 3: 18-20, he thinks that Christ preached to perhaps all the dead, and so gave them a chance for salvation.

St. Cyril of Alexandria, says J. N. D. Kelly, "was voicing universally held assumptions when he wrote [in Ps 30:22] that 'mercy is not obtainable outside the holy city'."[16]

St. Fulgentius of Ruspe clearly follows in the train of St. Cyprian:

> Not only all pagans, but also all Jews and all heretics and schismatics, who finish their lives outside the Catholic Church, will go into eternal

---

[12]Lactantius, *Institutiones* 4. 30. 11. PL 6. 542. *Cf.* also Damboriena, *op. cit.* p. 30.

[13]Augustine, *De natura et gratia* 2. 2. PL 44. 248-49.

[14]*Cf.* Burns, *art. cit.*, pp. 608-14.

[15]Augustine, *Contra Iulianum*, 4. 3. 25. PL 44. 750.

[16] Kelly, *op. cit.*, p. 403.

> fire. . . . No one, howsoever much he may have given alms, even if he sheds his blood for the name of Christ, can be saved, unless he remains in the bosom and unity of the Catholic Church.[17]

Fulgentius also is at least close to the error of Cyprian on invalidity of baptism given by heretics: "Baptism can exist . . . even among heretics . . . but it cannot be beneficial [*prodesse*] outside the Catholic Church."[18] He likewise believes, with Augustine, in the damnation of unbaptized infants.[19]

Restrictive Magisterium Texts

There are several Magisterium texts that seem quite stringent. The Profession of Faith prescribed by Pope Innocent III in 1208 A.D. for the Waldensians says: " We believe in our heart and confess in our mouth that there is one Church, not of heretics, but the holy Roman Catholic apostolic Church, outside of which we believe no one is saved."[20] Similarly, the Fourth Lateran Council in 1215 A.D. defined, against the Albigensians and Cathari: "There is one universal Church of the faithful, outside of which no one at all is saved."[21]

Pope Boniface VIII in his famous *Unam sanctam* of Nov. 18, 1302 spoke strongly: "Outside of which [the Church] there is neither salvation nor remission of sins. . . . But we declare, state and define that to be subject to the Roman Pontiff is altogether necessary for salvation."[22]

The texts of Innocent III and IV Lateran do not go farther than the patristic texts we have seen. But the second sentence from Boniface VIII does raise a further question. However, the difficulty is easily handled; for the critical line is quoted from St. Thomas, *Contra Errores Graecorum*: "Ostenditur etiam quod subesse Romano Pontifici sit de necessitate salutis"[23] ("It is also shown that to be subject to the Roman Pontiff is necessary for salvation.") But in the context, shown by the two quotes St. Thomas gives at this point, it means merely that there is no salvation outside the Church. In that sense one must come under the jurisdiction of the Pope.[24]

---

[17]Fulgentius, *De fide ad Petrum* 38. 81. CC 91A, p. 757.

[18]*Ibid.* 36. 79. CC 91A, p. 756.

[19]*Ibid.* 27. 68.

[20]DS 792.

[21]DS 802.

[22]DS 870.

[23]Thomas Aquinas, *Contra errores Graecorum* 36. #1125.

[24]The text on the two swords seems stronger than it is. It was explained

An Epistle of Clement VI, of Sept. 29, 1351, makes just a simple statement: "No man . . . outside the faith of the Church and obedience to the Roman Pontiff can finally be saved."[25] The sense is as above.

Finally, the Decree for the Jacobites from the Council of Florence in 1442 seems specially vehement:

> It firmly believes, professes and preaches, that none who are outside the Catholic Church, not only pagans, but also Jews and heretics and schismatics, can partake of eternal life, but they will go into eternal fire . . . unless before the end of life they will have been joined to it [the Church]; and that the unity of the ecclesiastical body has such force that only for those who remain in it are the sacraments of the Church profitable for salvation, and fastings, alms and other works of piety and exercises of the Christian soldiery bring forth eternal rewards [only] for them. "No one, howsoever much almsgiving he has done, even if he sheds his blood for Christ, can be saved, unless he remains in the bosom and unity of the Catholic Church."[26]

The internal quote at the end is one we saw above from Fulgentius. Does the Council endorse all the implications of Fulgentius? Hardly. As we saw, Fulgentius also teaches the damnation of unbaptized infants, and seems to contradict the teaching of Pope St. Stephen on baptism given by heretics. But, more importantly, we can see from the vehemence of Patristic attacks on heretics, *e.g.*, St. Cyprian *Ad Demetrianum*, that the Fathers have in mind those who are in bad faith, who culpably reject the Church. They do not seem to think of those who inculpably fail to find the Church.[27] So from this point on, it becomes largely a question not of doctrine but of objective fact: how many are culpable? Further, this statement was made in 1442, before the 1492 discovery that there was a whole other world. The writers thought that the Gospel had actually reached every creature—it had not—and supposed, as we said, bad faith on the part of those who rejected it.

So we need to think again of the remarks on brinkmanship in the introduction to this appendix.

---

by Boniface VIII himself (DS 870): "For 40 years now we have been a legal expert, and we know that there are two powers ordained by God. . . . We say that in nothing have we wanted to usurp the jurisdiction of the king. . . ."

[25]DS 1051.

[26]DS 1351.

[27]*Cf.* Augustine, *De natura et gratia*, cited above at notes 13 and 14.

Broad Texts of the Magisterium

That our interpretation of the Councils is not forced is guaranteed for us by the fact that the same Magisterium, equally guided by the same Holy Spirit, who does not contradict Himself, also made statements which require this interpretation. As we shall see, these Magisterium texts, by their repetition even on the Ordinary Magisterium level, can be considered infallible, in line with the general teaching of theologians about such repetitions.

Thus Pius IX, in *Quanto conficiamur moerore* of August 10, 1863, taught:

> God ... in His supreme goodness and clemency, by no means allows anyone to be punished with eternal punishments who does not have the guilt of voluntary fault. But it is also a Catholic dogma, that no one outside the Catholic Church can be saved, and that those who are contumacious against the authority of the same Church [and] definitions and who are obstinately [pertinaciter] separated from the unity of this Church and from the Roman Pontiff, successor of Peter, to whom the custody of the vineyard was entrusted by the Savior, cannot obtain eternal salvation.[28]

This is a most significant text. For in it Pius IX stressed both the broad view, and the need of membership. Further, Pius IX is noted for his insistent condemnation of indifferentism, as we see in this passage just quoted, and in his strong-sounding *Quanta cura*. So Pius IX does not deny the obligation to formally enter the Church if one knows the truth—that would be indifferentism—but he still could give a very broad statement which means that if one keeps the moral law as he knows it, somehow the other requirements will be met—though the Pope does not explain how. (At the end of this appendix we will try to explain how.) Yet he does help us by the words "contumacious ... obstinate" which clearly show he has in mind those who culpably reject the Church.

On August 9, 1949, the Holy Office, by order of Pope Pius XII,

---

[28] DS 2866. *Cf.* also W. Most, "Religious Liberty: What the Texts Demand" in *Faith & Reason* 9 (1983) pp. 196-209. Further clarification of the fact that Vatican II does not clash with Pius IX (*cf.* p. 206) is this: Vatican II, in # 7 did make provision for more than just public order when it said that the state must exercise "due custody for public morality," and in #4 it said that the churches must abstain from any action that would involve "improper persuasion aimed at the less intelligent or the poor." Pius IX had said (*cf.* p. 201) that the state must do more than merely defend public order in regard to excesses in religious liberty.

and basing itself on the teaching of Pius XII in his Mystical Body Encyclical (we shall cite the text presently), condemned the error of Leonard Feeney who held that those who failed to enter the Church formally, even with no fault of their own, could not reach salvation. The decree says:

> It is not always required that one be actually incorporated as a member of the Church, but this at least is required: that one adhere to it in wish and desire. It is not always necessary that this be explicit . . . but when a man labors under invincible ignorance, God accepts even an implicit will, called by that name because it is contained in the good disposition of soul in which a man wills to conform his will to the will of God.

Pius XII had said that a man can be "ordered to the Church by a certain desire and wish of which he is not aware [*inscio quodam desiderio ac voto*]," that is, the one contained in the good dispositions mentioned by the Holy Office.[29]

Vatican II taught the same in *Lumen gentium*:

> For they who without their own fault do not know of the Gospel of Christ and His Church, but yet seek God with sincere heart, and try, under the influence of grace, to carry out His will in practice, known to them through the dictate of conscience, can attain eternal salvation.[30]

We note that Vatican II said they need to act under the impulse of actual grace. This grace is always provided for those who do what they can. Further, we notice that Vatican II says they can attain eternal salvation—it does not say they would reach just a sort of limbo of adults, which some who wish to follow Feeney propose, though the Church knows nothing of such an intermediate state for adults.

Broad Texts of the Fathers

Many of the broad texts of the Fathers were given in response to

---

[29]DS 3870 and 3821. Some followers of Feeney insist that the fact that he was finally reconciled to the Church without retracting indicates the Church admitted Feeney had been right all along. This is not true: (1) The broad Magisterium texts (with repetition, so that we can claim infallibility for them) are incompatible with Feeney; (2) He was reconciled when quite old. The fact that he was not pushed to do more is an example of the widespread permissiveness that has done so much harm to the Church in our times.

[30]Vatican II, *Lumen gentium* #16. *Cf. Unitatis redintegratio* #3.

a charge by the pagans: If the Church and Christ are necessary, why did He come so late, and neglect countless millions born before His time? The first attested instance of this claim comes from the pagan Celsus, in his *True Discourse*, probably to be dated 178 A.D. Origen quotes Celsus: "Did God then after so great an age think of making the life of man just, but before He did not care?"[31]

We cannot help thinking of St. Paul himself, who in Rom 3:29-30 asks: "Is He the God of the Jews alone? Is He not also [the God] of the gentiles? Yes, also of the gentiles. For it is one [and the same] God who makes righteous the circumcision [Jews] on the basis of faith, and uncircumcision [non-Jews] through faith." In other words: If God had not provided for those who did not come to know His old revelation, He would seem not to act as their God. The same, of course, applies to the period after Christ, for St. Paul insists with repeated vehemence in Rom 5:15-19 that the redemption is much more abundant than the fall. If God had made provision before Christ, and then left men worse off after Christ, the redemption would be, for such men, not superabundant, but a harsh disaster.

Long before Celsus and before any known literary pagan attacks on Christ, Pope St. Clement had written to Corinth c. 94. A.D.

> Let us go through all generations, and learn that in generation and generation the Master has given a place of repentance to those willing to turn to Him. Noah preached repentance, and those who heard him were saved. Jonah preached repentance to the Ninivites; those who repented for their sins appeased God in praying, and received salvation, even though they were aliens [*allotrioi*] of God.[32]

That is, they did not formally belong to His People of God.

The most suggestive texts come from St. Justin the Martyr, who also wrote before Celsus, but anticipated the objection of Celsus. In his *First Apology* he says he will answer in advance the claim that those who lived before Christ were not answerable: "Christ is the Logos [Divine Word] of whom the whole race of men partake. Those who lived according to Logos are Christians, even if they were considered atheists,

---

[31]Origen, *Against Celsus* 4. 7. PG 11. 1037. For a general view of Celsus, remarkably sympathetic, *cf.* W. den Boer, "La Polemique anti-chrétienne du II Siecle: 'La Doctrine de Verité' de Celse" in *Athenaeum* NS 54 (1976) pp. 309-18. *Cf.* also P. de Labriolle, *La Reaction Païenne,* L'Artisan du Livre, Paris, 1942.

[32] First Clement 7. 5-7. Greek text in Ruiz Bueno, *op. cit.* BAC, pp. 183-84.

such as, among the Greeks, Socrates and Heraclitus."[33] Light on what Justin means by this comes in his *Second Apology* 10:8: "Christ . . . was and is the Logos who is in everyone, and foretold through the prophets the things that were to come, and taught these things in person after becoming like to us in feeling." Similarly in *Second Apology* 13.3, after speaking of Plato, the Stoics and others: "For each of them, through part of the Divine Logos, seeing what was cognate to it [*syngenes*] to it, spoke well."[34]

Danielou gives a helpful interpetation. He holds that Justin borrows Stoic termonology, so as to say that in each man there is a "seed of the Logos" [*sperma tou logou*], resulting from the action of the Logos which gives the seed [*spermatikos logos*]. For the Stoics, the Logos is the immanent principle of all reason, of which the rational faculty in each man is a manifestation: "It is the action of this Logos which gives to each man the capacity to form certain moral and religious conceptions.... That which Socrates and Heraclitus knew is in fact the Word."[35] They knew it partially and obscurely. But yet, Justin does not mean a difference in the content of the truth they saw and the truth that came through revelation. Danielou adds: "The difference is solely one of fulness, certainty, clarity."

We can certainly agree with Danielou that Justin the philosopher utilized the language and even to some extent the framework of ideas borrowed from Stoicism. But we believe, as we shall say later on, that there is still greater depth to Justin's thought. He had seen many philosophies, and now wants to use them in the service of Christ,[36] but without being a merely natural philosopher. The real basis of Justin's thought is probably Romans 2:14-16, in which Paul tells us that God, or the Spirit of God, or of Christ, writes the law on hearts, even the hearts of pagans, *i.e.*, makes known to each one what he should do. (Anthropology today agrees: pagans do know the moral law surprisingly well.) Those who follow the law written on hearts by the Spirit, do follow the Logos, and so can be saved, as Rom 2:16 says. Hence Hacker is not right in saying: "Justin is silent on the possibility for pious gentiles to

[33]Justin, *First Apology* 46. Ruiz Bueno ed. BAC pp. 232-33. Cf. J. Daniélou, Gospel Message and Hellenistic Culture, tr. J. A. Baker, Philadelphia, Westminster, 1973, p. 41. On p. 44 Daniélou says he thinks Socrates and others knew the Person of the Logos.

[34] *Cf.* also N. Pycke, "Connaisance rationelle et connaissance de grâce chez Saint Justin" in Ephemerides Theologicae Lovanienses 37 (1961) pp. 52-85. See also Justin 2. 10. 1-3.

[35]Danielou, *op. cit.* p. 42.

[36]Luneau, *art. cit.*, p. 837 cites *First Apology* 22. 2 where Justin goes so far in using pagan resources as to compare the Logos to Hermes.

reach final consummation in eternity."[37] If Justin says Socrates was Christian, and lived by the Logos, how can such a Christian fail to reach the goal? Again, Rom 2:16 speaks of this final consummation at the judgment.

We saw above that Hermas gives us the odd view of baptism after death. Yet in *Vision* 2.4.1 he shows a much broader view. The angel asks Hermas who he thinks the old woman is from whom he received the little book. Hermas opines it is the Sibyl. The angel corrects him: "You are wrong. . . . It is the Church. I said to him: Why then an old woman? He said: Because she was created first of all; for this reason she is an old woman, and because of her the world was established."[38] So the Church has always existed. Creation itself was carried out, it seems, in anticipation of her coming to be.

The so-called Second Epistle of Clement—regardless of its authorship (it seems to have been written about 150 A.D.)—agrees: "The books of the prophets and the apostles [say] that the Church is not [only] now, but from the beginning. She was spiritual, like also our Jesus. She was manifested in the last days to save us."[39]

St. Irenaeus, as we saw, has one passage which might be considered restrictive. But in many other places he takes a very broad view: "There is one and the same God the Father and His Logos, always assisting the human race, with varied arrangements, to be sure, and doing many things, and saving from the beginning those who are saved, for they are those who love God, and, according to their age [*genean*] follow His Logos."[40]

We note Irenaeus speaks of the human race, of the various time periods, of various arrangements, not just of the Hebrews and the arrangement God made with them. Further, although Irenaeus was not fond of speculation, yet he wrote that those who follow the Logos are saved. This of course sounds like Justin's *First Apology* 46, cited above. Grillmeier observes: "In his view, the incarnation is merely the conclusion in an immense series of manifestations of the Logos, which had their beginning in the creation of the world."[41]

---

[37]Hacker, *art. cit.*, p. 258.

[38]*Cf.* Patrick V. Dias, *Kirche in der Schrift und im 2. Jahrhndert*, in *Handbuch der Dogmengieschichte*, Herder, Freiburg, 1974, III. 3a, pp. 118-19; and Kelly, *op. cit.*, p. 191.

[39] Second Clement 14. 2. Ruiz Bueno ed. BAC, pp. 366-67.

[40]Irenaeus, *Against Heresies* 4. 28. 2. SC 100, p. 759. *Cf.* also Ignacio Escribano-Alberca, "Die Heilsökonomische Enthaltung des Glaubens bei Irenaeus und Tertullian" in *Das Dasein im Glauben*, *Handbuch der Dogmengeschichte*, Herder, Freiburg, 1974, I, 2a, pp. 32-38, esp. p. 33.

[41]Aloys Grillmeier, *Christ in Christian Tradition* (tr. J. Bowden) John

In the same vein, we also read in Irenaeus: "For the Son, administering all things for the Father, completes [His work] from the beginning to the end.... For the Son, assisting to His own creation from the beginning, reveals the Father to all to whom He wills."[42] And similarly, as if answering Celsus:

> Christ came not only for those who believed from the time of Tiberius Caesar, nor did the Father provide only for those who are now, but for absolutely all men from the beginning, who according to their ability, feared and loved God and lived justly ... and desired to see Christ and to hear His voice.[43]

Clement of Alexandria has many statements of a broad nature: "From what has been said, I think it is clear that there is one true Church, which is really ancient, into which those who are just according to design are enrolled."[44] Similarly: "Before the coming of the Lord, philosophy was necessary for justification to the Greeks; now it is useful for piety ... for it brought the Greeks to Christ as the law did the Hebrews."[45]

Daniélou makes incisive comments. First he observes that while Justin spoke of a common action of the Logos before Christ, Clement distinguishes two patterns: "Clement presents philosophy as representing for the Greeks a counterpart to the Law." So that some Greeks received only a common knowledge derived from reason, while others received the action of the Logos proper. So Daniélou cites *Stromata* 7.2: "To the one he gave the commandments, to the others, philosophy ... with the result that everyone who did not believe was without excuse."[46]

Hacker, however, says: "To attain final salvation it is indispensable that the souls of the righteous gentiles in Hades should do penance

---

Knox, Atlanta, 2d ed. 1975. I. p. 103. *Cf.* Luneau, *art. cit.* p. 832: "Faut-il rapeller comment, pour Irénée, la connaissance de Dieu demeure inscrite au fond du coeur humain et prépare sa venue." ("We should recall how, for Irenaeus, the knowledge of God remains inscribed in the depth of the human heart and prepares for His coming.") Strangely, A. Orbe, in an otherwise excellent study, *Antropologia de San Ireneo*, BAC, 1969, although he devotes pp. 502-15 to answering the objection of Celsus, does not seem to notice this point. *Cf.* also Danielou, *op. cit.* pp. 361-64; and P. V. Dias, *op. cit.* p. 161.

42 *Against Heresies* 4. 6. 7. SC 100, p. 453. *Cf.* also *ibid.* 5. 18. 2.

43 *Ibid.* 4. 22. 2. SC 100, p. 689.

44 Clement of Alexandria, *Stromata* 7. 17. PG 9. 552.

45 *Stromata* 1. 5. SC 1965 ed. (no number given) p. 65. *Cf. Stromata* 1. 20.

46 Danielou, *op. cit.* p. 52.

and accept faith in ChriSt. "[47] To be consistent, he should have added a requirement of baptism, thinking of *Stromata* 2.9, where Clement quotes at length the passage we saw above from Hermas. But it seems that Hacker here has made a methodological slip, in trying to force disparate statements in Clement into a synthesis. As we have been seeing, two kinds of texts are found in many writers, Clement included. Clement, like the others, did not really make a synthesis of the two series; he just stated each separately.

Clement, however, does seem to mean final salvation for gentiles, for he also says in *Stromata* 1.20.99:

> Philosophy of itself made the Greeks just, though not to total justice [*ouk eis ten katholou de dikaiosynen*]; it is found to be a helper to this [perfect justice], like the first and second steps for one ascending to the upper part of the house, and like the elementary teacher for the [future] philosopher.

We notice two things here: (1) Philosophy once did make the Greeks just; (2) it was not total justice. What this means is made clear by the comparison of the steps for one ascending to the upper part of the house. Philosophy really did make just, but it did not lead the Greeks to the highest levels, that to which Clement's "gnostics" (perfect Christians) attain.

Hacker later [48] helps our interpretation by saying that Clement is bringing out the implications of what St. John means in the opening of his Gospel, "when speaking of the light of the Logos that illuminates every man." We think again of Romans 2:15. Escribano-Alberca adds that for Clement, "Eternal life is reached through an obedience according to the Logos."[49]

Origen, Clement's great pupil, goes farther in the same direction. J. N. D. Kelly observes [50] that at Alexandria interest tended to focus on the invisible Church of the perfect Christian, whom Clement would call the true gnostic, and to identify this spiritual Church with Christ's mystical body. Kelly adds that in Origen: "In this mystical sense, Christ's

---

[47]Hacker, *art. cit.* p. 261.

[48]*Ibid.* p. 264.

[49]Escribano-Alberca, *op. cit.* p. 50. *Cf. ibid.* p. 51: "Gott wird durch keinerlei apodiktisch-beweisende Wissenschaft sonder nur durch die Gnade seines offenbarenden Logos erkannt. " ("God becomes known not by any kind of apodictically proved knowledge, but only through the grace of His revealing Logos.") *Cf.* also A. Brontese, *La Soteria in Clemente Alessandrino*, Universita Gregoriana, Roma, 1972, p. 283; *cf.* also p. 278.

[50]Kelly, *op. cit.* p. 201.

body comprises the whole of humanity, indeed the whole of creation."[51] Origen even becomes so bold as to assert that the heavenly Church existed since and even before creation: "Do not think I speak of the spouse or the Church [only] from the coming of the Savior in the flesh, but from the beginning of the human race, in fact, to seek out the origin of this mystery more deeply with Paul as leader, even before the foundation of the world."[52] Origen[53] has in mind Ephesians 1:4, in which he interprets the Greek *katabole* as meaning a fall from a better state. He thinks we were all in a world of spirits before this life. According to diverse merits, some became men, angels, devils, or stars in the sky. Origen feels he needs to suppose a sin on our part even before this life to account for human afflictions.[54]

It is Origen who gives us the objection of Celsus: "Did God then after so great an age think of making just the life of man, but before He did not care?"[55] To which Origen replies:

> To this we will say that there never was a time when God did not will to make just the life of men. But He always cared, and gave occasions of virtue to make the reasonable one right. For generation by generation this wisdom of God came to souls it found holy and made them friends of God and prophets.

Similarly, in his commentary on Romans 2:14-16 Origen said that the law written on hearts was not the law about sabbaths and new moons, but:

> that they must not commit murder or adultery, not steal, not speak false testimony, that they honor father and mother, and similar things . . . and it is shown that each one is to be judged not according to a privilege of nature, but by his own thoughts he is accused or excused, by the testimony of his conscience.[56]

The remark about the "privilege of nature" means that it does not matter whether they be Jews or not. There is no respecting of persons with

---

[51] *Ibid.* p. 202.

[52] Origen, *In Cant.* 2. 11-12. PG 13. 134.

[53] This accords with the belief of Origen that eventually all will be saved—for which membership in the Church is required.

[54] *Cf.* Hermann Josef Vogt, *Das Kirchenverständnis des Origenes*, in *Bonner Beiträge zur Kirchengeschichte* 4, Böhlau Verlag, Koln, Wien, 1974, pp. 205-10, and Damboriena, *op. cit.* , pp. 33- 37. *Cf.* also Origen, *In Matt.* 51. 870. PG 13. 1679.

[55] Origen, *Against Celsus* 4. 7. PG 11. 1037.

[56] Origen, *On Romans II. 9-10.* PG 14. 892-93.

God.

Origen also has a remarkable line on pagan sacrifices: "Since God wants grace to abound, He sees fit to be present. . . . He is present not to the [pagan] sacrifices, but to the one who comes to meet Him, and there He gives His word."[57] We have only the Latin text of Origen here; the Greek presumably would have read *Logos*, a thought reminiscent of his teacher Clement, and, more remotely, of Justin.

The objection voiced by Celsus is faced most explicitly in the so-called *Acts of Archelaus with Manes*, which Quasten[58] thinks really did not take place, but were composed by Hegemonius of Chalcedon, of whom we know nothing further. The date is the first half of the 4th century, probably after the Council of Nicea. Archelaus argued with Manes about the fate of those who lived in ancient times. As to these Archelaus asserts:

> From the creation of the world He has always been with just men. . . . Were they not made just from the fact that they kept the law, 'Each one of them showing the work of the law on their hearts. . . ?' For when someone who does not have the law does by nature the things of the law, this one, not having the law, is a law for himself. . . . For if we judge that a man is made just without the works of the law . . . how much more will they attain justice who fulfilled the law containing those things which are expedient for men?

As we shall see later, it is especially significant that Hegemonius ties his belief to Romans 2:15, "They show the work of the law written on their hearts"—written, really, even though the pagans did not know it, by the Logos, of whom Justin spoke.

The same objection about God's care in former times is answered also by Arnobius:

> But, they say: If Christ was sent by God for this purpose, to deliver unhappy souls from the destruction of ruin—what did former ages deserve, which before His coming were consumed in the condition of mortality? . . . Put aside these cares, and leave the questions you do not understand; for royal mercy was imparted to them, and the divine benefits ran equally through all. They were conserved, they were liberated, and they put aside the sort and condition of mortality.[59]

---

[57] Origen, *Homily on Numbers* 16. 1. PG 12. 691. *Cf.* Luneau, *art. cit.*, p. 835.

[58] J. Quasten, *Patrology*, Spectrum, Utrecht/Antwerp, 1966. III. pp. 357-58.

[59] Arnobius, *Against the Nations* 2. 63. PL 5. 909-10. *Cf.* Damboriena, *op. cit.* p. 29

The first Church historian, Eusebius of Caesarea, takes a similar stand:

> But even if we [Christians] are certainly new, and this really new name of Christians is just recently known among the nations, yet our life and mode of conduct, in accord with the precepts of religion, has not been recently invented by us; but from the first creation of man, so to speak, it is upheld by natural inborn concepts of the ancient men who loved God, as we will here show.... But if someone would describe as Christians those who are testified to as having been righteous [going back] from Abraham to the first man, he would not hit wide of the truth.[60]

Christian concepts, then, according to Eusebius, are as it were inborn, and so one could even say there were Christians from the beginning. This is possible, we may infer, since these early people, without recognizing the fact, were following the Logos—we think again of Justin's First *Apology* 46. The large, even cosmic role Eusebius assigns to the Logos, as shown by Muñoz Palacios[61] seems presupposed.

In his oration at the funeral of his father, a convert who became a bishop, St. Gregory of Nazianzus, said:

> He was ours even before he was of our fold. His way of living made him such. For just as many of ours are not with us, whose life makes them other from our body [the Church], so many of those outside belong to us, who by their way of life anticipate the faith, and need [only] the name, having the reality [*ergon*].[62]

In a similar vein, in his oration in praise of his sister Gorgonia, he said: "Her whole life was a purification for her, and a perfecting. She had indeed the regeneration of the Spirit, and the assurance of this from her previous life. And, to speak boldly, the mystery [baptism] was for her practically only the seal, not the grace."

St. John Chrysostom, in commenting on Romans 2:14-16, explains that the words "by nature" mean "according to natural reasoning":

> For this reason they are wonderful, he says, because they did not need the law, and they show all the works of the law.... Do you not see how again he makes present that day and brings it near ... and showing that

[60]Eusebius, *Church History* 1. 1. 4. PG 20. 77. *Cf.* Orbe, *op. cit.* p. 507.

[61] R. Muñoz Palacios, "La Mediaci6n del Logos preexistente a la encarnacion en Eusebio de Cesárea" in *Estudios Eclesiásticos* 43 (1968) pp. 381-414.

[62]Gregory of Nazianzus, *Oration 18*. 6. PG 35. 992; and *Oration 8*. 20. PG 35. 812. *Cf.* Luneau, *art. cit.*, 831-32.

> they should rather be honored who without the law hastened to carry out the things of the law?.... Conscience and reasoning suffice in place of the law. Through these things he showed again that God made man self-sufficient [*autarke*] in regard to the choice of virtue and fleeing evil.... He shows that even in these early times and before the giving of the law, men enjoyed complete providence [*pronoia*]. For "what is knowable of God" was clear to them, and what was good and what was evil they knew.[63]

In his Homilies on John, Chrysostom takes up the recurring objection of Celsus: "When, then, the gentiles accuse us saying: What was Christ doing in former times, not taking care... ? We will reply: Even before He was in the world, He took thought for His works, and was known to all who were worthy."[64] Here Chrysostom does better than in the previous passage, where he seemed to say men knew moral requirements through reason. For now he seems to mean that as Logos He made Himself known interiorly. Really, the knowledge pagans have of the moral code can be called a knowledge of the natural law, but they do not really reach it by explicit reasoning, but by a mysterious inner knowledge, which is the effect of the work of the Holy Spirit, who is the Spirit of ChriSt. Further, that natural law does coincide with the will of God.

In his comment on Romans 2:29 Chrysostom adds: "He means clearly not an idolatrous Greek, but a God-fearing one." He seems to think all idolators are culpable; a factual, not a doctrinal conclusion. He is perhaps influenced by the words of Rom 1:20-22.

The thought of St. Ambrose is less sharply focused: "Our price is the blood of ChriSt. ... Therefore He brought the means of health to all so that whoever perishes, must ascribe the cause of his death to himself, for he was unwilling to be cured when he had a remedy.... For the mercy of Christ is clearly proclaimed on all."[65] Ambrose hardly means that in general God has set up as it were a reservoir of salvation: if someone without personal fault should not reach it, he would be loSt. That was the view of some Thomists many centuries later. Instead, Ambrose says that the one lost "must ascribe the cause of his death to himself, for he was unwilling."

St. Augustine[66] shows remarkable fidelity to the point of method

---

[63]John Chrysostom, *On Romans II*. 5. PG 60. 428-29. *Cf.* Damboriena, *op. cit.*, pp. 52-53.

[64]*Idem*, *Homilies on John* 8. 1. PG 59. 67.

[65]Ambrose, *On Cain and Abel* 2. 3. 11. PL 14. 364-65.

[66] *Cf.* Kelly, *op. cit.*, pp. 411-12, 416; Damboriena, *op. cit.*, pp. 41- 48; Patout Burns, *art. cit.* pp. 608-10.

we stressed at the start of this study, in that he has clear examples of texts of both kinds, as we shall see presently. But it is helpful to notice what he does similarly, on a closely related question, that of predestination. His *massa damnata* theory is well known, in connection with which he writes that most humans are lost: "In it [punishment] there are many more than in [grace] so that in this way it may be shown what was due to all."[67] Further, he insists that which side a person will be on does not at all depend on prevision of merits.[68] Yet at other times, he teaches that the negative decision, reprobation, depends first of all on personal demerits, not just on original sin. (He nowhere, however, makes the positive decision, predestination, depend on merits.) Thus in *De diversis quaestionibus* he says that those who came to the Gospel dinner could not have come without being called, but yet, "those who were unwilling to come should attribute it to no one but themselves"[69]—therefore, not to God's prior desertion. Again, in his debate with Felix the Manichean, Felix asked why the lost sinners were not cleansed. Augustine replied: "Because they did not will it." Felix, surprised, asks: " 'Because they did not will it'—did you say this?" Augustine replied: "I said this: Because they did not will it."[70] In the *massa damnata* context the basic reason would have been desertion by God, followed by their deserting Him. So in *De correptione et gratia* he speaks of sinners who do not persevere: "They desert [God] and are deserted."[71] In *massa damnata*, he would have said: God deserted them, then they deserted Him. Thus Augustine implies a theory quite different from *massa damnata*, one in which predestination is without merits, but reprobation depends on demerits.[72]

In his *De civitate Dei*, Augustine also shows two different images of that city, which, as J. N. D. Kelly points out, he never reconciled.[73] On the one hand, in the final book 22, especially in chapter 30, he speaks of heaven as the final end of the City of God. Yet in 16.2 he identifies the Church and the City of God, though he knows that not all in the Church will be saved (18.28;20, 5, 9). Further, in 18.47 he insists:

---

[67]Augustine, *De civitate Dei* 21. 12, ed. B. Dombart, Lipsiae, Teubner, 1877, II. p. 514.

[68]Augustine, *De praedestinatione sanctorum* 17. 34. PL 44. 985-86.

[69]*Idem, De diversis quaestionibus* LXXXIII 68. 5. PL 40. 73.

[70]*Idem, De actis cum Felice Manichaeo* 2. 8. PL 42. 540.

[71]*Idem. De correptione et gratia* 13. 42. PL 44. 942.

[72]For analysis of all texts of Augustine, *cf.* W. G. Most, *op. cit.*, pp. 234-42.

[73] *Cf.* Kelly, *op. cit.*, p. 416; R. F. Evans, *One and Holy. The Church in Latin Patristic Thought*, S. P. C. K. London, 1972, pp. 100-01; and J. O. Meara, *Charter of Christendom. The Significance of the City of God*, Macmillan, N. Y. 1961, pp. 52-53.

> Nor do I think the Jews would dare to argue that no one pertained to God except the Israelites, from the time that Israel came to be.... they cannot deny that there were certain men even in other nations who pertained to the true Israelites, the citizens of the fatherland above, not by earthly but by heavenly association.[74]

He cites the case of Job, and earlier, in 18.23, the Sibyl of Cumae.

In *Retractations* Augustine explains this, following the tradition begun in First Clement:[75] "This very thing which is now called the Christian religion existed among the ancients, nor was it lacking from the beginning of the human race, until Christ Himself came in the flesh, when the true religion, that already existed, began to be called Christian."[76] Earlier, in his Epistle 102, Augustine takes up the objection of Celsus, repeated by Porphyry:

> Wherefore since we call Christ the Word [Logos] of God, through whom all things were made ... under whose rule [was/is] every creature, spiritual and corporal ... so those from the beginning of the human race, who believed in Him and understood Him somewhat [*utcumque*] and lived according to His precepts devoutly and justly, whenever and wherever they were, beyond doubt they were saved through Him.[77]

And further on in Epistle 102.15: "And yet from the beginning of the human race there were not lacking persons who believed in Him, from Adam up to Moses, both in the very people of Israel ... and in other nations before He came in the flesh."[78]

We notice how Augustine, in line with so many earlier writers, ties his answer to the Logos who administered all things even before the incarnation, so that those who followed Him, the Logos, were saved—we think again of the words of St. Justin on Socrates and Heraclitus, whom he even called Christians.

As Jurgens says,[79] the *De vocatione omnium gentium* is now widely admitted to be by St. Prosper, secretary to Pope Leo I, and an ardent disciple of St. Augustine. It is debated whether and to what extent Prosper modified Augustine's ideas on predestination. De Letter thinks

---

[74] Augustine, *De civitate Dei* 18. 47. Dombart II pp. 330-31.

[75] *Idem, Retractations* 1. 13. 3. CC 57. p. 37.

[76] *Cf.* Hacker, *art. cit.*, p. 272.

[77] Augustine, *Epist.* 102. 11-12. PL 33. 374. Cf #15; De Labriolle, p. 274.

[78] Augustine, *Enarrationes* Ps 57. 1, CC 39. 708-09; *De peccatorum meritis et remissione* 1. 10-11; *Enarr. in Ps.* 118. 25. 4. CC 40. 1750.

[79] W. A. Jurgens, *The Faith of the Early Fathers*, Liturgical Press, Collegeville, 1979, III, pp. 194-95.

Prosper did not clearly break: "St. Prosper ... is struggling to break away from the influence of the Augustinian predestination.... [O]wing to his inability to free himself fully from it, his idea of the general grace, universally given to all, fails to solve the problem."[80] De Letter adds that if Prosper had said that the sole reason why the special graces were not given to some would be because they refused them, Prosper would have made a great step forward.

Jurgens on the other hand holds Prosper did break with Augustine: "For Prosper, election is the result of God's foreknowledge of the elect, and is the only answer to the mysterious question of why God chooses, elects or predestines...."[81]

Let us see the texts of St. Prosper himself: "... according to it [Scripture] ... we believe and devoutly confess that never was the care of divine providence lacking to the totality of men."[82] And also: "To these however [who have not yet heard of Christ] that general measure of help, which is always given from above to all men, is not denied." We confess these texts are not fully clear, for De Letter can claim that Prosper means merely that general grace is offered to all, but that without cause, the added help needed for salvation is denied to some.

But Prosper does become clear elsewhere: "For this reason they were not predestined [namely] because they were foreseen as going to be such as a result of voluntary transgression.... For they were not deserted by God so as to desert God; but they deserted and were deserted."[83] Within Augustine's classic *massa damnata* theory the first step is God's desertion of a man—then man's desertion of God comes second. But Prosper[84] inverts that order. Really, as we saw above, Augustine has two theories[85]—the one, the massa damnata, which is often stated explicity; the other, never stated explicitly, but only implied, in several texts, ranging in date from 388 to 426, and at many points in between. St. Prosper is really breaking with the *massa damnata*, but is being entirely faithful to the implicit theory of Augustine, who also wrote, in *De correptione et gratia* 13.42: "Either they lie under the sin which they contracted originally by generation ... or they receive the grace of God, but are temporary, and do not persevere. They desert and are de-

---

[80] St. Prosper of Aquitaine, *The Call of All Nations*, translated & annotated by P. De Letter, Newman, Westminister, 1952, p. 17.

[81] Jurgens, *op. cit.*, III. p. 195.

[82] Prosper, *op. cit.*, 2. 5. PL 51. 652; and *ibid.* 2. 17. PL 51. 704.

[83] Prosper, *Responsiones ad capitula obiectionum Gallorum* 3. PL 51. 158-59. *Cf.* Hacker, *art. cit.*, pp. 277-78.

[84] More texts and analysis in W. G. Most, *op. cit.* pp. 242-43.

[85] On the two theories of Augustine, *cf.* again Most *op. cit.*, pp. 225-43.

serted." Prosper too said, as we saw: "They desert and are deserted." Again, Augustine wrote, in LXXXIII.68.5: "Nor should they who were unwilling to come [to the banquet in the Gospel] attribute it to anyone but themselves." But in *massa damnata*, the ultimate reason would be God's decision to desert. Similarly, Augustine wrote, in *De peccatorum meritis et remissione* 2.17.26: "It is from the grace of God which helps the wills of men that what was hidden becomes known, and that which did not please becomes sweet. The reason why they were not helped is likewise in themselves, not in God."

Hence it is proper to take the first text we saw of St. Prosper (at note 82) as opening salvation in some way to all, so that, by implication, the requirement of membership in the Church will be provided for.

We do not know whether St. Nilus was a former officer of the court of Theodosius who later withdrew to a monastery on Sinai, or whether he was superior of a monastery at Ancyra and a disciple of St. John Chrysostom. However, the following passage from St. Nilus is at least partly in accord with the thought of St. John Chrysostom which we saw above:

> In every nation, the one who fears God and does justice is acceptable to Him. For it is clear that such a one is acceptable to God and is not to be cast aside, who at his own right time flees to the worship of the blessed knowledge of God. God will not allow him to die in ignorance, but will lead him to the truth, and will enlighten him with the light of knowledge, like Cornelius.[86]

St. Nilus does, it seems, think salvation in each case is to be accomplished by being brought to the visible Church.

St. Cyril of Alexandria has a very significant passage:

> For if there is one over all, and there is no other besides Him, He would be master of all, because He was Maker of all. For He is also the God of the gentiles, and has fully satisfied by laws implanted in their hearts, which the Maker has engraved in the hearts of all. For when the gentiles, [Paul] says, not having the law, do by nature the things of the law, they show the work of the law written on their hearts. But since He is not only the Maker and God of the Jews, but also of the gentiles . . . He sees fit by His providence to care not only for those who are of the blood of Israel, but also for all those upon the earth.[87]

[86] Nilus, *Epist.* 1. 154, to Maximian. PG 79. 145.

[87] Cyril of Alexandria, *Against Julian* 3. 107. PG 76. 665. *Cf.* Kelly, *op. cit.*, p. 403.

St. Cyril bases his thought on Romans 3:29, where Paul argues that God, since He is God of the gentiles too, must have made provision for them. Cyril suggests that it seems that He did this by way of engraving the law on their hearts (Rom 2:15).

Theodoret of Cyrus, in commenting on Rom 2:14-16, makes clear that he holds, with St. Paul, that some gentiles, even though not members visibly of the People of God, are saved:

> For they who, before the Mosaic law, adorned their life with devout reasonings and good actions, testify that the divine law called for action, and they became lawgivers for themselves. . . . . He [St. Paul] shows that the law of nature was written on hearts. . . . According to this image, let us describe the future judgment and the conscience of those accepting the charge and proclaiming the justice of the decision.[88]

Theodoret also takes up the classic objection of Celsus. In his *Remedy for Greek Diseases*, he writes:

> But if you say: Why then did not the Maker of all fulfill this long ago? You are blaming even the physicians, since they keep the stronger medicines for last; having used the milder things first, they bring out the stronger things laSt. The all-wise Healer of our souls did this too. After employing various medicines . . . finally He brought forth this all-powerful and saving medicine.[89]

While he holds that God did not give such great helps before Christ, Theodoret yet holds God did take care of humans, by way of "different medicines."

Pope St. Leo the Great is a bit less clear than some, yet, when we consider his words in the context of the tradition we have seen developing, they seem to mean that there always was a Church:

> So God did not take care of human affairs by a new plan, or by late mercy, but from the foundation of the world He established one and the same cause of salvation for all. For the grace of God by which the totality of the saints always has been justified was increased when Christ was born, but did not begin [then].[90]

---

[88]Theodoret of Cyrus, *Interpretatio Epist. Ad Rom.* 2. 14-16. PG 82. 70-72.

[89]*Idem, Remedy for Greek Diseases* 6. 85-86. SC 57, pp. 284-85. *Cf.* Hacker, *art. cit.*, pp. 268-70.

[90]Leo the Great, *Sermon* 23. 4. PL 54. 202. *Cf.* also *Sermon* 31. 7 and 76. 3. *Cf.* also Damboriena, *op. cit.*, pp. 48-49.

Pope St. Gregory the Great, a strong admirer of St. Augustine, also speaks of Christ preaching to the dead: "When He descended to the underworld, the Lord delivered from the prison only those who while they lived in the flesh He had kept through His grace in faith and good works."[91] But Gregory does not mention a baptism in the underworld, nor does Augustine. Yet his conviction is clear that God somehow made provision for those who did not formally enter the People of God.

But Pope Gregory also follows the tradition we saw in Augustine and earlier, of making the Church exist from the beginning:

> The passion of the Church began already with Abel, and there is one Church of the elect, of those who precede, and of those who follow. . . . They were, then, outside, but yet not divided from the holy Church, because in mind, in work, in preaching, they already held the sacraments of faith, and saw that loftiness of Holy Church. . . .[92]

Primasius, Bishop of Hadrumetum, writing about 560 A.D., in his commentary on Romans, does not explicitly mention the Church, yet he makes clear, with Paul, that some who were not visibly members of the first people of God were just, and will be saved at the judgment:

> "By nature they do the things of the law. . . ." He [Paul] speaks either of those who keep the law of nature, who do not do to others what they do not want to be done to themselves; or, that even the gentiles naturally praise the good and condemn the wicked, which is the work of the law; or, of those who even now, when they do anything good, profess that they have received from God the means of pleasing God. . . . "And their thoughts in turn accusing or even defending, on the day when God will judge the hidden things of men." He speaks of altercations of thought . . . and according to this we are to be judged on the day of the Lord.[93]

St. John Damascene, often considered the last of the Fathers, gives us a possibly helpful text:

> The creed teaches us to believe also in one holy Catholic and Apostolic church of God. The Catholic Church cannot be only apostolic, for the all-powerful might of her Head, which is Christ, is able through the Apostles to save the whole world. So there is a Holy Catholic Church of God, the assembly of the Holy Fathers who are from the ages, of the pa-

---

[91]Gregory the Great, *Epist.* VII. 15. To George and Theodore CC 140, p. 465. *Cf.* Damboriena, *op. cit.*, 49-50.

[92]*Idem, Homilies on Ezechiel* 2. 3. 16. CC 142. p. 248.

[93]Primasius, *On Romans* 2. 14-16. PL 68. 423-24.

> triarchs, of prophets, apostles, evangelists, martyrs, to which are added all the gentiles who believe the same way [*homothymadon*][94]

We note St. John says that the power of Christ can save the whole world, and that it extends even to "the Holy Fathers who are from the ages" before ChriSt. He may mean the power of Christ even before the incarnation worked inasmuch as the Logos was present to all.[95]

Without pretending to give at all a complete survey, yet it may be worthwhile to give two samples from the post-patristic age.

Haymo, Bishop of Halberstadt (died 853), in his commentary on Romans 2:14-16, says that the words of Paul that the gentiles show the work of the law written on hearts can be understood in two ways. First:

> They show surely that they have the natural law written on their hearts, and they are the law for themselves: because they do the things that the law teaches, even though it was not given to them. For example, the Saracens who have neither the law of Moses nor of the Gospel, while by nature they keep the law, do not commit murder, or commit adultery, or other things, which the law written within them contains; they are a law to themselves.... In the second way: When the gentiles ... naturally do the things ... because they have the same law of Moses written on their hearts by the inspiration of Almighty God ... "their conscience bearing witness to them, and their thoughts in turn accusing or even defending." And when will this be? "On the day when the Lord will judge the hidden things of men" according to my Gospel.[96]

So, Haymo thinks even some Saracens of his day are being saved!

Similarly, Oecumenius, commenting on the same passage of Romans, around 990 A.D., gave the same explanation:

> "They do the things of the law" using the reasonings of nature for just actions. These are wonderful, not needing a teacher, being their own lawgivers and fulfillers of the legislation.... "Their conscience bearing witness to them," for it is enough in place of the law to have their own conscience testifying for them.... At that judgment we do not need external accusers or witnesses ... but each one's own reasonings and conscience either accuses or defends.[97]

---

[94]John Damascene, *Against Iconoclasts* 11. PG 96. 1357.
[95]*Cf.* Damboriena, *op.cit.*, p. 85.
[96]Haymo, *Exposition on Romans* 2. 14-16. PL 117. 381.
[97]Oecumenius, *On Romans* 2. 14-16. PG 118. 356-60.

Summary and Conclusion

We found restrictive texts in Hermas, St. Justin, St. Irenaeus, Clement of Alexandria, Origen, St. Cyprian, Lactantius, St. Augustine, St. Cyril of Alexandria, and St. Fulgentius. There are also five Magisterium texts that seem restrictive.

We found broad texts much more widely. Only three of the above ten Fathers who have restrictive texts lack broad texts: St. Cyprian, Lactantius, and St. Fulgentius. All others, plus many more, do have them.

Broad texts are found in: First Clement, St. Justin, Hermas, Second Clement, St. Irenaeus, Clement of Alexandria, Origen, Hegemonius, Arnobius, Eusebius of Caesarea, St. Gregory of Nazianzus, St. John Chrysostom, St. Ambrose, St. Augustine, St. Prosper, St. Nilus, St. Cyril of Alexandria, Theodoret, St. Leo the Great, St. Gregory the Great, Primasius, and St. John Damascene. We added two samples of later writers with broad texts: Haymo and Oecumenius.

We find many of the Fathers specifically answering the charge of Celsus (why did Christ come so late)—St. Justin, St. Irenaeus, Origen, Hegemonius, Arnobius, St. John Chrysostom, St. Augustine (though not all explicitly mention Celsus).

Very many speak of the Church as always existing: Hermas, Second Clement, Clement of Alexandria, Origen, Eusebius, St. Augustine, St. Leo, St. Gregory, St. John Damascene.

The idea that theophanies in the Old Testament times were really by the Logos is very common among the Fathers. So it is not strange that we find many of the Fathers speak of the Logos as present to men to save them: St. Justin, St. Irenaeus, St. John Chrysostom, St. Augustine.

Closely related is the idea that pagans can be saved if they follow the law written on hearts by the Spirit of Christ, or the Logos, as in Romans 2:15:[98] Origen, Hegemonius, St. John Chrysostom, St. Cyril of Alexandria, Theodoret, Primasius.

What is the common denominator? Though not all mention Celsus specifically, it seems that underlying all broad texts is the conviction that somehow in the past, God did provide for all men—this is something sometimes explicitly tied to Romans 3:29-30 (He is not the God only of the Jews). This is the fact of which all seem convinced. But just how that provision is worked out is less clear, and often the writers do not attempt to explain.

Yet we can build on these data to reconcile the two kinds of texts,

[98]On the general problems of the exegesis of Romans 2. 14-16 *cf.* W. Most, "Focusing in St. Paul. A Resolution of Difficulties," in *Faith & Reason* II. 1976, pp. 47-70, esp. pp. 57-61.

so as to solve the problem of "Extra Ecclesiam nulla salus." St. Justin gives the best starting point. He says that those who followed the Logos, who is in each person, were Christians, even though they were considered atheists, such as Socrates and Heraclitus. As we said above, Justin was using the language of Stoicism—part of the usual tactics of apologists, who were eager to show the similarity of Christian thought to that of the best philosophers. But does Justin really mean to give us just Stoicism or to play on the vagueness of the word Logos (Word/reason)? Of course not. So if we ask in precisely what way the Logos was present to Socrates and others, we could utilize the insights of many other Fathers: The Logos was there to write the law on hearts (cf.Rom 2:15). Modern experimental anthropology concurs; pagans do know the moral law surprisingly well. How do they know it? It seems to become known in some interior way, though not by mere reasoning. That interior way, even though the pagans did not recognize what it was, is God, or the Spirit of God, or the Spirit of Christ, or the Logos—all mean the same. St. Paul clearly has this thought, for in Rom 2:15 he obviously echoes Jeremiah 31:33 (prophecy of new covenant): "I will write my law on their hearts."

So God did and does indeed write His law on the hearts of men. Objectively, this is done by the Spirit of God, the divine Logos, as we said. As Justin says, those who follow the Logos were and are Christians.

Now if we add still other words of St. Paul in Romans we can go further. In Rom 8:9: "Anyone who does not have the Spirit of Christ, does not belong to Him." So, those who do have the Spirit of Christ, and follow the Logos as He writes the law on their hearts, do indeed belong to ChriSt. But still further, according to the same Paul, to belong to Christ means to be a member of Christ (*cf.* 1 Cor 12:27). Again further, to be a member of Christ, is also to be a member of His Church for the Church is the Body of ChriSt.

So we seem to have found the much needed solution: Those who follow the Spirit of Christ, the Logos who writes the law on their hearts, are Christians, are members of Christ, are members of His Church. They may lack indeed external adherence; they may never have heard of the Church. But yet, in the substantial sense, without formal adherence, they do belong to Christ, to His Church.

They can also be called sons of God, for Romans 8:14 adds: "All who are led by the Spirit are sons of God." As sons, of course, they are coheirs with Christ (Rom 8:17), and so will inherit the kingdom with Him.

We can even add that objectively—though probably those who

drafted the text or voted for it did not realize it—Vatican II taught the same thing: "For all who belong to Christ, having His Spirit, coalesce into one Church."[99]

In saying this, we are not contradicting the teaching of Pius XII (Mystical Body Encyclical). He spoke of some as being ordered to the Church by a certain desire which they did not recognize. We admit that. To add to truth is not to deny truth.

Three possible objections remain. First: is our solution indifferentist? Not at all. For we insist that even these people who belong without formal adherence have the objective obligation to formally enter the Church. It is only their ignorance that excuses them. As we saw, Pius IX, so strong against indifferentism, concurs in our conclusion that somehow these people can be saved.

Second: are we proposing mere naturalism, *i.e.*, if one is naturally good, that is enough? Not at all. First the natural law is God's law too; second, these people objectively follow the Spirit of God, and so are on the supernatural plane; finally, they also have available actual graces, and use them, as the Vatican II's broad text said. God always offers actual graces to those who do what they can.

Thirdly and finally: some would say that the Fathers and the Magisterium speak only of people before Christ—after He came, formal entrance into the Church is necessary. We reply: First, the Magisterium texts speak in the present tense, not the paSt. Thus, Pius IX: "God by no means allows anyone to be punished with eternal punishments. . . ." And the Holy Office said: "It is not always required. . . ." Vatican II similarly: "They who without their own fault . . . can attain eternal salvation." Second, the statements of the Fathers show a basic conviction that God must have made provision for men before Christ: the same thinking applies to those afer ChriSt. Further, St. Paul in Romans 5:15-19 insists strongly and over and over again that the redemption is more abundant than the fall. But if the coming of Christ caused countless millions to lose in practice all chance of salvation, then the redemption would not be superabundant—it would be a tragedy, a harsh tragedy for these persons. And God would not act as if He were their God—as St. Paul asserts in Romans 3:29-30.

---

[99]Vatican II, *Lumen gentium* #49. *Cf. Unitatis redintegratio* #3.

Scripture Index

Index